DAVID CAMPBELL has been a lover of sto[r] an early age. These passions have directe teaching, broadcasting, writing, performi Edinburgh, he spent his childhood in the story-and song-rich North-East of Scotland. After graduating with Honours in English from the University of Edinburgh, he worked as a producer with BBC Radio Scotland for many years devising, scripting and directing a wide variety of radio programmes. Mentored in storytelling by Duncan Williamson, David has gone on to mentor many others in the craft. One of Scotland's finest storytellers, he has toured worldwide with his repertoire of talks and stories and currently lives in Edinburgh.

By the same author:

Tales to Tell I, Saint Andrew Press, 1986
Tales to Tell II, Saint Andrew Press, 1994
The Three Donalds, Scottish Children's Press, 1996
Out of the Mouth of the Morning, Luath Press, 2009
A Traveller in Two Worlds Vol I, Luath Press, 2011
A Traveller in Two Worlds Vol II, Luath Press, 2012

Minstrel Heart
A life in story

DAVID CAMPBELL

Best wishes,

enjoy the jaunts,

David Campbell

Luath Press Limited
EDINBURGH
www.luath.co.uk

First published 2021
Reprinted 2021

ISBN: 978-1-910022-25-2

The paper used in this book is recyclable.
It is made from low chlorine pulps
produced in a low energy, low emission manner
from renewable forests.

Printed and bound by
Severn, Gloucester

Typeset in 11 point Sabon by
Main Point Books, Edinburgh

Contents

For my brother John

A Man

A man held out a promise
 that he could not keep:
A promise, hope, illusion that he held,
 a dream that love could compass all.
But his defeat was that it was,
   as once his father said, so long, so long ago,
 that he was 'in love with love'.
And he pursued it all along the decades of his life,
Tore off deception as a layer
 of love's onion skin
And married truth
 thinking this was the golden ring,
But found truth
 was too stern an inquisitor at many fleshes
For it needed wisdom and compassion
 to find half an ounce of worth,
And these were weighty companions,
 not easy to fall in love with
But to be earned by patience and humility.
So on he trudged, the boy in love with love,
And every meeting was a joy,
  and pain,
Not one without the other.
So, he came to know, as age came on
That all he'd found was still,
 as a rough stone on the shore,
In need of tides of time
 To smooth it into something beautiful.

(David Campbell, 2010)

Preface

A SURPRISING OMISSION from David Campbell's memoir is any mention of his hair. When he was my English teacher in 1966, he wore it short at the back and sides and with a long, falling quiff. It was gingerish then, as I recall and, when he returned work to us, he swept his hand back through it, before he delivered a comment. It was a micro-performance from a handsome man, fine featured and with the strong body of an athlete, a good centre I would have thought if he had been a rugby player. He has remained a handsome man – even into his 80s. The pony tail he has worn during the 'storytelling years' is now white, but his delight in the moment and an awareness of how it might be best shared have been constants from those flop-haired times.

A 'performance' of course presupposes an audience and the memoir shows how David found his at an early age among his playmates, while he in turn was drawn to elders who could tell a story or a joke. Now he can look back and share the moments – the texture of a tale – the future storyteller instinctively saved. Of course, the performer is helped immeasurably by the extent to which he or she has 'charm'. *Minstrel Heart* tells the story of someone who I have witnessed charm audiences of school students, university students, family, friends and folk with whom he just happens to be sharing space. Some readers may question his assertion that he has pursued, through his many relationships, an understanding of the nature of love. However, I think of Edwin Morgan's late collection, *Love and a Life,* in which long term relationships and the briefest encounters are alike viewed by the poet as manifestations of love.

Lest 'performance' sound too egocentric, it has to be balanced – even for an audience of one – with a sense of welcome. As a storyteller, David saw how, with Duncan Williamson and other Travellers he came to know well, this quality is bred in the bone; *Minstrel Heart* shows the extent to which David himself has always welcomed people into his life and into his flat. Whether they were needy, in want of encouragement, or merely passing, they were welcome to the ceilidh. There is then a depth to his charm; the minstrel heart may have wandered, but it has always been capacious. In fact, a defining feature of the poems which thread through *Minstrel Heart* is their welcoming tone, the desire to invite the reader to share a memory of a moment or of a person.

One of the attractions of the memoir is its buoyant sense of forward propulsion. ('Every age has its compensations,' he once told me.) Blessed with confidence from a young age, David has trusted his inner voice to make the decisions that have shaped his life – and to defend what is important to him. Discarding what no longer held him, thrusting himself towards fresh experiences and new people, we can see how the life 'understood backwards' has resulted in a coherence which his blind choices could not have foreseen. His memoir is, as we would expect from a storyteller, an engaging tale; the story of a richly satisfying life. What makes it of greater value, as a historical and cultural document, is what it says about the times it was lived though: most especially, Scotland in the last 50 years. Through inclination, choice and chance, David has been a central figure in the cultural and political shifts that have seen Scotland's identity move decisively from a British/Scottish accent to a Scottish/British one in which the British element is more and more diminished.

His interests in folk song, poetry and drama, at a time when there was a sense of rediscovery of Scotland's past and present contribution to each, swept him up in Hamish Henderson's 'carrying stream' of song, story, music and dance. *Minstrel Heart* vividly gives us a portrait of the excitement of the young teacher whose active interest in drama led to a BBC posting which brought him into contact with Scotland's foremost writers, among them Norman MacCaig, Iain Crichton Smith and George Mackay Brown; whose interest in live events led to his involvement in intimate and large scale readings; whose interest in Scots and Gaelic culture deepened into the appreciation and practice of storytelling, which has absorbed him, as practitioner, teacher and writer, over the last 30 years.

In *Minstrel Heart*, you will read portraits of many of the significant figures in oral and print literature over the last half century. I began this preface with my own brief portrait of the poet/storyteller as a young man. Alastair Reid told how, when his prose pleased Mr Shawn, the legendary editor of *The New Yorker*, it caused a spot of joy to blush on Shawn's cheek. I once wanted to see something similar in Mr Campbell's comments, *after* he swept his hair from his face. It seems so unlikely therefore that I am writing this about him in my 70th year. Yet, from what better point to observe that *Minstrel Heart* is testament to the many lives he has enriched along his way. I consider it most fortunate that mine has been one of them.

Tom Pow,
May 2021

Prelude

Memory

One had a lovely face
And two or three had charm
But charm and face were in vain
For the mountain grass
Cannot but keep the form
Where the mountain hare has lain.

THIS WB YEATS' poem expresses for me how place and date and detail fade like a 'glimmering girl' 'into the brightening air', but the emotions remain like the hare's indentation in the soft grass.

When I reflect over the eight decades of my life, I can see from my earliest years a boy in love with words and with stories, with poetry, with people – loves which were to connect me with singers, poets, writers, actors; with writing and performing myself. I recall in my early teens overhearing my father saying to my mother, 'Our David is in love with love.'

Sing not the song that others have sung. Sing only what you
yourself have realised in your own heart. (Guruji)

What I've realised in my own heart is that its song is for many, that it sings for whom it meets on its way. It does not remain at home, but is a wandering minstrel heart.

I started falling in love when I was at Fraserburgh Primary School, aged five. I was in love simultaneously with three girls in my class. No one knew except myself. They were Nadine Soutar, Vivien Stafford and Norma Bissett. Nadine's face was soft and pear-shaped. I suppose she became June Allyson, the film star of my adolescent infatuation. Vivien was definitely Rita Hayworth, and Norma a sultry Gina Lollobrigida. I had no difficulty in adoring each of them equally and separately.

This 'falling in love', being inexplicably drawn to someone, has been a constant in my life, as has the tendency to be in love with more than one person at a time. In my mature years it has evolved into the conviction that we are married to the person, or persons, that we are with at the present moment. Right now, it is to myself as I make this entry into my life stories.

This seemingly inborn, karmic, or whatever, tendency was to become the source of great loves, pleasures, vexations and complexity, as well as a pilgrimage in search of understanding my own nature, and the nature of love itself.

David Campbell,
Edinburgh,
May 2021

I

A Charmed Life

WHEN I WAS a baby, our family lived in a house in Craigleith Hill Avenue in Edinburgh. I slept in a cot adjacent to the room of my mother and father.

One day when my father returned from his work in the then labour exchange, my mother insisted, 'We have to move David into our bedroom.' There was no apparent reason for this except my mother's intuition and adamant insistence, but my cot was moved into their bedroom.

That night the ceiling came down in my room. Lumps of heavy sodden plaster fell directly where I had been lying.

2

Little by Little

HOW COULD I know how big the world was? Why would I need to know? It was simple. I had a big brother and a big sister, a wee brother, an old comfortable granny and a mum who made breakfast every morning, except Sundays when Dad brought everyone breakfast in bed. This was the world. Our house was white and had a garden. These houses, built in the '30s, occupied only one side of the street since we were so far on the outskirts of Edinburgh that we still had a farmer's field in front of the house and the playground of a disused sand quarry at the back. It was a cosy cradle of childhood, nourished by bedtime stories my dad told my wee brother but that I eagerly eavesdropped to hear. They were always about a boy adventurer called Johnny Morey who travelled the world.

I remember how I loved my sister's tortoise. He was a small explorer. I can see him still, brown and pondering on the green back lawn. He lived under a hard smooth shell; the shell seemed to be made of pieces glued together, brown as chestnuts. This tortoise sometimes poked his head from under his shell house. His neck was as long as my three-year-old middle finger, but dry and crackly as if it would creak when it came out of the shell. But it didn't; it was completely quiet. Sometimes he would go for a walk across the lawn on his four padded feet. He was very, very slow. I called him Little by Little and loved watching him moving always as if he knew where he was going. I was very fond of Little by Little. He was my friend.

One day Little by Little seemed especially clear about where he was going and I watched a long time as he made his way out of the garden gate into the field across the road. The field was vast, full of sun-ripe tawny barley, and into that vastness Little by Little made his way watched by my affectionate eye.

When my sister enquired where he was, I innocently replied – so I am told – 'Oh, he went for a walk.' This, a preface to sister's horror and tears when she discovered where he'd taken his walk.

The family, except Granny, searched the field for what seemed ageless hours until dark fell and the harvest moon rose. That talismanic tortoise still visits me, his lone and fearless journeying to adventure, freedom and danger.

Like my father's Johnny Morey and the tortoise, I was from my earliest days an explorer. I was an explorer because I knew that always I could return to that cossetting cradle, unlike my friend the tortoise. Even aged three, the toddler me would stray along the road to the neighbours, some 300 yards away, who would phone my mother to say, 'Mrs Campbell, don't worry about David, he's visiting us.'

3

Across the Border and Back Again

IT WAS OUT of this cosy world that my father's temporary position in the Civil Service drew our family to the village of Sprotbrough in Yorkshire, a difficult and alien world for five-year-old me. A photo of my face and posture eloquently expresses an anxious, fraught child. Not only was the language at first unintelligible, but as a stranger I was harried and ran from the school gates, first to the brief sanctuary of my father's office and then, the coast clear, home.

Two memories of Sprotbrough indicate an early sense of empathy. One day brother John, in helping to clean the brasses in the house, had inserted his finger into the tin to gather some scrapings. In no way could he extract it. This filled me with tears and inconsolable alarm as I had visions of a lost finger or a brother with a Brasso tin appended to his hand forever. Huge relief when it was removed, I don't recall how.

My mother did not like living in England and longed to be back in Scotland, and so with my little brother she returned to stay temporarily with her mother in Pitlochry. During this time, my father took me to a circus. I still recall my eyes streaming with tears. The ring master smartly dressed in red tunic and white trousers sacked a little clown for some misdemeanour. As the little disconsolate figure in floppy jacket and baggy trousers was walking away, stooped and sad, the ringmaster called him back,

'Hey, where did you get that jacket?'

'From the circus,' said the clown, taking it off and handing it to the ring master.

'The shirt?'

And so on it went until the little fellow trooped out and away wearing only loose floppy underpants, leaving my father to put his arm around me, dry my flooding tears and explain that he was not really sacked but would be back for the next show.

My childhood propensity and desire to entertain and do tricks found an exemplar in a cheery, rotund, *eeh by gum*, Yorkshire friend of my father, Sam Leadbetter, who intrigued me with his bowler hat trick. He would put on the hat, stick his middle finger in his mouth, puff his rubicund cheeks and strenuously blow, and lo the hat would tip up from his head. Magic! Despite my huffing and puffing till red in the face, my efforts were in vain until he revealed the secret. He stood back to the wall, and the brim being firm, leaned gently back simultaneously with the blowing and elevated the hat!

It is interesting how early these personality characteristics manifested themselves and how different the nature of siblings. Neither my little brother nor my sister had any desire to entertain, and brother John was a talented but modest pianist playing for pleasure, and not an entertainer like me!

It was also at this time that my love of words was ignited. I briefly had a marvellous teacher who introduced poetry by reading it and encouraging us to listen. A poem that moved me deeply with a sense of compassion and joy was 'Abou Ben Adhem':

Abou Ben Adhem

Abou Ben Adhem (may his tribe increase!)
Awoke one night from a deep dream of peace,
And saw, within the moonlight in his room,
Making it rich, and like a lily in bloom,
An angel writing in a book of gold:–
Exceeding peace had made Ben Adhem bold,
And to the presence in the room he said,
'What writest thou?' – The vision raised its head,
And with a look made of all sweet accord,
Answered, 'The names of those who love the Lord.'
'And is mine one? Said Abou. 'Nay, not so,'
Replied the angel. Abou spoke more low,
But cheerily still; and said, 'I pray thee, then,
Write me as one that loves his fellow men.'
The angel wrote, and vanished. The next night
It came again with a great wakening light,
And showed the names whom love of God had blest,
And lo! Ben Adhem's name led all the rest.
Leigh Hunt

I include this poem since its sentiments went so deep at that age; I learned it and still recall it.

My father's application for a transfer back to Scotland had him posted as manager of the local labour exchange in Fraserburgh, where amongst his other duties was the placing of evacuees from the war.

In Yorkshire, my mother had vigorously made clear my adoption of the local dialect was certainly not for home use, and when I arrived in Fraserburgh aged five, I rapidly had to learn Doric, that highly distinctive North East dialect so different that not even Lowland Scots can understand it. But I can still fall into it with a fluent and congenial ease like meeting a long-lost friend. This language too had to be abandoned as soon as I crossed the doorstep into our house.

Learning the language was not the only challenge. In Primary One Fraserburgh Infant School, I was rapidly acquainted with the fact that on the next Friday I was to fight the class champion, Charlie MacDonald, a sturdy, well set up, local fisherman's son! Luckily my big brother John was home on leave from the RAF and took it upon himself to give me boxing lessons, and the advice to attack rather than defend.

On that Friday, a circle surrounded Charlie MacDonald and me with cheering encouragement for Charlie from classmates. He seemed formidable but five-year-olds are not capable in fisticuffs of inflicting serious damage. Anyhow, by luck or by John's advice, I landed a blow on Charlie's nose which gushed with blood, the sight and realisation of which brought tears to the champion's eyes concluding the combat with me as victor and new class champion. The threat however remained of the 'best of three'. Fortunately, that was never realised.

Inside the classroom things were peaceful. We had a beautiful young Polish teacher called Miss Petroshelka. One day, reluctantly I suppose, she took me out from my seat at the back of the class to be belted for talking. It was then a universally accepted part of school life that this was the punishment for misdemeanours: to be strapped on the held-out hand by a leather belt.

I returned to my seat and continued talking – perhaps in part a result of the leniency of Miss Petroshelka in delivering the strokes. Asked why I still continued to talk, I apparently replied, 'I hadn't finished what I was saying, Miss.'

This charm and leniency did not prevail in the Central School, to which we graduated aged seven. Our Primary Three teacher was to be the grisly Miss Cranner. In today's teaching world, she would not have survived – one of her habits was to hurl the leather belt across the room at miscreants. How she failed to injure or escape censure is a mystery.

My younger brother and I were too young to appreciate the dangers of frequent German bombing raids on the targets of VASS's munitions factory, Maconochie's food tinning factory or the prosperous and important fishing fleet. During the raids, my mother turned the sofa upside down and put my little brother Eric and I under it until the long shrill blast of the all-clear. My brother's red and black Pinocchio-like gas mask seemed more fun than my standard black pig-snouted model.

Because of the importance of the fishing, the crews had extra rations so as a bonus we had plenty meat and endless supplies of fish from the seaport. On our Sunday walks with my father, farmers would supply him with fresh-laid eggs. At a time of severe rationing, we were never short of food. At the top of our road was an anti-aircraft gun site where we kids visited and the soldiers gave us chocolates.

We children were happy, unafraid and unconscious in any deep way of the perils around us. The presence of the war was a daily reality. When our mother took us down to the harbour, we'd see the herring girls with their lightning fingers at the quayside gutting the fish and throwing their innards into the air where the swooping, shrieking gulls would snatch and gobble them before they neared the ground. On Sundays, the harbour was thronged with little fishing trawlers in bright primary colours bearing mysterious women's names, and smelling of tarry rope and fish, but above them floated huge barrage balloons to protect the little boats from enemy dive bombers.

In wartime Fraserburgh, life for a child growing up was wonderful. There was space and freedom – space and freedom except on Sundays when we could watch the families in black, like big crows followed by docile little crows, making their doleful way to church. None of our family attended church. My father, who had seen a woman's name struck from their family Bible because she had conceived out of wedlock, vowed at an early age he would never attend a church which could do such a thing. Hence, we didn't go to Sunday School or church. My mother's sole stated religion amounted to the wise dictum, which she exemplified, 'Do as you would be done by.'

The swings in the playground were chained, like the local children, into silent obedience to the Lord's Day of rest, but my father took my brother and me on wonderful walks along the sand dunes, and one of the longest and most beautiful beaches in Scotland. We were also warned not to go near the big awesome pronged enemy mines beached on the shore that could blow us to smithereens, wherever that was! We also walked the lighthouse wall breathtakingly exposed to the wild waves and dramatic sea sprays.

An occasion which wakened delight in me was a family visit to Aikie Fair. At this fair was a stall in which you rolled a penny down a little chute and it had to land centrally on coloured squares with numbers or blanks on them. My penny landed on the unthinkable riches of a ten shilling note! I was wealthy beyond dreams.

But I was wakened to a wealth of the heart in a tent where a dark-eyed, black-haired tinker woman stood still and solid and singing. The ballad she sang was 'Son David'. her name, Jeannie Robertson. I was mesmerised. The rest of my family were completely unmoved by her voice, and oblivious to the electric effect it had had on me. Something was kindled. I love that ballad. It was a foretaste of the great Traveller singer-storytellers I was to admire, meet and become friends with later – Lizzie Higgins, Sheila Stewart, Stanley Robertson, Duncan Williamson, folk who were to take me into the treasury of their tradition, lore and ways of thinking. Duncan Williamson was to become a friend, teacher, companion, pain and inspiration and part of my life for 20 years.

4

Granny Howling

MY FAMILY, LIKE countless others, was scarred by the sufferings of two World Wars, the deaths and wounds, the legacy of grief and psychological trauma.

When my brother John was 18, he was a Flight Engineer in the RAF. My sister, Anne, 17, was working in the office of the munitions factory. My father, too old for a call-up, had been transferred to Fraserburgh as manager of the local employment exchange. He was also in the ARP, the Air Raid Precautions service. He returned from one of the frequent night bombing raids to tell us of a wall blown clean off a house, leaving a bed miraculously suspended on high by its two bottom legs – an old woman perched on the headboard. She refused to be rescued without the mattress. Sewn into it were her life's savings.

At the time, my mother kept open house for the British, Commonwealth and Polish air crews stationed for training at nearby Cairnbulg Air Base, so our home was always abuzz with what seemed to us kids giant laughing men in uniforms, men who were in or hardly out of their teens. Two young Australian airmen who were both fond of my sister Anne, then 18, were to feature in a surprising way 50 years later.

I remember aged seven being in high excitement because I was allowed to go along the road myself to the station to meet my big brother who was coming home on leave. Intent on meeting him, I didn't recognise him in his uniform and hurried past. He called me back,

'Hey, DD, where are you going?'

'I thought you were a big air man,' I said.

'I am,' he replied, 'I'm a Sergeant now.'

John loved his kid brothers and used to play with us and sing current War chants like 'Hitler, boy, what a funny little man you are'. When he was stationed close by my mother's sister in Rickmansworth, near London, he could take short leaves. From there he sent my mother a letter:

I've never been able to do much for you. Let me pay your fare and the boys' to London and you can come down for a while.

My mother was certain he had a premonition of his death. My mother and I and little brother, Eric, took the train there for a visit. My granny was staying there at the time.

It seems that the moment he died, my mother was walking down the stairs at my aunt Nan's house, and said, 'Something has happened to John.'

It was the morning of 21 July 1943. I woke up in my aunt's house to the sound of my grandmother's wailing, and when I came from my bedroom, saw her twirling her thumbs, pacing to and fro, wringing her hands. My mother was pale and silent. She once told me that John had loved her more than any other human being ever had, and to me this seemed reciprocated.

His plane, a Stirling Bomber, had crashed in England killing the crew. His funeral was in a church in Rickmansworth. In the chapel, I saw his coffin, shining polished wood with glittering brass handles. I wanted to see him, but somehow I can't remember how, I gathered that he was too broken for me to see. This baffled me – I imagined him lying there in his smart RAF uniform but his face unrecognisable. To the drowning sound of the organ, we sang 'Eternal Father Strong to Save,' his favourite hymn.

The shock of John's death killed the child my mother was carrying. We would have had another wee brother. In a way, I think my mother never recovered. The love between her and her firstborn was deep and intense and full of fun, as I found when I came across a letter he wrote to her shortly before his death. Every year until she died aged 94, I could feel the tacit pall of grief when I visited her on 20 July. In 1981, when I visited my mother at her home on Armistice Day, I saw lying under the photograph of John wearing his uniform, his 19-year-old face and clear eyes, a poppy; I found it hard to keep back tears.

My father was equally devastated by the death of his stepson John whom he loved fully as much as he did Eric and myself. He arranged a family holiday on a farm called Balnealach, Perthshire, by way of helping the recovery I suppose. By now, the nearby woods were ready for the hazelnuts to be gathered and so he took myself and my brother hazelnut gathering.

Late one afternoon, now aged eight, I went to this hazelnut wood alone and there sat beneath the trees in dappled sunshine and wept inconsolably for the death of my big brother. When I returned to the farmhouse, my family – mother, father and brother – were already sitting to eat supper. Although nothing was said, I think they sensed from my silence and the red eyes something of my sadness, and I was grateful to be allowed that privacy. Years later, and still now, the words of Dylan Thomas speak to me:

After the first death there is no other.

By now, my father, my mother, my sister and younger brother have all died and I recall these deaths with equanimity, but I'm still brought to involuntary tears when I remember or tell anyone of the death of my big brother John. And in my memory, I always recall that hazel wood where my eight-year-old self grieved alone and privately. The first two lines of WB Yeats's poem 'The Song of Wandering Aengus' resonate with that childhood memory:

I went out to the hazel wood
Because a fire was in my head.

I always associate this poem with its enchanted sense of another world, invisible but a mere glimpse away, with that childhood experience in the woods, that private last farewell. This sense of privacy of grief has made me avoid participating in communal ceremonies of grief, and uniforms and militarism became anathema to me. Aged 12, at George Heriot's School, I resisted every overture to join the Combined Cadet Force. My conviction was confirmed when I heard the raucous, saw-edged bullying schoolboy Sergeant bawling at young recruits. It didn't help that my incompetent Maths teacher was in charge of these recruits. There were rumours too of queer goings-on in the tent on CCF summer camps.

On Armistice Day when I was 12, in my first year at George Heriot's School, all the staff and boys were gathered before the Cenotaph for a service commemorating the dead former pupils of two World Wars. All the cadets and staff in charge of them were in uniform. All the boys who had lost a father or brother were expected to form a line in the front row.

I hid, even at that age being horrified at the idea of being drawn into a uniform lament when my own sadness about the loss of my brother and all that it meant was totally private. This sense I shared with my mother who never made any public show of the deep and devastating grief of the loss of her first son. The only thing she made clear was that she wished the casket of his ashes to be scattered along with her own when the time came. When the time did come, my brother and I threw them both to the wind on top of the Braid Hills in Edinburgh where my mother and brother John had walked.

Ashes

April fourth 1994
you died mother.
After the cremation
I phoned the undertaker
to ask for your ashes.
The undertaker lady told me they were safe
in a plastic bag
not a casket.
I thought you might smile at that.

Under my bed lies a casket.
It contains the ashes of your son, John,
killed on his twentieth birthday.

The clumsy bomber he was engineer of
bursting into the ground.

You wished these ashes of fifty years
to be scattered with yours;
We will find a place for such a wedding.
Confetti of ashes,
and each flake will be our gratitude for you
and the grown seeds
you left to follow you
into the dust.

With her family's experience of the sufferings and traumas of two World Wars, in which Germany was the enemy, it was understandable that my mother had an extreme dislike of Germans, a dislike confirmed by the horror stories of the Concentration Camps. Yet the effect on me in my 20s was signally different.

5

A Windy Boy and a Bit

Now as I was young and easy under the apple boughs
About the lilting house and happy as the grass was green,
The night above the dingle starry,
Time let me hail and climb
Golden in the heydays of his eyes…

('Fern Hill' Dylan Thomas)

TWO YEARS AFTER the end of World War II, my family returned to Edinburgh. Before finding a place to rent, we stayed at the house of my mother's sister, Aunt Nan, at 29 Pentland View, where I'd lived for the first four years of my life. My father had sold it to her at a knock-down price – providence in money matters not being one of his qualities – and so my mother, father, myself and brother were now living with my aunt and two cousins. The house had three bedrooms, a lounge and dining room. The lounge was now converted into a bedroom for my mother and father, and somehow this temporary arrangement passed congenially.

A playground paradise in the form of an extensive disused quarry was at the back of the house. No advanced thinking adventure playground designer could have planned a better environment for fertile adolescent imagination and physical activities, endless ingenious games, physical challenges and creative enterprises.

At the top of the main road was a row of shops. The quarry extended from there for a quarter of a mile in one direction and was probably 300 yards across. This wonder world contained many hillocks, one precipitous incline, a stream, a small pond (sometimes frozen), a turret hill that had contained a wartime shelter, many banks, trees, elderberries and rhubarb growing wild, and a forest of hemlock. The dried stalks of these lofty plants made ideal spears and makeshift javelins.

29 Pentland View was the first house in the row, there being 200 yards of unbuilt land between it and the main road. On part of this was a section of the old farm road by the side of which grew a sturdy mountain ash which we christened 'the aeroplane tree'. There we each had our appointed perch, and this was the place to plot, plan and devise our enterprises. There we'd climb and talk – my gang. This was the very tree where on one occasion my cousin Alex, two years older than me, climbed to a branch above. This branch broke, tumbling Alex on top of me, and me to the ground where I broke my wrist.

The core members of my gang were myself, my brother Eric, neighbours Ali and Tubby, and we also had a tomboy, Anne, whom we admired for her pluck and readiness for everything. I'd be 12 when the gang was formed, my brother nine, Anne and Tubby 11.

Later, further members were enlisted and we amalgamated with another gang. The *raison d'être* of our gang was not the usual activities associated with the word 'gang', but more akin to the gang of 'outlaws' in Richmal Crompton's *Just William* books. We devised and built a variety of huts, held Olympic Games, produced plays, invented a Quarry Broadcasting system and cooked over campfires.

Perhaps it was the imminent coming of the Olympic Games to London that in 1948 made me decide that the gang should hold the Quarry Olympic Games. These were customised to our equipment and surroundings, as well as to the individual abilities of the gang members. In the flat space between the old farm road and 29 Pentland View were two shallow sandpits, the one ideal for long jump and hop step and jump, the other for high jump and pole vault. The vault was dangerously executed at first by using a clothes pole! Later we discovered bamboo. We also invented a springboard jump. This consisted of creating a springboard from a thin plank and a box. The contestant would sprint up to the springboard and leap airborne, it seemed to me, to dizzy heights of six feet and over.

Each gang member had for each event his best performance assiduously noted. We improvised our own hurdles and stone shot put. Our gang had a marathon emulation in a race to Hillend Park and back, about five miles, for which my brother Eric had the inbuilt stamina to win. We had also cycle races of that distance in which I didn't participate since I had concluded that cycling developed the wrong muscles. And I didn't have a bike.

From the individual 'record' performances, I calculated handicaps and when I look back it was a measure of my inbuilt desire to encourage that, although I was the best athlete, I never won the Olympic Games, nor was the all-over champion.

By the second year of this great enterprise, we had gathered the 'Springers', the kids from Comiston Springs Avenue. One of these, Gordon, was neither a good runner, jumper or thrower, but he was the clear champion in two of our unique events. In the 'hanging on to a branch by hands for the longest period', he could easily outlast any of us. We also had a crazy endurance event. Tubby, our precocious scientist, had invented an electric shock machine activated by turning a handle. Gordon seemingly could endure endless amounts of electric current, again for periods far exceeding any of us. Gold for stamina and endurance in each of these events.

Another scientific contribution of Tubby's presaged an important phase of my future. In a farther-from-houses part of the quarry was a little hill.

Out of that hill we dug an earth hut covered not with corrugated iron but, inauspiciously, with corrugated asbestos sheeting, which in turn was covered with turf, and the gang of four or five could enter from the door dug in the side and sit there cosily. Tubby rigged a microphone some 50 or 60 yards away in a glade where, by a fire, I sat of an evening and told stories, mostly mystery or ghost. These, by the wonder of Tubby's knowledge, were relayed to speakers in the hut on the QBC, Quarry Broadcasting Corporation. I remember especially putting the chill of fear into both myself and my audience by telling a story I had found. It concerned a Dr Morris, a sinister doctor-hypnotist who experimented with his patients by exploring the threshold of pain under the hypnosis. Meantime we had cooked rhubarb with purloined sugar!

This hut collapsed because of the unsuitable brittleness of asbestos as roofing, not known then to be a health hazard, but probably a fortuitous collapse. The hut was soon replaced by a well-built structure of wood stakes with corrugated iron nailed on: an ideal den.

My popularity as a gang leader was seriously dented when I fell in with slim, beautiful, fair-haired and pigtailed Izzy, or more romantically 'Isobel' in my early love-struck attempts at verse. This distraction and her incorporation into the gang did not at first go well. Izzy was lean, confident, and right! I was stricken, blind, and delighted. She was less than enthusiastic about the Olympics, although swift and adept enough in the chasing games and the 'hido' – hiding illicitly in the stooks of the corn field where I had carelessly lost my sister's pet tortoise, Little by Little, as a three-year-old.

What devotion, what sweet innocence and what romantic notions infused my love for Izzy, the guileless poetry and dizzy daydreams; I was a musketeer who'd rescue her from desperate perils. Heroic fantasies! The reality was somewhat different and the passion was expressed by no more than holding her hand as I walked her home sharing glucose tablets, which I imagined improved my athletic prowess.

And then came a moment of enlightenment. Izzy and I were alone in the quarry and we decided to make a fire. We were aged 13. I said I would make the fire.

'No,' said Izzy, 'I'll make the fire. We learned how to make fires at Girl Guides.'

'I know how to make them. I make them all the time,' I countered.

'Well,' said she, 'we'll make two fires and see whose is best. Three matches each!' She stood a slim figure of complete assurance.

Two then it was.

We gathered our kindling, twigs and wood, and were ready, mine built by experience, hers by the *Girl Guide* book!

My fire was soon aflame; hers, despite the three matches, remained dead.

'So,' I said, 'mine's best.'

'No,' said she, 'mine is the proper way to make a fire. It's the best way!'

I was completely baffled by this confident alien logic, a bewildering psychology. There she stood, a lean figure of certainty by the dead fire. Rendered totally incapable of words as I looked at her, so complete and dauntless and wrong, that in my bafflement I aimed at her a brief clumsy kiss, so that we stood back from one another in astonishment. However ineptly, we had crossed a threshold: our first kiss. We roasted two potatoes on the fire.

By the time I was 14, I decided that I would learn to dance, take ballroom dance lessons. I suppose this was at least partly inspired by the realisation that there would be girls in the class, and somewhat influenced by the debonair grace of Fred Astaire and Ginger Rogers. This decision was to have many consequences. Another impetus was that by that age I was a member of George Heriot's athletics team and, as such, could attend the school annual dance, and take a partner!

Diary entry, 8 December 1950: I met Isobel in the tram and went to her house and I asked her, with her mother's permission, to the school dance. She accepted.

20 December 1950: Isobel and I went to the school dance – in evening dress. Super! Overstayed our time but got a taxi home at 12.30am. The evening was bliss. I gave her a pound box of chocolates.

The dance class I attended was run by a remarkable woman, Doris Cowie. She was at that time in her 30s, red-haired, slim, energetic and punctilious. She was full of fun, married to John, an amiable accountant, far too fond of drink. They had a fair-haired daughter of nine years called Shirley. In that small dance class of six pupils, I was at first the only boy. These five girls were pals and paid me little attention, but I was learning the waltz, quickstep, slow foxtrot, tango! I loved it and subsequently not only did I progress from bronze to gold but, easily persuaded by Doris, I took the qualification as a teacher in ballroom, Latin American dancing. With this qualification I became Doris's assistant and in these days of thriving ballroom dancing I thereby earned considerable pocket money whilst I was at Edinburgh University.

Meantime, I had started my education at George Heriot's School. My brother John had been a pupil there. This school had been founded in 1620 by Heriot who was money lender and jeweller to King James VI and I. His legacy and will was still maintained in that the school had so-called 'Foundationers' so that the children of single parents would be educated free of charge.

My mother was determined that her children should have the best education possible. At that time the fees at Heriot's were modest, but our family was struggling for money. My father thought, for several reasons, not least his egalitarian socialist principles and in-built thrift, that we should go to the free corporation school. Despite our financial struggle, my mother would have none of it. In such matters she was insistent. Her conviction that the prestige of a 'good' school, and my brother John's having been there, were unanswerable arguments, and so I found myself at Heriot's. My mother had made a personal appointment with the then Vice-Headmaster, Eddie Hare, who'd known my brother, and lo, I was whisked into Class 1B, for reasons that were not clear. That class had German as a second language. Apparently, this was a time when that language was useful in Science, and Heriot's had a tradition of producing scientists and doctors from a school timetable heavy with Chemistry, Physics, Zoology and Botany. Learning German, however, was to influence a decision later in my life.

It was inevitably something of a shock to come from a primary school in the small north-east fishing town of Fraserburgh to secondary school in Edinburgh. There was a little bonus. The tram car I took from Fairmilehead passed the stop where Izzy would board – if she wasn't late. I would keep her a seat in the round upstairs compartment at the front of the tramcar. For these precious morning meetings, I would save up jokes, innocent and doubtless corny, but this was my method of courtship, the beginning of a lifelong addiction to joke telling and, in a way, an apprenticeship for a future career as a storyteller. When I was 14, at Christmas time, I presented Izzy with a poem I had written for her. This romantic liaison became more sporadic when we moved from my aunt's house and rented a flat in Mardale Crescent. It was there aged 14 that I developed pneumonia.

My crude diary of the time records that my fever was so high, the pain in my back so invasive, that I had no sleep during the night. And on Friday 13 March 1949, I was admitted with an alarmingly high temperature to Edinburgh Royal Infirmary. There, I received penicillin injections and a painful hole was bored in my back. My mother visited to find me at an open window surrounded by several students being examined and addressed on my conditions by the professor. She asked the physician to explain why I was at this open window. He suspected an underlying chronic condition in my lungs.

'You only need common sense,' said my mother, 'to know that you address a critical condition before a chronic one. I want my son to be removed from this window at once.'

I found myself moved to a bed in the middle of the ward.

On 9 April, after nearly a month in hospital, I took farewell of my friendly nurses and some of the patients and was glad to return to my family.

School was to further my interest in words, story and drama in several significant ways. Despite the curriculum bias to Science, there was a thriving school play tradition, a 'Lit', Literary and Debating Society, and two compelling English teachers, both of whom I was lucky enough to be taught by.

The most remarkable was 'Chinkie' Westwood who derived his nickname from the fact that, as he himself announced to new pupils, 'Although I know very well how much I resemble an oriental gentleman, I would prefer that you call me "Spats."' He habitually wore spats, sported a boater hat and carried a Malacca cane walking stick. His appearance was the least of his uniqueness.

His room was next to the top of the turret staircase in the quadrangle corner of the spectacular 17th century stone school. Its high walls were shelved with books. I remember one day our class trooped in without seeing our unpredictable English teacher and one of us said, 'Where's Chinkie?' From the top of a ladder looking out a book came the answer, 'Your oriental friend is aloft.' At that time, we had no feeling that the nickname was derogatory and we certainly had great regard and admiration for our eccentric English teacher. It was long before the age of political correctness.

He taught with what seemed to be the principle of constant surprise. Later in life, when I became a teacher of English myself, I followed this example, realising that when the students couldn't predict what was coming next they had to stay awake and attentive.

If you happened to be in our oriental friend's class, mid-morning he would summon a boy to his desk, which was slightly elevated at the front of the class, with a sharp, 'Ha lad!' and beckon him to his side, mutter in his ear, and the boy would disappear downstairs. He would return with a tray, tea and biscuits and our unconventional teacher would spread his morning newspaper, drink his tea, and instruct us, 'Seven minutes free conversation with your neighbour, lads.' Tea drunk, the lesson would proceed.

He was a wonderful reader and had us, as 17-year-olds, hiding our tears at the tragic conclusion of the poem, 'Sohrab and Rustum'. He also branded that poem permanently on our minds by once more whispering an injunction to a classmate who vanished while 'Spats' startlingly impressed upon us the omnipresence of the Oxus River in the poem. Down the turret stairs came a mini deluge, the cascade carried by the messenger emptying two buckets of water from above. From below a minute or so later came a bewildered History teacher under whose door downstairs some water of the Oxus had seeped!

Another way in which the imaginative 'Spats' extended our thinking and capacities to express ourselves was that he would command every boy to propose a five-minute speech without notes on any subject that interested him. I recall regaling the teacher and class with the intricacies and relative effectiveness of different styles of high jumping. I myself, pre-Fosbury Flop days, favouring the Western Roll.

Our English teacher also conducted an after-school 'General Purposes' club in a small room adjoining his. In that room he taught shorthand and typing to prepare us as future journalists or writers. This he taught along with knitting, holding that this should not be the preserve of education for girls. He also had in this room a small billiard table!

Very unusually for the time, a black boy, Olu Ogunro, came to Heriot's whereupon 'Spats' made sure he was welcome, announcing to his class,

'We have a black boy in our class from Africa. His name is Oludotun Ogunro. We will call him Olu for short. To make him welcome we will sing a Scottish song for him, 'Roaming in the Gloaming'. Ready?'

Everyone sang heartily and laughed loudly, and Olu had instant acceptance; brilliant psychology from an enlightened teacher. Olu incidentally became a high jumper in the athletics team, where I was the captain.

The conclusion of this inspiring teacher's career was as crass and unenlightened as he was enlightened and wise. He took a small group to Greyfriars Bobby's pub to expound its history and explain the traditional measures! Crime of crime, boys in a pub. This much-loved and brilliant man was sacked.

One day I met him on The Mound, clad as ever – boater, spats, Malacca walking stick – and he informed me that, amongst other things, he was now studying Theology at New College.

Our extra-curricular education at Heriot's, apart from the inspired English classes, probably taught and formed me more than the standard timetable. The tradition of debating at the 'Lit' was a marvellous nursery for public speaking and thinking on your feet. Even as timid first year pupils, aged 12, on a Friday evening we would be amongst the stars of the Upper School and encouraged to stand up, formally address the Chair and make a bold, if hesitant, contribution to the debate. From this, we progressed to win inter-scholastic debating contests which I later continued at university level.

As well as taking part in school plays, those of us in the echelons of the upper forms devised variety shows, performed for the public in the school hall. For these, we gathered the best singers, musicians and script writers. My fellow creator and producer in this was a close companion at the time, Ian Gloag, always top in English to my second top! He wrote like Raymond Chandler and together we devised comic and satirical sketches. The well-known actor, film and television performer, Roy Kinnear, was cradled here. These activities and my love of poetry presaged my future as an English teacher, radio producer, writer, storyteller and sometime poet.

My sporting career at Heriot's did not include the iconic rugby. This was by an odd circumstance. When as a 12-year-old I arrived at Heriot's as a first year pupil, I discovered that after lunch on Wednesday afternoon all my classmates had mysteriously disappeared, and so I took the tramcar home. The same thing happened on the second Wednesday. By the third, I learned that they had gone to a place called Goldenacre to play a mysterious game called rugby. In Fraserburgh, I had never heard of this game.

So it was that I continued with my free Wednesday afternoons, my presence at Goldenacre seemingly not missed. However, I subsequently discovered that my ignorance of this vitally important game relegated me to a sub-species.

One of my English teachers was Charlie Broadwood and one day he said, 'Hands up all the boys who saw the FPs trounce Watsonians at Goldenacre on Saturday.' There was a healthy show of hands. 'Now (pause), stand up all the keelies who didn't.' Ignorant of what an FP was, who Watsonians were, what a keelie was – although the derisive tone indicated it wasn't a good thing to be – I rose to join the ranks of inferior beings.

However, I was to be redeemed, though not in Charlie's opinion.

Having discovered that this Goldenacre was a place for cricket and athletics in the summer term, I took myself there where I found a shed of athletics equipment – high jump stands, javelins, discuses and shot puts. There were also sandpits.

Being devoted to high jumping, for what reason who can tell, I was a sole figure practising on my own, raising the bar incrementally to my best height, and unconsciously, being observed by the new games master appointed by the Head Master, William Dewar.

Donald Hastie, this games master, realised that I was jumping high enough to be included in the under-14 section of the athletics team, and could have won that event in the inter-scholastic championships. He also informed me that I had somehow devised an economic form of jumping called the Eastern Cut-off, with which style an Australian had won the high jump in the 1948 London Olympics with the now modest height of six feet, six inches. That was the beginning of my 'official' athletics career, fostered by our homemade Olympics. Donald Hastie had been a pole vault competitor and so became a splendid mentor and coach. It was soon clear, however, that some of the old guard volunteer rugby coaches on the staff resented him, at the least. I loved several events and by my dedicated and tireless practice, excelled in them, and was delighted to be elected by the boys as Captain of the athletics team. This role totally suited that strong part of my own nature as teacher and fosterer of the younger and talented members of our team.

I was twice school games champion and for a while held the school record for high jump, pole vault, and shot put, as well as being Scottish junior pole vault and high jump champion in 1954. Subsequently, I represented the Edinburgh University team as a pole vaulter.

Outside all of this, my greatest teachers were my father and mother.

My father was born in Greenock in 1887. He left school at the age of 12 with a little green pamphlet-sized document called the Scotch Leaving Certificate testifying to his proficiency in Reading, Writing, and Arithmetic. I still have that document. With these qualifications, he became a shipping clerk, starting work at five in the morning. His attempt to enlist for the army in 1914 for World War I was refused because he had flat feet. He belonged to the tradition of those Scots who valued education and read widely, and he became the youngest manager of a branch of the Labour Exchange in Scotland, the early incarnation of the DHSS, but without the bleak reputation that organisation has now.

My father was an avowed and idealistic socialist, supporter of the Labour Party. This idealism and the principles of egalitarianism were a persuasive part of my own political education, and from an early age my father taught me how to argue, how to argue persuasively.

I remember I was taking part in a school debate and was putting my arguments to my father. At a certain point, I countered him by saying: 'Dad, that is absolute rubbish.' His mild reply was a measure of his wisdom as a teacher. 'Well, David, you'll need to find something more persuasive to express that if you want to win your school debate.'

I realise now how aware he was that he was nourishing a young mind. Amongst other gentle lessons I learned from him was the occasion when my granny was staying with us, and she said to 12-year-old me as she prepared for bed,

'Now David, you'll not forget to say your prayers.'

'I don't believe in God, Granny.'

My father said nothing at the time, but later, 'David, your granny is an old lady. She has said her prayers all her life. You can discuss your beliefs in God with me or anyone else, but by telling Granny you don't believe in God, you are just upsetting an old lady.'

My father was deeply interested in spiritualism, and his view of life beyond death could be summed up by Hamlet, 'There are more things, Horatio, in heaven and earth than are dreamt of in your philosophy.'

Our family never went to Church. My father, as I mentioned, totally dismissed it for his own reasons. My mother wasn't interested. Perhaps it was not surprising then that when I was 17, I became not only interested, but obsessively involved in a form of Christianity. Three people fostered my interest – two boys from school, Tommy Mayo and Stuart MacGregor, and Sandra, with whom I'd fallen devotedly in love!

Tommy Mayo invited me to the highly evangelical Bristo Baptist Chapel, hearty singing and the perils of not listening to the still small voice, or the sacrifice of the blood of the Lamb. Stuart, a fine orator, was a perfervid and persuasive evangelical preacher from a soapbox on The Mound by the Galleries in Princes Street. This was at that time a Speakers' Corner of political and religious zealots, such as the fiery, tweedy Scottish Nationalist Wendy Wood, and the rabidly anti-Catholic McCormack who promulgated tales of every corrupt miscreant priest that ever was.

The *coup de grâce* in my conversion was my falling in love with Sandra, a fervent Christian. With her, I attended West Mayfield Church led by a fine minister and preacher, the Reverend James Whyte (later Moderator of the General Assembly). With Sandra, I also attended St George's West in Shandwick Place where the Reverend Murdo Ewan McDonald was an erudite and charismatic preacher whose poetic Highland eloquence thrilled me and packed his church on a Sunday evening. These influences, along with my own nature, made me not only a convert but, like St Paul, a zealous convert, and leading light in the Youth Fellowship.

So I decided to become a minister. My father's response to this characterised his enlightenment. He took no objection to this ambition, but delighted in the arguments we had in my abortive attempts to persuade him of the Christian message. He, of course, stayed of the same opinion, still echoing his affection for Fitzgerald's translation of the *Rubaiyat of Omar Khayyam*:

> Myself when young did eagerly frequent
> Doctor and saint, and heard great argument
> But ever and anon came out at that same door as in I went.

In many ways, my father's behaviour epitomised Christian values. For a man born through the time when homosexuality was seen as an obscene perversion – witness the ugly hounding and sad tale of Oscar Wilde and disastrous fate of Alan Turing, the brilliant wartime codebreaker – my father would say to me, 'You know David, if you knew the story of these people [homosexuals], you would not be able to judge them.' That, amongst other of his utterances, became for me a conviction and later a mantra 'By their stories shall you know them.'

I still frequently hear my father's voice. If I misplace something, he says, 'David, a place for everything and everything in its place.' This perhaps after he'd lent me one of the little useful treasures in his waistcoat pocket as an injunction to return it: the handy little pair of scissors in a wee red leather case, a rubber, a pencil. And, 'If a job's worth doing, it's worth doing well.'

He led by example. On Sunday mornings he brought the whole family breakfast in bed: bacon, egg, tomato and toast. The one price my brother and I, who shared a room, had to pay was, as he surveyed the disarray in our room: 'It would be a great help to your mother if you boys would tidy this room.' A small price.

He taught us to play golf, chess, table tennis, whist and solo whist, throw and kick a ball. The card games and the table tennis my brother and I played with our parents in foursomes, bearing in mind dad's adage, 'Never grumble when you lose and laugh like blazes when you win.' My father told jokes which I still sometimes tell!

My mother's teaching, as her love, was practical. Neither of our parents ever struck us. I remember hearing my mother sayng that when she was invited to the minister's house for tea in Fraserburgh, the minister's wife had told the assembled company of women, 'So when he misbehaved, he got a good thrashing and then he came and hugged me, and said, "Mummy, I love you."'

'Yes,' said my mother, 'because he is afraid of you!'

She was not invited back, which would have been a delightful relief. I doubt if she would have gone.

She was totally thirled to her children. She had been married before and when she discovered that, out of jealousy or whatever, her husband had taken John, as an infant, out of his cot and left him lying on the cold floor, my mother left.

My father's income from a meagre Civil Service pension and a poorly paid job as an unqualified accountant meant that we were poor. I remember the embarrassment of having to conceal that my shoes' soles were worn through and that my Heriot's school uniform was patched, tricky things for an adolescent whose appearance was important at a time when one might wish to impress a young lady.

One day my mother saw a notice on a church which read, 'God feeds the birds, but he does not bring food to the nest.' As a practical step to address our poverty, she applied for a job as supervisor in Mackie's Restaurant, Princes Street, and four months later boldly applied for the post as manageress of one of Edinburgh's largest restaurants, in Patrick Thomson's department store on the Bridges. Her success was soon evident and she took the restaurant from a financial liability to a healthy profit in one year. But her priority was to look after her family.

In this way, my brother and I came by the luxury of running spikes, tracksuits, new clothes and the odd meal in her restaurant where a little sedate band played chamber music. My mother's example was her teaching.

My mother, in bringing us up, had a great understanding of the value of surprise and distraction. When we were small and up to some activity that she felt inappropriate in some way, she would suddenly, 'Bazooka!', go to the chimney and, as if by magic, produce some object by holding her hand up the flue. I think I inherit both that sense of the use of surprise and her sense of mischief. I remember the whole of our family being in a state of alarm when she convinced us that she had been caught shoplifting. Her account culminated with her attempting to flee from the shop, the manager in pursuit, hauling her back by pulling her leg... just as she was pulling our leg. But she had us aghast.

I was her disciple. When she was manageress of the Patrick Thomson's Restaurant, I used to phone up in an adopted voice and accent and make preposterous bookings until she tumbled to the total improbability of the excess. One day she arrived home and said, 'David, you've to stop these phone calls.' A customer with a quirky voice had phoned to make an extremely large booking to which request she retorted, 'Just stop your nonsense at once, will you? I'm extremely busy.' My own spontaneous, elvish pieces of nonsense are, I'm sure, a legacy from my mother.

My mother was practical, my father canny. One evening recently as I lay in bed darning my kilt socks, I wrote a poem celebrating this inheritance:

Darning

Going to bed
I throw my kilt socks
Neatly before me on to the floor and see
They have been darned and darned
And carefully darned by me.
The skill and neatness
Learned, mother, from you,
The frugality, father, from you,
A perfect marriage,
A perfect inheritance of skills,
And as I pat and smooth
The final patch,
Just as you showed me, mum,
I celebrate you both.

Both of my parents instilled considerate rules of courtesy and manners that have lasted a lifetime. Granny was never allowed to be called 'she' or 'her', but respectfully 'Granny'. You didn't leave the dining table whilst people were still eating, and if it was necessary required a reason and an 'Excuse me'. You stood for the elderly, held open doors: these became the habits of a lifetime.

A lasting legacy I have from my parents is a huge sense of gratitude, gratitude for how they each strove to nourish the family by their tireless work in taxing jobs and by encouraging us to follow our own interests. That money was short was a strong incentive for us to help.

As a result, my brother and I would always take holiday jobs when we were at school and university. I had casual Christmas Post Office work, summer grouse beating, factory work, and my ballroom dance teaching and English tutoring.

All these were an education in different ways.

On a school Christmas holiday, aged 16, I was attached to parcel delivery with a driver and his mate who hired their van to the Post Office. We started delivery at eight in the morning. At 11 the driver said to me, 'Alright, ginger, see you at two o'clock.'

'Are we not doing another delivery?' asked the innocent.

'Two o'clock, ginger!'

This was not my father's teaching.

I worked also in Crawford's biscuit factory in Leith, digging dough, cleaning floors and dealing with the colourful jibes and teasing of the women workers! My co-worker was Bob. He was recovering from a stomach operation when he told me he had been told to work on night shift; a hazard to his need for small regular meals. Naively, I approached Mr Conlan, the foreman, and suggested this was not conducive to Bob's recovery.

'Collect your books from the office at four o'clock!'

I got the sack.

At least, my father applauded my solicitude.

A congenial job was as odd-job man and labourer in the construction of a new C&A store in Princes Street.

In all these I made new, if temporary, friends.

The next chapter of my holiday employment was to be strange, exacting, fraught, unpredictable and rewarding.

6

A Boyhood Fantasy

'Be cheerful sir. Our revels now are ended.'
(*The Tempest*, Act IV, Scene I, William Shakespeare)

IN MY LAST year at school I was about to enter a story that was to have a profound effect, not only on me, but on my family.

One day, the Careers Master at George Heriot's called me and my friend and fellow prefect, Iain Gloag, into his office with the offer of an unusual summer holiday job.

The job description was that we were to act as prefect companions to a 16-year-old boy whose health had been damaged by excessive smoking and drinking, which had caused a premature ageing process. A large house, 'Barscobe', on the banks of Loch Lomond, had been acquired for six weeks to function as a mini boarding school with tutoring and domestic staff, and three 'prefects'. The pay was modest – £4 per week – but all travel, food and keep were included, with the bonus of free tuition in English and History. This, as I recorded in my diary at the time, seemed an ideal way to pass the summer, enjoying a country holiday and earning money!

As I had been pole vaulting for the Scottish Schools in England, I arrived a day late. Feeling nauseous from the bus journey, I went up the driveway and came to the entrance hall, where I was met by a tall red-headed man who looked about 40, wearing long red stockings, grey shorts and a grey long-sleeved woollen windcheater.

'You'll be David Campbell,' he stuttered in a Home Counties accent.

I was somewhat unnerved and asked where Iain was.

'He is, eh, having his bath. I'll show you to your room.' He lifted and carried my bag before I could think.

We ascended the stairs and he indicated my room and the adjacent bathroom, where Iain was 'having his bath'. I thanked him and looked briefly into my room. On the bed was a pair of grey shorts, a pair of white flannel shorts, red stockings and grey jersey.

I knocked on the bathroom door and called Iain's name.

He immediately unsnibbed the door. I entered as a dripping Iain climbed back into the bath.

'Who was that person?' I fondly believed he was the butler or a house servant.

'Mike,' said Iain. 'He's the one we're here for. He's a bit odd as you see, but he's okay. We start the timetable tomorrow. Dinner's at 6.30, in half an hour, we're expected to wear white flannels and red socks.'

And so began an unimaginable journey that deserves a place in the margins of 20th century history – and incidentally got me a job in the BBC, my brother his medical fees, and my mother a house.

To the newly appointed 'prefects' – Iain, myself, and Robert from George Watson's College, Edinburgh, all from day schools – the public school-style timetable was unfamiliar and something of an insight into boarding school life.

As an 18-year-old athlete, I found the morning exercise routine with which we started the day rather comic, consisting as it did of nothing more strenuous than elementary arm swinging, toe-touching and brief run-on-the-spot exercises to accommodate Mike's limited physical capabilities.

There was then a brief – could we believe it at the time – Bible reading and blessing for the day. No singing, Lord be thanked.

Then the first discomfort – breakfast, a pleasant meal of porridge followed by scrambled egg on toast, served by an amiable cook but rendered indigestible by what we took to be signs of Mike's rooted antagonism to authority – criticising with unsubtle rudeness the eating manner of Mr Stewart, the tutor. Mike ostensibly addressed his hardly *sotto voce* remarks to us, such as: 'Some people apparently don't find it vulgar and offensive to speak with their mouth full.' The ensuing silence was brittle. A lean, athletic man of about 40, Mr Stewart was clearly dismayed and at a loss as to how to deal with these expressions of contempt.

Lessons began with readings from HAL Fisher's *History of Europe*, an erudite tome. (My brother Eric, on a later occasion attended a session of this itinerant 'boarding school' and so benefited from his reading as to astonish his History teachers at George Heriot's with his display of knowledge gained from Mr Fisher, knowledge which indeed helped him to a good pass in Higher History.) The lesson was basically the task of reading sections and in 'prep' time writing an essay. A short dictionary quiz followed, then English – Shakespeare's plays (most welcome). Thence to an uneasy lunch, a compulsory rest in our rooms, an afternoon walk by Loch Lomond and prep. At an even more stressful dinner, Mike 'hinted' that Mr Stewart was 'nibbling like a myxomatosised rabbit'. This fraught evening meal was followed by more prep time before lights out.

As I have said, from primary school in Fraserburgh through to my secondary education, the use of the tawse (a leather strap) on the hands for punishment was accepted as a custom and hazard of school life.

The instrument of chastisement in our mini boarding school, however, was foreign to us: the cane. As part of our role as prefects, Mr Stewart, exhorted by Mike's guardian, instructed us that, for the good of his damaged health and as a deterrent to further impairment, if we caught Mike smoking or drinking or in possession of cigarettes or alcohol, he should be caned:

six strokes. The unpalatable reality is that following these instructions, this is exactly what we did and after the initial grue of distaste, continued to do. My own acquiescence left me uneasy. Someone bending over a chair to receive these strokes of the cane seemed worse than holding out one's hand to receive 'the belt'. That Mike never evinced any grudge about receiving these punishments surprised me at the time.

Years later, I forgave myself a little, or at least understood myself better and by implication a whole generation of German youth, when I heard a story from a wise and beautiful old man, who became for me a guru of sorts.

Mr Kovacs was an Austrian Jew who fled the Nazis and fought for the British in the North African desert in World War II. He was a wise and peaceful man, lauded and revered by successive generations of his pupils in Rudolf Steiner schools. Like these pupils, I became a disciple of his insight and wisdom. I first visited him in the mid-'70s – visits which became Friday evening habits. My girlfriend Barbara McLean had written to him expressing her fascination with a lecture he had given. He invited her to visit him. Her accounts of their talk were so interesting that I asked her if he would invite me as well, and so he did.

The story he told which came to deepen my understanding of myself and others, was this. When the British Army took prisoners during their advance across North Africa, these prisoners were commanded to stand to be counted. According to Mr Kovacs, the German prisoners stood to attention at once, the Italians more randomly, while the North African tribesmen refused. Whereupon, the Sergeant would instruct his men to strike them with the butts of their rifles to make them stand.

Mr Kovacs said that he soon became accustomed to what had initially seemed alien to his nature and upbringing, something repugnant. 'You just get used to it,' he said. The honesty and matter-of-factness of this account by my peaceful and esteemed friend affected me deeply.

Mike's response to Mr Stewart continued to be ingeniously, wittily antagonistic. Our establishment was managed at a distance by letter and telegram with Mike's guardian, a Mr McLeod, his lawyer, Mr Greenlees, and his uncle, R Bracken. I thought Mike must have expressed his dissatisfaction when the bewildered Mr Stewart was peremptorily despatched after only three weeks in post. No doubt he was grateful to be gone. He was supplanted at short notice by the housemaster of an English boarding school familiar with our routine.

During our exercise afternoons, nothing more than a leisurely walk by the side of Loch Lomond, Mike was curious to learn about my life in Edinburgh and my family. Out of the classroom, he was likeable and interesting company, telling us about his visits to his guardian in South Africa... his sick cousin, Jamie... a broken love affair.

Shortly after my return to Edinburgh, a letter arrived from Mr McLeod expressing how much my influence and friendship had benefited Mike:

> When David and Mike began work under Mr Stewart, they became friends at once. David's high spirits, good nature and capacity for friendship won loyalty and respect from Mike. It is because of the increasing value of David's work with Mike that I felt we should agree to assume the financial responsibility for his brother's university education.

He would consequently be grateful if I would return during the next vacation, for which Mr Greenlees had hired Lochnaw Castle in Wigtownshire. Would I also set enquiries afoot to hire two further study companions for Mike, boys who would benefit from additional tuition, holiday employment and the countryside?

I spent two more such periods with Mike, by which time I was studying for an Honours Degree in English at Edinburgh University – and lavishly, excessively enjoying the social side of university life. I had found the vacation period at Lochnaw Castle hugely stressful because of Mike's incessant tutor-baiting and I was reluctant to return when the plea came from Mr McLeod and R Bracken saying how redemptive was my presence. The new location of the 'school' was to be on the island of Scalpay, adjacent to Skye.

My mother, aware of my reluctance and the stress it was causing me, advised me not to go. My father appealed to me to continue the help and friendship I was providing for a distressed and unhappy boy. After all, Mike's people had kindly bought my English course books for me and, helped with my brother's medical course fees. These were clearly kindly people concerned to do the best for their charge.

Reluctantly, and now 'promoted' to assistant tutor, I agreed to go. However, Mike's behaviour towards the tutor followed the familiar pattern of derision and it took only four days before he packed his bags and left. Such was the magic of influence, another tutor appeared, Mr Green, an ex-army chaplain.

I remember with clarity the drama and distress of of what ensued – the collapse of an extraordinary fabrication.

Shortly after his arrival, the new tutor, Mr Green, had sought a private conversation with Mike. Outside, the rain was falling and I felt the isolation of the island. The house was intensely silent. I was sitting nervously smoking in my study when Mr Green knocked on the door. He came in, lips tight. We both sat down. There were no preliminaries.

'This has to stop,' he said. 'Do you know who Mike actually is? He is Lord Brendan Bracken, who was Churchill's wartime Minister of Information. You can imagine the feast the press would make of the set-up here, the nature of the implications they would draw. I've spoken to Lord Bracken and he has, of course, agreed. The matter is at an end.'

Part of me was stunned, part already began to unpeel the cataract of credulity that had let myself, tutors, companions, cooks and housemaids in successive Scottish grand house 'schools' to become part of the masquerade.

Not even the villagers or congregation in churches we had attended had blinked or, whatever they thought, said anything as to the astonishing truth of the identity of 'Mike'.

The multiple identities deployed to authenticate the fantasy were elaborate and skilful. The handwriting of each of the actors in the drama was distinctive: Mike's own a large, open-lettered scrawl; R Bracken's diminutive, tight and neat; Mr Greenlees' signature was an indecipherable squiggle appended to typewritten letters; and Mr McLeod's hand was precise and careful, often appended to a typewritten letter. These epistles, of which I have 34 in my files, had apparently come from different identities and locations: 8 Lord North Street London (R Bracken); Natal (Mr McLeod); Claridges, London and Grand Hotel Roma, and one scrawl from Mike addressed to Ricky (his name for my brother, Eric).

That evening after Mr Green spoke to me, I was bewildered by complex emotions. I sat in my room smoking cigarettes in quantities that made me dizzy and my lungs as raw and rasped as my thoughts. Easy now to see the degree of my myopia but equally the colossal ingenuity directed to the fabrication of this fantasy, the impeccable organisation and the psychology of the multiple personalities, worthy indeed of a man who had served at the right-hand-side of Winston Churchill as his Minister of Information during World War II, orchestrating a brilliant propaganda campaign.

That evening as dark was falling, 'Mike' knocked on my door and suggested we walk in the grounds. The role had been abandoned and yet the man I now knew to be Lord Bracken was not so very different from the person I had known as Mike. He wished me well in my studies and said he would ask his lawyer to set aside sufficient funds to purchase a house for my family. (At the time, we were living in renting accommodation.)

The next morning I packed. Mike was intending to leave after he had seen the household dismantled. When he saw me and two others off in the boat, I couldn't keep tears from my eyes. So strange to have a friend who wasn't who I thought he was. And yet, he was a friend, if we say 'by their fruits shall ye know them'.

What is certain was that at no time was there any suggestion of homosexuality in his relationship with any of us, though there was clearly an element of masochism in the creation of his fantasy world.

To give some idea of his punctilious care and generosity to my family, I quote here from the one letter he wrote and signed, not under the alias 'R Bracken', but as B Bracken:

8 North Lord Street,
Westminster, London SW1
26 August 1957

Dear David,
<u>House Purchase – Educational Arrangements</u>
... A contract is being arranged with a first-rate Insurance Company
to pay the family allowance for seven years as from the opening
of 1957. This will ensure that the allowance will not be subject to
the precariousness of human life and thus enables your family to
be freed from monetary anxiety during the years you are preparing
for and establishing yourself in your profession and your brother
is following the course which will enable him to enter the medical
profession.

This drew a conclusion to the strange drama. True to his word, Brendan
Bracken arranged to gift sufficient money for my mother to buy a semi-
detached stone house in the Braids district of Edinburgh, which delighted
her and relieved her of constant vexing worries about rent. It provided a
home for my ailing father and fees for myself and my brother when we were
studying at Edinburgh University.
    Later in that fateful summer of 1957, I received a letter from Michael
Green, the tutor who had identified Lord Bracken and realised the scandalous
implications of his deception:

Holmside Vicarage
Burnhope, Durham
25 August 1957

Dear Mr Campbell
    ... As far as Scalpay is concerned, I think we can look upon it as a
closed book now. It was an unfortunate experience, especially for you,
but like all experience it was perhaps not without value...
I do suggest that you keep an eye on the papers to see if any 'queer'
advertisements appear. Somehow, I feel it will not be necessary but it's
best to be on the safe side...
        Yours sincerely,
        Michael T Green

A year after this, Brendan Bracken was dead. He died on 8 August 1958,
at the age of 57. Yet I had believed him to be a schoolboy.
    I had not heard from him since our parting on Scalpay, and read of his

death in laudatory obituaries. He was reputedly a mystery man, his origins unclear and aspects of his life kept hidden.

For my part, I am grateful to him and that experience for many reasons, some clear from the above, but also because he bore out my father's edict: 'David, if you knew a person's story, you would not be able to judge them and you might understand them.'

Now, many years later, I see Brendan Bracken as a kind of Prospero, creating, literally, an island exile populated by actors of his casting and following a script of his devising. My own beginnings of an understanding of this complex friend comes, as my father had said, from gleaning something of his story. While he was alive and for a long after his death, I did not choose to talk about the strange circumstances of our acquaintance for fear of marring the reputation of a man of great generosity and kindness who I count as a friend, albeit a complicated one.

Rumoured to be an illegitimate son of Churchill, he was in fact born in 1901 in Tipperary, Ireland, the son of a builder-mason. His father died when he was four and from childhood he was a rebel. His mother found his ungovernable behaviour so distressing that she eventually decided to lodge him with a cousin who was a priest in Australia. There, he was a teenage vagabond, by all accounts hugely articulate and intelligent, an omnivorous reader – and a fantasist.

He returned to England aged 19 and succeeded in enrolling himself at Sedbergh Public School, having persuaded the Headmaster that he was a 15-year-old who had been orphaned when his parents died in a bush fire, and making an impression with his knowledge of History and his hunger to learn.

Winning a History prize and leaving after one term, using his Sedbergh tie equipped him with a new identity: that of a public school boy, a young gentleman. His ability and these credentials presaged an illustrious career. He became a Conservative MP, Editor of the *Financial Times*, ensured the future prosperity of *The Economist* and was Chairman of Sedbergh School and of a large South African mining company, the Union Corporation. He was Churchill's closest friend, confidant, and tireless advocate. Although he was later honoured as First Viscount Bracken, he never took up his seat in the House of Lords.

He ordered his faithful chauffeur to burn all of his papers after his death. He was cremated at Golders Green Crematorium in North London without a service, according to his wishes, and his ashes scattered on the Romney Marshes.

He left not a rack behind.

I suppose the brilliance of how he created his 'boyhood' fantasy, the theatrical extravagance and punctilious attention to detail, appeals to my sense of drama. Winston Churchill's son Randolph in the *Evening Standard* obituary wrote of Brendan Bracken that he was 'Perhaps a genius, an expert in the art of make-believe and fantasy.'

> Our revels now are ended. These our actors,
> As I foretold you, were all spirits, and
> Are melted into air, into thin air:
> And, like the baseless fabric of this vision,
> The cloud-capp'd towers, the gorgeous palaces,
> The solemn temples, the great globe itself,
> Yea, all which it inherit, shall dissolve
> And, like this insubstantial pageant faded,
> Leave not a rack behind. We are such stuff
> As dreams are made on, and our little life
> Is rounded with a sleep.
> (*The Tempest*, Act IV, Scene I, William Shakespeare)

7

To Be Young Was Very Heaven

INEVITABLY, PUBERTY BROUGHT its own pleasures, complications and habits.

My sister inadvertently introduced me to the pleasures of masturbation by pinning on her wall a photo of the iconic Hollywood sex symbol Jane Russell in a tight-fitting striped jersey which, in silhouette, accentuated her proud and tantalising breasts. This kindled in my thighs pleasurable sensations to become the first experiences of the sharp sweet delight of ejaculation, a joy not readily abandoned, so that it became as,

> There was a young woman from Spain
> who liked it now and again.
> Not now and again,
> but now, and again and again and again.

In my teens, in the early '50s, there was a shop in Bread Street which I would guiltily visit to purchase a small black and white publication called, I think, *Focus* by the photographer Howard Marks. This featured splendid nude models who, because of the censorship of the time, had demurely airbrushed pubic hair which for unfathomable reasons was considered lewd. Ironic that our age has ubiquitous pornography with clinically shaved models in poses that convert those of the early '50s into tracts of pre-Fall innocence.

Their discovery by my parents prompted an awkward conversation with my father. In so many ways hugely wise and enlightened, he found this 'talk' as embarrassing as I did. My recollection is that he considered this function to be reserved for the marriage bed. My response was rather akin to that of the wee lad whose mother found him masturbating and warned him that the practice would make him go blind. After a few days of considering this, the young boy said to his mother, 'Can I just do it a wee bit and wear glasses?' Anyhow, the pleasure once discovered was not to be relinquished.

Separate from this solipsistic activity, in the department of my heart was my lifelong tendency to fall in love; even, as I observed earlier, as a five-year-old in Fraserburgh Primary School. At 12, it had been Izzy, and then there was Diana.

I met her at a weekend residential conference of ESCA, Edinburgh Schools Citizenship Association. She was blonde, shapely, cuddly and flatteringly adoring. Returning to Edinburgh we attended dances, films and interscholastic debates together. She became by degrees not so much a companion, as an appendage: where I went, she came. Even when I would, of a Saturday morning, go to Goldenacre Playing Fields to practise my pole vaulting, she would embarrassingly appear to watch, applaud and wait to chum me home.

Diana was warm, kind and pleasant, but also adhesive and stifling. One evening, I knew I had to be free of the constancy of her ubiquitous presence. It was at a dance in the ironically named 'Happy Valley Dance Hall' at Craiglockhart, a popular teenage haunt. There I unhappily but resolutely said we had to part. The cataract of tears and sobbing and pleading did not stop as I walked her the seemingly endless way to her home. As we approached, she appealed for us to try again. My resolution collapsed and I agreed. Walking across the playing fields of Myreside homewards, my heart was stone and I felt defeated.

> He who binds to himself a joy doth the winged life destroy
> but he who kisses the joy as it flies, lives in eternity's sunrise.
> (William Blake)

We did 'try again'. I had, until this point in our relationship, made eloquent and enthusiastic overtures that we should 'make love'. Now, when she agreed, my heart's precocious wisdom counselled me to refuse, and so we didn't. It would have been my first time.

At 17, going on 18, came the lightning of my first profound and deeply romantic love affair.

Saturday nights were an excitement. Public dance halls in Edinburgh were hugely popular in the '50s. We Edinburgh schools' teenagers went to Glendinning's Dance Studio in the douce area of Marchmont. Like the Mardale, where I had learned ballroom dancing – it was a dance school which became a dance hall on Saturday evenings. Here, we danced waltz, quickstep, slow foxtrot, even tango.

It was at Glendinning's that I first met Sandra. Across a crowded room, I saw the turquoise shimmer of her dress. Probably she was not the most beautiful girl there, but 'when the dance ga'ed through the crowded hall / Tho' this was fair and thon was braw,' it was Sandra who had me in thrall. In tune with the marvellous courtesies of the day, when the next dance was announced, I crossed the hall, grey flannels, lovat sports jacket, white shirt and sea blue tie, and formally asked her if she would like to dance. The great thing was that I was a fine dancer and had learned from Miss Cowie at the Mardale School of Ballroom Dancing, and Sandra, too, could dance! We danced and talked: dancing made the sporadic talking easy. I remember the flow, the gliding and the giddy spins – showing off and exhilarated. The dance, the next one asked and accepted and, importantly, the last waltz. This was the beginning of my first big, significant love; a great learning was to come from it. How slowly and innocently it took its way.

At the time, I'd 'got' religion and Sandra was a card-carrying member, like myself, of the Christian Union. I still have a present she gave me, *Daily Light* Bible readings for every day, a pocket-sized green hardback.

Oh, the meetings after school. Walking her to the corner near her home, standing in the cold blasts of an Edinburgh winter, the sky darkening in the late afternoon, and we two fixed to the corner in the grip of east wind and first love.

We were lucky, lucky youngsters. We were both good athletes; both prefects and leading lights in our schools; we both loved literature, drama, poetry. Holding hands was still an excitement, the thrill of a reciprocated squeeze, eloquent. We had plenty to talk about – I wrote poetry; she much admired her English teacher, Mr McEwan. It was the time in the early '50s when the atom bomb threat prompted a poem from me. I read it to her and she took it to Mr McEwan for his approval. I don't remember learning much from this, so his remarks can have been neither painful nor hugely laudatory.

A giant nocturnal mushroom grows
The putty shade of death,
Earth sleeping below
Scarcely a tremor shows
But the deep gloom cast down seems to blot out God's sun.

This is a snatch of what I recall. The poem was later, amongst all my adolescent verse, to be lost in a disturbing way.

From freezing on street corners, we progressed to sitting on the cold doorstep of the ground floor flat where she lived with her mother. There I discovered the joy of breasts. I find the word 'breasts' always reminds me of the Glasgow lassie in the back row of the cinema with her 'lumber'. When his hand began to explore her thighs she at once admonished, 'Hey, hey, etiquette, etiquette! Tits first.'

Anyhow, from the cold doorstep I was invited into the drawing room to talk with Sandra's cosy mother, who would retire to bed and leave us by the fireside, where we inevitably, by slow degrees, progressed downward from the delight of the breasts. In these days – how the world changes – schoolgirls wore firmly elasticated regulation navy blue sturdy knickers, a formidable obstacle, but where there is a mutual will, there's a way. As the old-fashioned knickers said to the modern panties, 'Well, me girl, I've had me ups and downs, but I've never been pushed aside.'

Despite our qualms of guilt, set against the pulpit of the Presbyterian Church, we joyfully consummated our love in the fire-lit drawing room. Perhaps the frisson of the forbidden lent a sharper sweetness to our union.

Nevertheless, the whisper of guilt was ever-present and when, one day, Sandra's visiting brother-in-law came unannounced into the room to retrieve his cigarettes, caught *in flagrante delicto*, we leapt like scalded cats asunder and fretted nervously in case he should inform her mother, which he never did.

The other predictable scare was a late period, which temporarily persuaded us to 'tread the straight and narrow,' a resolution unpalatable to our glands and hearts. Yet this jolt was sufficient to compel us to resolve, like Holy Willie to pray:

> O may it ne'er be a living plague to my dishonour
> And I'll ne'er lift a lawless leg again upon her.'

How mores, manners, morality and behaviours have changed since those days, with the arrival of the contraceptive pill and radically changed attitudes! As we approached the '60s, the times already were a'changing. The idyll of our romance did not last.

Sandra was completing her sixth year at school, where she had become School Captain, and I was now at Edinburgh University studying English Literature, Moral Philosophy and British History. One bright sunny afternoon I decided to do my history exam revision in the back green of our family ground floor flat in Morningside Road. As I was reading, a black and white photograph fluttered down from above and rested beside me on the lawn. It was of an attractive young woman in a summer dress. Looking up I saw that the window above me was ajar and occupied by a black cat which I, naively, assumed had dislodged the photo.

It was no hardship to abandon my studies to take the photo to the door of the flat of my upstairs neighbour. It was she who answered my ring – Rose McLenaghan, an enterprising and mischievous young Irish nurse.

That I passed my History exam by the barest of margins was undoubtedly attributable to this meeting, as was the beginning of the crack in my relationship with Sandra. After that first meeting with Rose, I would leave my house in the morning, bidding my parents a habitual farewell, and instead of making my way to university, climb the next-door stairs to Rose's arms and bed. There, we would spend the entire day in making love with brief intermissions – the wonder of youth's appetite! I would leave her flat around teatime and return from my enlightening and exhausting day's education replete and with a headache, and no further knowledge of history.

Given my nature and convictions of the time, without the extravagant detail, I told Sandra of this liaison with Rose. I was still very much in love with Sandra and assured her so, and we continued it seemed much as before, but...

My escapades with Rose continued only briefly. She was as feisty as she was passionate and made it clear that I was giving her insufficient time and attention, and so that joyful interlude concluded as rapidly as it began, leaving delicious memories of initiation, excess, mischief, fun and exhaustion.

I think Sandra and I, at that time sharing the idea of Christian love, its sense of universality, inclusiveness and forgiveness, were both to encounter challenges to these precepts. My meeting with Rose was one such challenge. I was to encounter another.

During my first year at university, I also spent my final fraught vacation periods employed as a tutor in the fantasy private 'Boarding School' I described earlier. While I was thus employed, Sandra and I faithfully exchanged letters. In one of these she described how, through the church, she had befriended a young Malaysian student, Teh Uwa.

When she met me off the train at the then Caledonian Station at the west end of Princes Street, I failed at first to notice her reserve, but when I suggested we meet next day, she informed me that she had arranged to see her new friend, Teh. A dunt! However, imbued with the ideal of amor vincit omnia, I accepted the change and over the next few weeks Sandra shared her time with me and Teh.

Then, a pivotal evening. A mutual university friend, Paul Martin, a splendidly idle American Fulbright-funded ex-serviceman, whose main university study was keeping a coffee table in the Common Room free for his pals, was having a party. Sandra and I were invited. She was to arrive later, as she was to watch Teh playing squash in Glasgow. Meanwhile, I was to make a life-changing discovery at this party.

In these fresh days, I neither drank nor smoked, being devoted to my career as a pole vaulter in the university athletics team. Someone at the party assured me that cider was non-alcoholic and very soon I was euphoric, much I suppose as Gourlay's son was through alcohol in *The House with the Green Shutters*. My imagination was an eloquent butterfly, capturing a fascinated audience to a colourful tale, some of it even told in spontaneously rhyming couplets. This was a road of no return and before the evening was out, the drama was to take a darker turn.

Later I found myself sitting alone in the kitchen with a sharp carving knife in my right hand. My left hand was clenched with the thumb pointing vertically upwards while my right hand whistled repeatedly towards it as if to decapitate a prisoner. At the last instant the thumb would descend and dodge rapidly and so avoid being slashed and severed. At this moment, Sandra appeared. In vino veritas. The noble ideals collapsed before the hurt heart. With each sweep and dodge of the knife, I told her it was over. Not her tears, nor mine, changed the rhythm of this sad conclusion, exposing the underlying heart's truth and pain.

I recall little else of the evening, except that I was violently sick. Paul got me a black coffee and somehow, I made my way home, late and bereft. Both of us grieved as one can only grieve the loss of first love with its sweet, slow journey of companionship and initiation.

While I had been with Sandra, I was a fervent evangelist, a 'leading light' in the Youth Fellowship of North Mayfield Church. No Paul on the road to Damascus was more fervent than I. But the sense of guilt attached to the sin of pre-marital sex was an increasing vexation.

The occasion that Sandra and I broke up coincided with my accidentally discovering the joys and in vino veritas effects of alcohol. Thus, my Christian conviction that amor vincit omnia dissolved when alcohol spoke the truth. It was an end and a beginning. I now revelled in the endless student parties and dances, the various attractions of the Common Room: engaging women, jazz sessions and the frisson of playing poker, albeit for small stakes.

I had to make a ritual farewell to Jesus. One evening, boldly drunk, I decided to visit the minister of my church to announce my renunciation and my Devil's-disciple lifestyle. I rang his bell, clearly not sober. He invited me in, courteously informing me that he could offer me tea or coffee but, whimsically, not more of what I had already been imbibing. When I lucidly recounted my exploits gambling, roving and drinking, he matter-of-factly observed, 'You haven't yet aspired to spiritual pride in your catalogue of sins.'

The minister, James White, subsequently Moderator of the Church of Scotland, was a wise and good man. It was not till I later discovered Buddhism that this hiatus in my spiritual voyage continued.

Meantime, ironically, my next girlfriend was an American from Florida, a convinced Roman Catholic Christian with an iron-clad chastity belt which no key of my eloquence could unlock.

8

Varsity Meetings and Matings

SPONTANEOUS COMBUSTION. IT is strange but certain that something akin to joyful recognition characterises our first meeting with some people. It is a mystery to accept, celebrate and not bother to question. Such a meeting I had with Mick Ridings. I was the first person he encountered as he arrived at Edinburgh University as a student from Yorkshire, and the recognition and pleasure was immediate with him, as with me.

We met in the Common Room of the Old Quadrangle, the meeting place for Arts students to drink coffee, make assignations, dodge classes, talk – casually, politically or culturally – listen to Johnny Winter's jazz band on a Friday afternoon and attend Friday evening dances with a band and a bar. It was a cornucopia of student delights. To me at the time, 'to be alive was very heaven'.

In this heady environment, Mick and I met and began a lifelong friendship, a friendship which was to have extreme consequences for Mick but in these first heady days, we were drunk with excitement, with the shared joy of friends, dazzling young women, literature, theatre and the dizzy frequency of parties and beautiful Edinburgh.

Mick lived in a flat in Circus Place, in the New Town, which he shared with three other male students – two Americans and an English medical student. More significantly for me as it turned out, four female students lived in the flat below.

My involvement with Valerie, an attractive, warm, willing and knowing Yorkshire girl, had two particularly regrettable consequences. The first was that as a devoted idealistic athlete, whose father's cousin was the legendary Eric Liddell who famously would not run in the Olympic Games on a Sunday, I foolishly followed Valerie's encouragement and started smoking. As my lungs were already weakened by a prolonged bout of pneumonia, described earlier, this led to sporadic chest infections and a phlegmatic cough that has never left me.

The second was that I was pole vaulting for the Scottish student team at a student games held in Hull which was the home town of Valerie, so she invited me to stay with her folks during the course of the games while the rest of the team lodged in a hotel. Her father was a genial but suspicious man, rightly surmising that his daughter was no better than she should be. Her mother was a nosy evangelist.

When I returned to Edinburgh I phoned Valerie to ask her to bring back or send my notebook containing the poems I had written since my early teens. There was a thundering silence: 'My mother burned it.'

This was an emotional record of my teens in ashes. The poems, or verses, were of no great literary quality, but they were a diary of my adolescence. They included, odd for me to think of it now, an anthem I'd written for the Coronation of Queen Elizabeth. This had been set to music by our talented and temperamental Heriot's Music Master, Percy Smith, and sung in the Usher Hall by the whole school choir at the annual concert. It was in itself nothing shattering and carried sentiments that now would make me cringe, but it was me, then.

The notebook also included simple nature poems, a first naive love poem, 'To Isobel', and subsequent effusions for other young ladies. I suppose, perusing these along with some innocent compliments to the attributes of her lovely daughter, compelled the perfervid evangelist to condemn the book to the flames.

That, for a while, stopped my poetry. Odd though it may seem, the book gone, I felt I had nowhere to put a new poem.

One extravagant jaunt with Mick remains a vivid memory. So extravagant and unlikely was this, that Mick's family did not believe it had happened until, when years later he and I were reminiscing, I corroborated his version of our student daftness.

Drinking in the Golf Tavern by the Meadows one evening, we fell in with a loquacious old salt who invited us to join him on his ship, which was berthed in Leith Docks. Intrigued by the invitation, we rolled down to the docks and climbed a long rope ladder to the lofty deck, from whence we descended deep down to his cabin which, unbelievably, had a vociferous parrot occupant. His tales needed to be taken with salt, and were accompanied by glasses of rum, but we were both credulous, wide-eyed and captivated. One of his yarns involved his visit to a South American land where the local delicacy was the thighs of a virgin!

In the early morning, I decided to make my way precariously down the ladder and take the long walk home. Mick, however, awoke to the throb, throb, throbbing of the ship's engine, a reluctant stowaway and it was a week before he made his way back to Edinburgh – from Denmark.

Mick and I met up with two bosom pals, Alison Drever and Anne Dunlop, meetings with dramatic different consequences. I was hugely fortunate to fall in with, and fall in love with, Alison, when I was in my third year, she in her first. She was sunny, clever, agile and swift to learn jive. I was an expert, having taught jive at Mardale, and she a more than apt pupil. We were athletic and flamboyant, executing whirls and throws and dazzling sequences in the Empire, now the Festival Theatre, at Varsity Vanities. In an unconscious joy, we would spin on the dance floor, frequently gathering a circle around us to watch.

Meantime, I was finding the English Department lecturers, apart from one or two exceptions, a desiccated crew, particularly Professor Renwick, Head of the English Literature Department, who entered the crowded first year class, glanced at no one, read notes I imagined to be crumbling with the dust of ages, and then left.

Belonging to the arid crew like an anachronism was Doctor A Melville Clark. He was a nice man, spruce, pedantic and Presbyterianly moral.

For fun and to keep awake, I'd synchronously translated his lectures on 18th century literature into rhyme:

The Spectator

Volume after volume came
For Addison a lucrative game
In number ten, I note for a lark
Is highly regarded by A Melville Clark.
Ah Melville Clark what makes you thus dilate
In simple pomp as empty as your Pate
Lists and catalogues, diverse and sundry
And useful as a list of laundry.
So fresh and lively is your metaphor
That where could such be met before
Except when primal man first spoke
And even then so trite, used but as a joke
But sure no man has genius more
In saying worse what oft was said before.
Your head contains an epic catalogue
Of common places which must set agog
To see a mind so plunder bent
On clichés, hackneyed phrases, all that's old
Or long decayed and crusted o'er with mould.

Expecting largesse and high ideals, I was further disillusioned when Professor Renwick found a pretext to extract Alison from a part she had in the departmental play in which I was performing. I took this to be the result of his friendship with her father, the Dean, who disapproved of me.

Another struggle for me was Old English. It was in that class that I met and got to know George Mackay Brown, who was devoted to Anglo-Saxon grammar and poetry; *Beowulf, The Dream of the Rood, The Battle of Maldon* and such, which were all great trials to me.

George would say, 'Well, you see, David, I always like to get to the roots of things.' He was very shy and hovered at first on the periphery of the coterie of poets who frequented Milne's Bar, a gathering celebrated in Sandy Moffat's painting of the group. George would say, 'The menu in Milne's was very limited but very nice, pies and beans, half pie and beans, half pie and peas' and so on.

At any rate, it was Alison, not the English Department, who introduced me to the exuberance and lyricism of Dylan Thomas. In my later career as teacher and storyteller, these entered my lessons and performances. Heriot's had failed to inform me that Higher Latin was a requisite to enter the Honours year in English Literature. Alison tutored me in my late and laborious attention to this deficiency and enabled me to pass while I was midway through the English Literature course.

When my two chums in the English Department, Alastair Walker, Bill Stirling, and myself got the results of the 'Finals', we were all pleased to have an Upper Second, there being but one elusive 'First' in our year. Bill Stirling suggested that we invite three unattached girls from our class to the Graduation Ball and I felt it churlish to refuse. Of course, Alison was deeply hurt and I still have a guilty regret when I remember her. Now and then, that betrayal still visits me.

I do not recall how my relationship with Alison ended but I suppose it can be no credit to me. She met up with a scholarly American and lives in the States.

Alison's big pal was Anne Dunlop and that is how Mick, Anne, myself and Alison came to be an adventurous foursome. Mick used to impress me even then with his wide knowledge of contemporary theatre. He was an avid reader of *The Observer* and *The Times* and the reviews of Kenneth Tynan and Harold Hobson. So theatre visits were a huge excitement, as was the Edinburgh Fringe and International Festival. This enthusiasm was to give both of us pleasurable work later. Mick was to gain the title of 'Mr Edinburgh Theatre' when he gave talks to devoted groups of followers, previewing productions at the Lyceum. When I filled in for Mick on one occasion, it was clear that the class adored their 'Mr Edinburgh Theatre'. I gave classes in Contemporary Drama for Edinburgh University Extramural Department. Both Mick and I would take our students for a drink and spend more in the pub than we earned from the classes, but the friendships formed and the talk were more than commensurate.

The consequence of Mick's meeting Anne was that they married, but Anne's tendency to be suspicious of any of Mick's friends became an obsessive and clinical condition of unfounded jealousy, to which Mick became a victim, a prisoner, the condition culminating in her refusal to let him touch their baby boy whom she kidnapped so that Mick had no contact with him till the boy was in his 30s.

After our university days, Mick and I met only sporadically until we were to catch up later in our lives.

Mick's second marriage ended in heart-wrenching betrayal, delivered in a stunning blow where the door of his house was locked against him and his money gone.

Desolate in a rented room, he had a heart attack, the first of a succession. I knew of this only in retrospect, but as in the fairy tale, at the lowest ebb when the protagonist is washed up on the shore, the helper comes. When I caught up with Mick after a hiatus, he had met and married Jane; they were ideally suited, sharing amongst other things a deep love of theatre and literature, and offering a mutual healing and haven of loving companionship. Jane was a balm for Mick's hurt heart. She, like Mick, was immediately attractive, warm and welcoming.

In the days when Mick's heart was weakening, they were less able to make the theatre excursions that were their joy. In these days I visited them in their Marchmont flat. As Mick's health declined, they came to see a performance I was giving about Dylan Thomas, a poet Mick and I loved. His response was suffused with warmth and light. The flame of the combustion of our first meeting was burning strong and, not surprisingly, I found when visiting him in a care home in Leith where he died that all the carers loved my old shipmate:

Shipmates
For Mick

Do you remember?
how can you forget?
The Long John Silver evening,
you and I, innocent roisterers
meeting the old salt
whose tales needed a pinch.
And sailing forth with him
clambering who knows how
up the drunken high rope ladder
to his lofty ship.
Then sinking down, down, down
to his cabin den,
drinking more than was more
than sense.
And awed when a real parrot
sat on his shoulder
and he widened our eyes
with the tale of tastiest flesh,

virgin's thighs from a jungle tribe
in South America.
Then rescued by some buoy
of sense I somehow
who knows how
ascended from the depths
descended the ladder to the pier
and somehow
got home
while you, Ancient Marinered
fell under his spell
and out of consciousness.
Wakened to the throb, throb, throb
of the ship's engine,
and you at sea indeed
returning a week later
from Denmark.
Do you remember?
How would you forget?

9

The Tin Room

MY PRE-FINALS TERMS at university were occupied by constant study: mornings in the library, brief coffee break, library, snatched lunch, library, home, endless coffees and reading till midnight. Only Friday and Saturday evenings were dancing and party time; the rest of the weekend, work. I was living at home and had a secluded room at the top of the house for a study.

Things at home were vexing. My father's arthritis had become more painful and limiting, which for a man who had prized his agility and capacity to run even in his late '60s, was distressing.

Prompted by his belief in spiritualism, he and my mother had made a trip to see the faith healer, Harry Edwards in the south of England. He returned eased from pain and with a renewed capacity to walk freely. Unfortunately, after several months, this remarkable effect wore off.

Now the rheumatoid arthritis so painfully inflamed his joints that he was largely bedridden and in constant pain. In evening study breaks, I would visit him in his bedroom downstairs. He had a lively mind, acute and clear thinking, reflected in the clarity of his hazel eyes. These were mutually engaging breaks.

To alleviate the severe pain of his condition, my father was prescribed an opium substitute, pethidine. In retrospect it seems unwise that he administered these pills himself. In a semi-sedated state he took an overdose and passed into a coma, with sad consequences when he recovered consciousness.

Unaware of this, I visited him one evening as usual for our habitual chat. With tears, and in obvious distress, he looked me in the eye and said, 'David, David, how could you stand by and let these men treat your mother like that? David!' and he sobbed uncontrollably.

To hear these words from the father who had taught me so much, witness the distress speak in the face I knew so well, was bewildering and, at that moment, incomprehensible. It was to see a whole fabric of my life collapse. It was to stand behind a glass wall, incapable of helping, incapable of reaching through. These fearful hallucinations would come and go, but their onset meant that my mother could no longer cope, and our doctor, hopefully at first, to give her respite, had my father admitted to a ward in the Royal Edinburgh Hospital in Morningside.

It was there, on a radiantly sunny day, the day I graduated from university, that I visited him. Fresh from a graduation photo session, I was gowned and carried the precious scroll in a red tube container. Through several locked doors, attendants conducted me to his ward. He was sitting in bed and his face lit with the brightness and clarity I knew so well, when I appeared. He was the proud father and I was the son proud to make him happy, and grateful in a way no words could say then, or ever. It was as good a visit as the circumstances made possible.

With the vividness of slow motion, I recall that as I walked in the sun along the gardened row of houses on the way to meet my family and girlfriend Alison for a graduation lunch, as if a hand held my shoulder, I stopped. Into my mind there came a voice, 'You are never going to see your father again!' It was so strong and clear that I could not move. Physically, my father, apart from the arthritis, looked healthy and well-taken-care-of. And then I thought, even if this premonition is true, what can I gain by returning, and anyhow... so I joined my mother, brother, sister, brother-in-law and my girlfriend Alison, for lunch in the Wee Windaes on the High Street.

On this particular summer vacation, I worked in a place called Culty-braggan in Perthshire, said by some to be one of the last outposts of the Romans, the site of Mons Graupius, a battle between the Picts and the Romans recorded by the historian Tacitus. During the Second World War, it was named POW Camp No. 21, built to house 4,000 prisoners categorised as the most fanatical Nazi supporters. We were employed by the NAAFI to feed between 1,500 and 2,000 cadets. We students were kitchen wallahs, humble unqualified kitchen workers.

The hours were long, the tasks menial and there was a definite hierarchy. The least desirable task was working in the 'tin room', where two rather troll-like men, whom we pitied, scoured remnants of bacon, bangers, porridge and custard from vast pots, pans and vessels. In two huge deep sinks they laboured in a steamy scullery adjoining the main kitchen. Strangely, one of the top jobs was the tattie peeling. This simply involved choosing potatoes of similar sizes, emptying them into the top of a machine, replacing the lid, switching on a button and the potatoes were rumbled round a metal drum. When you judged they were scraped, you opened a hatch and out they flew, white and clean. While the process was taking place you could nip out the back door and have a smoke.

I made a great friend during this time, a man named Bob Paton. He was 54 and had been a translator in Belgium until his wife left him, taking everything with her. It was a mystery why she should have left this urbane, amiable and fun companion. However, that was a subject we did not pursue. One day, in a sneaky smoke break outside the hut, he was telling me the story of his marriage. I was so engrossed that when I returned to the potato machine, it spat out its large potatoes the size of pan drops. I almost lost my easy job over this.

Simultaneously, the two tin room trolls took ill and who should be sentenced to take their place but my friend Bob and myself. I learned something wonderful one day. I was cleaning parts of the mincing machine over the waste bin filled with the grease, beans, eggs, porridge of the day – a sludgy swill – when the metal component of the machine fell into the bin.

With a childlike naivety, I said to Bob, 'We'll need to get another part.' His face told me the absurdity of my conclusion. So, I stripped off my shirt and began to grope down through the greasy swill. As I descended further and further, Bob was overtaken with mirth. Then I realised that once you are in, you are in, and grease and beans are just grease and beans. And so as my fingers found the object, my chin almost on the surface of the grease, I continued as if in a desperate foray for the lost part so that Bob ultimately was lying on the floor, howling with uncontrollable laughter. Tom Sawyer style, I had turned toil to the coinage of fun.

Long hours as we worked through the day in that camp, as many hours did we drink and frolic in the night, occupying the hayloft of a farm's barn outside the grounds of the camp. There, Stuart MacGregor, a former schoolmate who was to play an important part in my life, used to join us with his guitar, singing folk songs.

At Cultybraggan we male students occupied a wartime Nissen hut adjacent to one for the female students and some young local female workers. We worked hard and played hard, full of capers and high spirits. On one occasion, answering a challenge, I raced naked round the women's hut to shrieks of horror... or was it delight? An early 'streaking' adventure that presaged later capers.

One evening, we all walked the mile or so to Comrie Village Hall – to the weekend dance. Interrupting the dancing, an announcement invited David Campbell to come to the front door. My father was dead. I did not want to hear it. Several folk offered to walk me back to the camp. I took Margaret's offer. She and I had become close. She was at teacher training college.

When we returned to the camp, it was an evening of bright moonlight. The Nissen huts were constructed in two parts, with a brick wall between. The larger part housed our gang of students, the smaller part, which originally billeted the two sergeants, was unoccupied. It was to this part we retired.

This night is clear in my memory. We lay in the bed together and the moonshine glistened through the glazed glass window above us. As we lay there quiet, I silently said to my father, 'Dad, I don't know if you will understand this. I am not going to think of your death now. I am going to be here with Margaret.'

There were very few people at the crematorium for my father's funeral. He was not a Christian, but lived by deep spiritual convictions that made a beautiful man. My mother had seen him in good physical health shortly before she was informed that he had died. She was convinced that one of the patients, a big man who alarmed my father, had killed him. Her thoughts were that the consequences of pursuing and investigating the matter would only extend the pain of his death. In those days, people were not infected by the disease caught from America of litigation and the notion that compensatory money is any substitute for the loss of a loved one.

10

Highland Frolics

RONNIE WOOD, A friend of my brother from school days at Heriot's, was a regular visitor of our family and asserted that our dad was the first adult to listen to him and gain his confidence. His own dad was difficult and critical. Ron became a big pal of mine, being more a gallivanting spirit than my brother Eric, and so it was that together in the early '60s we planned a Highland jaunt in my ancient Morris 8, bought second-hand in pre-MOT days for £50. Now it would have failed the test on many counts.

In the friendly vehicle, we arrived at Newtonmore, fortuitously on the night of a dance in the local hall. With the traditional half bottle of whisky tucked in a pocket, we arrived in the hall where a small local band was warming up and the dancers gathering, women against one wall, men against the other.

In high spirits, dauntless and inventive (I was later reminded by Maureen who was to become a golden thread in my life), I exuberantly organised a spontaneous dance, possibly a social mixer I'd learned from my teacher Doris Cowie in my ballroom dancing days. Soon my eye and fancy were caught by Maureen McKenzie, whom I'd first seen in the university library. There, her eye had also fallen upon me!

'The nicht drave wi' sangs and clatter,' and Ron fell in happily with Maureen's friend from the Hebrides, Kenina.

Ron and I had pitched our ancient canvas tent in a field on the outskirts of town. To this cosy nest we invited Maureen and Kenina, the pleasure of the night recalled for me by waking with the dew and the sun, and a joy-flushed dawn photograph of myself and Maureen, taken outside the tent before she and Kenina departed for their early holiday job at the Richmond Hotel.

This was the beginning of a great lifetime love and friendship of two mischievously consanguineous spirits!

After this Highland meeting, we were both fully occupied with our own lives, she with her boyfriends, I with my girlfriends, but this did not preclude occasional rendezvous and later zany role-playing evenings with my friend Gordon and his girlfriend Beth.

One hiatus in our meetings was when Maureen and her husband Alan spent some years in Australia. When they returned, Alan helped as accountant in our Fort Knox enterprise. By 1972, my marriage to Ina, and Maureen's to Alan, had come to an end.

A spontaneous, clattering kiss in my photographic darkroom during a wild Hogmanay party in 1980 reignited a new phase in our relationship.

Her son, Lindsay, was nine and I introduced him and Maureen to mountain climbing and camping in the beautiful Glen Etive. By a little pool, he swam and gloried in having his own tent. Sure-footed and fearless, he scrambled up the narrow sharp peaks of the Aonach Eagach Ridge, Glencoe. But my most vivid memory of Lindsay is of a walk along the River Etive. It is a memory of the purest and most beautiful sound I ever heard.

One early summer's evening, he was running along the course of the river in front of us, disappearing round bends, when the air was split by an indescribable, wild, high-pitched scream.

The Boy

Buachaille Etive Mòr,
The great Shepherd of Etive
Crouches and humps above his glen
Rock flanks glistening in the sun
An ageless guardian
We follow the river's
Meandering
Ahead the boy moves
With its moods,
Listening to water
Saunter, slouch, scamper, skip
And he vanishes around
A bend
The air is hushed a moment
Then
A shrill wild cry
Splits silence open
And we come upon
A statue child
Arms high and eyes
On fire
Agaze in wonderment
At where
A diamond avalanche
Plummets down
Into a pool of seamless black
And nine years of wonder
Makes awe a sound
A rapture
And the whole glen sings.

The darkest chapter was when Lindsay, as a handsome young man, part-time fashion model, from experimenting with LSD became schizophrenic and haunted. His demons were so clamorous and insistent that not all his courageous efforts, not the love of his mother, the support of friends or the psychiatric care he received, could silence the torment. One day he walked into the River Forth and drowned.

Maureen asked me to conduct his funeral service. I'd known Lindsay from his childhood. Together we'd played and explored, and as he grew older, laughed and talked. I'd also seen at close quarters his struggle, his pain and his courage. I realised that if I were to conduct the service without breaking into tears, I had one overriding task and that was to celebrate – celebrate Lindsay and all his beauty and qualities. That conviction and love carried me successfully through the ceremony. Doing it for Lindsay and Maureen and putting all else from my mind.

And now, as I look back 60 years from that sun-flushed beginning of a lifelong love and friendship through the vicissitudes of our lives, mischievous intrigues, adrenalin-spiced clandestine assignations, challenges of emotional and physical mountains, we find, however long the interval, we meet as if it were yesterday.

The Why and How of Faces

When you meet a face that
your soul recognises,
for God's sake, say 'Hello'.
For whatever reasons that
your education cannot explain,
or understand,
in that face is written
a tomorrow for
your life's story,
And for the story of the one
behind the face.
Be pleasantly, simply bold. Say 'Hello'.
The rest will follow.

(David Campbell)

11

The Tug of Curiosity

AFTER COMPLETING MY Honours English degree, having abandoned my intention to become ordained as minister in the Church of Scotland, I took a shortened two-term course at Moray House in Edinburgh. Moray House was a dreary teacher training college, its lecturers, with rare exceptions, pretentious. All my friends from that course found themselves teaching posts in comprehensive schools; this was the educational egalitarian trend of the time. Fecklessly, I had failed to apply for a post.

It was then that Bob, my tin room companion at Cultybraggan, set my life on a different course. We were accustomed to meet in Edinburgh for a drink and he invited me to give ballroom dance classes in the East Lothian village of Pencaitland where he lived, so we met at least weekly.

One day he informed me that there was a position for an English teacher at his old school, Melville College. That was a small private boys' fee-paying school where the pupils' uniform was pillar-box red. He was fulsome in encouraging me to apply.

A week later, when he came to my house and discovered that I had done nothing, he supplied me with the advertisement for the post and information about the school, and chid me on my lack of resolve. And so I applied for this job in a school for the privileged and well-off while all my pals were already employed in comprehensive state schools. I applied and, largely because of my sporting credentials, impressed the moody headmaster and was appointed. I wonder what my father would have said, a man who had inculcated in me the ideals of socialism? But I had valuable lessons to learn and saw at first hand the poverty of the rich and the unenlightened attitude of not all, but several of the staff.

I was still living at home and on more than one occasion, expressed to my mother the certainty that I was going to be sacked. I was expected, like the rest of the able-bodied male staff, to assist in the rugby training afternoons. On one such icy cold afternoon, a burly Maths teacher drew aside a slender boy, who happened to be a fine sprinter in the athletics team I had formed, surrounded him with the rest of the team and roundly condemned him for being 'yellow and gutless' for avoiding tackling a giant running at speed. I fully believed that this master was going to hit me when I articulated the injustice, and lack of understanding in his damaging and bullying behaviour. Not for the first time, the matter came to the attention of the headmaster. Some pupils were boarders and their loneliness, sadness and victimisation by some of the prefects was all too evident.

When I look back now on my life of 80-plus years, I see certain constants. One is that whatever the logic, I have always acted upon inner promptings. At certain stages has come the clear conviction: time to change, time to leave, time to give this up. So it was that after four years' teaching, I knew it was the time to leave Melville College and go to Germany.

My mother, of course, was distressed by the prospect but I needed to know what Germany and the Germans were really like. At this distance, that may seem immature and unnecessary but then, less than a decade after the war, it was different.

I applied for two posts, one in a High School near Hamburg and one as an assistant in the English Department in the University of Heidelberg. The latter felt the more enticing – the romantic setting, the history, the attractive young students. It chanced I was made an offer by both, but as I had sent an acceptance to Die Halepaghen Schule in Buxtehude, a small town near Hamburg, I honoured that when my invitation later came from Heidelberg. The road not taken.

And so, I prepared to leave family, friends and my dizzy Edinburgh life. During the Melville College, Jekyll & Hyde years, I was by day a highly charged devoted teacher, by night a rambling explorer of the pleasures of the town. With Gordon Allan, my carousing friend and companion of the time, I would go drinking, hunting, dancing and sharing the intoxication of poetry. I carried copies of Allen Ginsberg's *Howl* and collections by Charles Causley and Robert Service, bought from Jim Haynes' famous George Square bookshop. In Ancient Mariner mode, these I would spontaneously read to the sometimes surprised but surprisingly attentive pub- or party-goers.

Drink and high spirits, good company and fearless imaginations made fizzy champagne. Gordon and I both loved free dancing and with the right music we would rove the floor, each weaving his way in and out and around couples dancing more conventionally together. Ours was an uninhibited, playful, chasing, hunting, probably to bystanders rampant exhibitionism, but for us a game.

We were good at games. On one typical evening of fantasy and fun, myself and Maureen met up with Gordon and his chirpy girlfriend, Beth. Gordon's greetings were always more than effusive. He and Beth arrived at Milton House Hotel where we had agreed to rendezvous. With his usual prelude, he clasped Maureen wordily with warm hand-fondling poems of praise of her beauty, protestations of love, beseeching for counter-protestations and finally, 'Hello, dad,' to me. Maureen responded to all this with reciprocal charm. I have found that most people have resources of imagination, mischief and nonsense if they are assumed to have these characteristics. And so it was.

We sat outside the hotel on a terracing that looked over fields to the hills beyond the River Forth. With no prelude or introduction, we talked nonsense. Frodgedobolum was a giant. We spoke his language, big, bulbous, vowelly, full of softened bubbly plosives and syrupy labials. We made amorous conversation as cows, hens and cats. In another role, Maureen became a sleazy, downtown New York hardened, money-earning, good-time, knowing-where-she-was-going, taking men for a ride, gal. She met me, an innocent abroad, fresh from the provinces, eager for big town fun but daunted and overcome by the bold, assertive sexuality of women who called the shallow bluff of my veneer of cockiness and left me timidly retracting with excuses, objects of this new Maureen's contempt and derision.

Later in our role-playing fun when she was a pert office girl on a night out, she was horrified by my transformation into a dribbling senile, lustful, persistent and amazingly nimble reprobate bent on no good. We danced chasing and hunting dances. Immaculate Frank Sinatra young man with coy, but in the end winnable young lady dances, Latin, Ballroom, jive, close, apart, talkative, friendly loving dances and suddenly it was time to go to the empty flat of Gordon's unwittingly hospitable granny where, in a clutter of chairs, old magazines and hurriedly cleaned cups and glasses, we sat in the kitchen, drank whisky, read Robert Service, DH Lawrence, modern poets, Leo Aylen, Gregory Corso, Lawrence Ferlinghetti, nonsense poems. In the end, replete with words, we left Gordon and Beth, and sofa'd into a warm snuggle to find our delight in one another was mutual.

Once upon an early evening, with eyes ever alert for a beauty, Gordon and I were sitting, not as habitually in Deacon Brodie's bar, but in a café in Forrest Road, when across the crowded room we saw two attractive young Danes. With what spontaneous ingenuity I came to their table and engaged their interest I can't recall, but Friday was Ina's birthday and they would love to accompany us to the dance at King's Buildings. Little did I anticipate that Ina was to become my first wife.

It was certainly attraction at first sight and fascination at our second meeting at the dance at King's Buildings. She was 20 that day. Her fluency and command of English astonished me, her sense of vivacity, mischief and fun enchanted me. We glided and whirled on the dance floor. Ina was slim, tall, lithe, with a puckish beauty. 'Oh yes, it's me and I'm in love again,' goes the apt response of the pop song.

Ina was the au pair for a family with a stone-built house at the top of a road leading to the Braid Hills. I had borrowed my brother's tiny antiquated blue Austin 7 for the occasion of our second date. I rolled up to the front of the house, got out and crossed the garden path towards the door. Ina's ground floor room faced me and through the window I saw her, affecting to be unaware of my arrival, uncross her long shapely legs to adjust her skirt. Sweet wiles.

We took a little sightseeing jaunt in this already obsolete but charming little vehicle and I introduced Ina to the cuisine in Khushi's, my favourite Indian restaurant, in Lothian Street. At the close of the evening I drove her home. As we sat together in the close proximity of the front seats, the moment imperatively announced itself that it was time to kiss. I leaned eagerly towards her and was surely about to consummate this moment, when I was jerked backwards. The belt of my coat was trapped in the door. When Ina realised this, her laughter was a burst of champagne bubbles – laughter which quelled my discomfiture.

My mother, brother and sister loved Ina, who became a frequent visitor to our house. My father would have adored her. When she returned to Denmark some months later, we engaged in a lively and witty correspondence, her English facility always surprising and delighting, as was her imagination.

Meantime, my life in Edinburgh continued with jaunts into town with Gordon, teaching at Melville College, drinking with my gruff old philosophic fellow teacher Jimmy Doyle and living comfortably at home with my mother and brother Eric.

That home comfort was disturbed by the deep concern my mother and I shared about Eric's mental state. Several factors conspired to induce severe agoraphobia: he broke up with his girlfriend, the church persuaded him to support an unstable student who demeaned, diminished and derided him, and the dissecting rooms at university induced nausea and faintness. He would leave our house only to walk the short distance to the golf course and back.

My concern prompted me to ask the Fife Director of Education, whom I knew, if there were any temporary teaching jobs. Thanks to his sympathy and the shortage of teachers at the time, he arranged a post at Crossgates School.

Crossgates turned out to be a significant crossroads and beginning of my brother's lifetime successful career teaching Mathematics.

I well remember the morning he had to go. He left the house pale and shaking. But he went. He later completed a degree and was set.

One weekend I was attending a literary conference at Moray House. I decided to adjourn to Greyfriars Bobby's Bar for the duration of the lunchtime break and before the next session, which was to be on Lewis Grassic Gibbon.

In the bar I fell into conversation with Frauke, a young German woman studying Scottish literature. Frauke was short-haired, neat and intense but laughed readily and radiantly. She expressed her disappointment that she had not known about this conference.

'Come along with me anyhow,' I said.

'But I haven't enrolled.'

'No one will notice. Come along.'

With her experience of pernickety German bureaucracy, she was amazed by this idea but, assured by my insistence, along she came – the beginning of a relationship that was sporadically to continue in Germany and led subsequently to my role as a matchmaker, providing her with a husband.

Frauke's landlady in her Cambridge Street flat was deaf. Naughtily, I would make late night and all night visits, then in the morning Frauke kept her landlady in conversation in the kitchen whilst I crept silently forth. As well as our nocturnal meetings we shared a love of theatre, poetry and endless exploratory literary and philosophical chatterings.

She was a scholar who rejoiced in the freedom of study and mischiefs in Edinburgh after the fetters of German academicism. I was to learn much from Frauke, whose story was to lead to a profound transformational shift in my understanding. My meeting with her in Edinburgh furthered the nascent impulse to work in Germany.

Life in Edinburgh was full and frolicsome and filled with friends, but my curiosity and inner voice said, 'Time to go, time to leave', and so I did, to become an assistant teacher in Die Halepaghen Gymnasium, Buxtehude, a small town across the river Elbe from Hamburg. I took with me my schoolboy German and my mission to satisfy my curiosity.

12

Laying a Ghost to Rest

AT THE END of the war, when I was ten, I had seen in the long-gone illustrated magazine, the *Picture Post*, photographs of the emaciated survivors of Belsen and Auschwitz, the skin-drawn bones of corpses, and the grisly gas chambers. The stories of Hitler's 'Final Solution' and Nazi atrocities were ubiquitous.

My mother's pain, coupled with these stories and such evidence, were strong persuasion that the Germans were somehow cruel, bad and different.

Yet I had learned German at school from an elderly, gentle man and learned too of their culture, literature, poetry, and then in my teens through a schoolmate, Ron Wood, I met young Germans and particularly young German women who were evidently not discernibly different in nature from the young Scottish women I knew. These were the days of the innocent and romantic friendships of my teens – long talks, walks, going to the pictures, family visits to my suspicious, circumspect but courteous mother and openly welcoming father. My father was uniquely hospitable and understanding, talking at ease with all the young people who visited our house.

I suppose it was a combination of my father's influence and my own curiosity and a desire to find for myself what the Germans were like that prompted me to work there. Equally, my friend Ron was a Germanophile, liking numerous aspects of the land, and its young women, a predilection I enthusiastically shared.

As Edward Albee says in his play *The Zoo Story*, 'sometimes a person has to go a very long distance out of his way to come back a short distance correctly'. Answering my curiosity and inner promptings, I took farewell of my first teaching post. There I had learned that the only way to learn to teach is to teach.

My last day at Melville College brought some tears to my eye. My baby first year 12-year-olds pressed on me the royal sum of four shillings and thruppence, which they had hastily collected, having forgotten I was leaving. My 5G class, the rogues of the fifth year, all of whom had surprised Chunky Bain the head of the three-strong English Department because they had all passed Higher English, presented me with an emblazoned 5G silk tie in school colours, which they had commissioned. I was the only member of staff to have this honour. It is the only necktie that I still have in my wardrobe. But the event of that last school day which left me inarticulate and moist-eyed, was an invitation to visit my not remarkably academic class 3B. Robyn Aitchison, a boy whose poem the BBC had broadcast, stood up and made a little speech thanking me for I don't remember what, and then gave me a

Cassell's German dictionary signed by everyone in the class. I thanked them as best I could.

And so I arrived in *die kleine Stadt*, the little town of Buxtehude, where I found a room on the second floor of a two-storey building. Adjacent to my room lived Ishmael, a plausible Turk with contempt for western women and a mission to fuck as many as he could. There were two other rooms and a bathroom on our landing. I seldom saw the other occupants.

I was now an exchange teacher in a Gymnasium (High School). My diary of the time records:

I have some pretty descriptions of my new job, and Headmaster – Herr Oberstudiendirektor Dr Gütling. Piecing together conversational snatches, observations and impressions I appear to have landed here under the jurisdiction of a firmly corpulent middle-aged, cigar-smoking, externally charming, hearty, moody, pompous, bullying, grandly titled Herr Oberstudiendirektor, Dr Gütling, who is dotingly in love with one of his probation teachers, Fräulein Schenken. This comfortably attractive young Fräulein in public treats our big white chief with flirting blatant familiarity in the staff room, arrives at school when she will, sits in comfort in his office smoking, chatting, and treats her companion probationers with unveiled threats.

The comedy is in the 'old man, young maid' aspect of the affair, the extent of the Oberstudiendirektor's jealousy, and the fantastic bold openness of the student teacher: the whole school, staff, students, town, country round knows of this wild scandal, and the protagonists make no secret.

Before I had taught a single lesson, I was introduced to something of the thoroughness of German pedagogy. On the first day at 7.45am I was summoned to the office of the great man and given an indecipherable German document to read. I explained the impossibility and he fetched his concubine who lifted his spirits, translated to me the crimes for which I could be thrown out of the German teaching profession, and then before the great chief I took an oath, repeated after him to be a good boy, shook hands and was thereafter dispatched forthwith for a Gesundheitzeugnis (health certificate) to the town of Stade without having taught a single lesson. Urine was taken in one room of a large, white official building, blood in another, an X-ray in a third, and an examination of eyes and ears in a fourth. Between each I sat in a waiting room and read Brendan Behan's *Borstal Boy*.

I was learning the human similarities and cultural differences. Each morning, in the North German fashion, the teachers assembled in the staff room, formally shook hands with a 'Guten Morgen, Herr Campbell,' and so on, and then, the grand entrance. The Herr Oberstudiendirektor appeared with his announcements and commands for the day. One morning, when I had been there for a month, the mighty Herr made a dramatic pause in his announcements. His gaze fell directly on me... silence. The following conducted in German:

'Herr Campbell, you did not attend school yesterday morning.'

'No, Herr Oberstudiendirektor. I was sick.'

'And yet you attended in the afternoon.'

'Yes, I had recovered.'

'That is not possible.'

The silence enlarges itself.

'In Scotland, it is possible to be sick in the morning and not in the afternoon,' I say.

The teachers are statues. A long silence is broken at last by the Oberstudiendirektor's sudden, loud guffaw.

'Aah, so!'

And the world returned to life as out of a frozen film frame.

I had attended staff meetings in Melville College, but none like the ones in Das Halepaghen Gymnasium, Buxtehude. The form was not dissimilar to how I imagined Hitler's Bunker Conference. We sat at seven in the evening at a long table in a long room with Führer Dr Gütling at the head of the table, his two deputies, one on each side, and the rest of the staff in order of precedence and seniority ranged down the table – at the lower end the *Referendare*, probationers, myself and fellow spirit Herr Düren, who was part-time. These conferences lasted for hours. The one surprising element of informality in them was that there was an adjoining room that stocked a beer refrigerator from which staff, particularly my old friend, Herr Düren, would from time to time collect a beer. One occasion particularly I recall. The evening was hot, the detailed analysis of the performances of classes endless.

'Fräulein Schmidt,' said the boss, 'in your class 7B, you have awarded only two students with an A pass. Why?'

'In that class, these are the only students with marks that merit an A pass.'

'Unmöglich. Impossible, in a whole generation of young Germans to have only two.' He laughs. 'Impossible. You will make more. Five.'

'But, Herr Oberstudiendirektor, that would not be a fair assessment.'

'Fräulein Schmidt, we stop the conference now. Until you change your mind.'

The Fräulein bursts into tears. Herr Düren slips outs for another beer. Otherwise there is silence. At length, 'Well, Fräulein Schmidt?'

Fräulein Schmidt, 'As you say, sir.'

Herr Düren has returned to his seat beside me, falls unnoticed and drunk onto the floor, and the discussion proceeds until midnight when the despot departs.

The formality in northern Germany, the punctilious bureaucracy, the hierarchies were informing me of the cultural differences between our countries but I was to meet more gemütlich, cosy elements.

In my comfortable little room I instigated the notion of the ceilidh, inviting a few of the teaching staff and successfully loosening their inhibitions and formality and morals with liberal supplies of whisky, dancing, music and song, and incidentally igniting one or two affairs, some open, others decidedly clandestine.

Herr Düren, my friend who had slid drunkenly onto the floor at the conference, was a whimsical character who mocked the bureaucracy and held a huge sadness for the blight on Germany and German culture of the Third Reich. I found also a firm friend in Rüdiger, one of the probationers whose temperament, attitudes and sense of fun made a fellow spirit. An amiable iconoclast, not of the polite North German mould, we shared a fondness for poetry, music, people, women, life! He suggested I get a guitar, and put a new joy into my life, a source of lasting amateurish inexpert pleasure.

Susie, the new exchange teacher from England, wished to learn the guitar and so we had our practice sessions in my room. Susie was embarrassed by the lecherous leers and insinuations that my neighbour Ishmael put on our sessions. The wall between my bedroom and his was thin, and Susie and I decided to simulate a spectacular orgy: we placed my bed next to the wall and provided a wailing, groaning, squealing, bed-bouncing extended soundscape. Sometime later, we emerged from our room and were not surprised to find him prowling the corridor clearly suspecting our ruse. We chuckled our way for a drink.

Susie and Rüdiger made a subsequent liaison of their own sort, and Susie and I continued our guitar practice without the intrusion of Ishmael.

Serendipitously, at the same time I had met Maria Carini, half-German, half-Italian, her father a teacher of guitar. It was by his advice that I had bought one.

Maria had silk-black hair, dark flashing eyes and Roman Catholic respectability inherited from her father. A conversation with Maria from my German journal:

Maria: 'I find I hate my body, do you?'

David: 'On the contrary, I love mine.'

Maria: 'Why, I don't know. Do you think it could be because I was once disappointed?'

David: 'No. I think it must go further. The body is us. We express ourselves through its eyes, voice, hands, movements. We speak with it.'

In parcels, I heard Maria's story of her 'lonely and kicked childhood', the guilty stricture of her religious upbringing, her distrust.

We talked and talked and talked. Her story, her courage compelled and moved me. One day to my surprise, in the dark, concealing the body of which she was ashamed, she invited me to my bed. And afterwards, I dressed and while I went for five minutes to the toilet, she dressed unseen.

When I was ill, she gave me – limitlessly – food, bedclothes and her secrets, and helped with the school geography lessons the wily Dr Gütling had persuaded me into undertaking.

As a diversion, I took up an invitation to a party in Hamburg by Frauke, who now lived there. It was a short train journey and, as it was Saturday and I was free, I decided to go early to explore the city in a vague quest for something of interest. This diversion is described fully in my journal of the time:

Having seen churches, lakes, university buildings and the like, the inevitable Reeperbahn, the famous street of prostitutes, draws me where I look with curiosity at the old, the fat, the young, the old and fat, the young and pretty, the all-shaped, and listen to their 'Komm mal hier', then I walk on. Casually walking up another street, I see a full-busted woman. I walk past and hear 'Komm mal hier'. I say, 'Danke, nein.' 'Nur zwanzig Mark' and I am intrigued more by an interest in how I'd perform in the interesting circumstance than anything else. And I am, I believe, a bit excited by the circumstance.

Together, we trawl through a narrow passage, up a narrow stairway, into a small room not much more than a bed. She undresses and encourages me to do the same. She says I can, for a modest five marks, have 'interesting pictures' to look at. This of course, in my reckless champagne frame of mind, I do, and there I am lying on a bed looking at pictures which I really don't take in at all, and she is squeezing a pimple on her rather full but otherwise pleasant breast. In a moment of panic, I ask 'And do you have health cards?' 'We must,' says she. She then puts a contraceptive on me with great deliberation and I'm interested and a little excited, not sexually but otherwise. Then, studying the task as a carpenter does the wood he is planing, manipulates John Thomas until she fancies him ready, which he is not. Then she lowers herself on to him and squirms up and down. All is in vain, since jellies have been firmer. She then reapplies herself to the job, gently, skilfully, and finally gives up in total disgust and says in an offhand way, something to the effect, 'You can carry on.' I do, and she finishes off the job, covers herself in eau de cologne and tells me to put my socks on, quickly, for the smell. This, after giving me a piece of paper to cover the prophylactic and indicating a receptacle for both. Affably then we part with the cheery enough mutual 'Auf Wiedersehen.' Unlikely indeed.

It was now time to make my way to the party, which was held in a cellar with a cement floor. Apart from the cheerful lighting the host had installed and the moody music provided by a trio of musicians and a singer, the place reminded me of a wartime air-raid shelter. Perhaps that's what it was.

The evening turned out to be a disaster for my health. I drank overmuch and later fell asleep on the floor, waking bitterly cold and with a rasping, cement dust induced, cough. Back in my little room in Buxtehude, John Keats sprang to mind as I coughed specks of blood into the sink. This was compounded by pain-pinching sinusitis, and the 'hell o' a' diseases' as Burns so aptly put it, a severe toothache. My condition occasioned a dramatic solace and a surprising meeting.

The urgent demands of the toothache meant that I got a lucky immediate dentist appointment, first thing Monday morning, and subsequently was referred to an ear, nose and throat doctor, who was to irrigate my troubling sinuses. Panic. A big needle. I felt all the blood churning, head swimming, ominous prelude to unconsciousness. Luckily, I sweated only and the operation was, apart from the moment when the needle cracked through the nasal cartilage, less troublesome by far than the anticipation.

I returned weak, nauseous and exhausted to my little haven, described in my journal as 'my 65 marks a month, paid and possessed womb of a room, den of my wicked cheerful private own'. Clear Dylan Thomas influence!

In the early evening, the doorbell rang. I rose from my bed and opened the door to a young woman, the doctor's assistant. 'Herr Campbell, you left your wallet.' I thanked her and she left. Later in the evening, the buzzer again. 'I brought you soup. You are not well.' I was not well, and hugely grateful to this attractive ministering angel, named Sylvia. I was too feeble for school and for the next week, each evening Sylvia came at the end of the day, and at the end of the week brought a surprise. 'I think you are well now,' she said, and produced a bottle of champagne. A photo of the time depicts my mother's greatest fear: a gaunt, lean figure, eyes intensified, hollow cheeks. 'You will be the sailor,' she said, 'I will be the prostitute.' She popped the cork, poured two ample fizzy glasses, took off her shoes. 'Zum Wohl!' Good health indeed! A bubble of mischief and astonishments. Sylvia loved words and play. Although her English was limited, her capacity to express was not. And so we took our roles and this playful adventure began, and my spirits and health revived. Sylvia was not only innovative, but unpredictable, teasing, tantalising, and at 20 years old, an education. No longer could I blunder in the idea that men are the great initiators.

One early evening as we lay in bed, she announced with her customary mischievous, half mocking seriousness, 'Now I am going to visit my girlfriend in Hamburg. Women are better than men at making love.' I could not argue with that. She dressed and parted, and said, 'See you soon, sweet bagger'. Her pronunciation, and also spelling, were as individual as herself, as I discovered in her subsequent letters on my return to Edinburgh.

For all her joy and vivacity, Sylvia could surprise also by sudden cloud-bursts of tears, when recalling her mother's grief abandoned by a wartime English father who didn't know of Sylvia's existence. As unexpectedly, the sun would shine and she would be teasing, laughing, playing, a tantalising young Cleopatra.

My life and emotional involvements were, to be euphemistic, complex at this time, and my health wretched. Sometime after the health disaster exacerbated by the party, Frauke solicitously visited me in my den. That same morning, I found to my joy a letter from Ina, opened it, rapidly read it and numbly, dumbly, slowly woke out of a splitting headache to the greater pain of comprehending its contents. Farewell. Tired by the directionless course of our relationship, and perhaps rightly suspecting my dallying amongst wayside flowers, she had concluded we were going nowhere. Strange indeed that a physical pain is so weak before an emotional one. I blinked and conversed with Frauke as if she were at the end of a phone.

Agitated, I told her the contents of the letter, and Frauke's response was to inform me that her feelings for me too had changed, lost their glow of romance. The chapter felt complete: farewell from Ina, this sea change in Frauke. I had no excuses for myself.

Over this terminal letter from Ina, in my diary I wrote: 'I feel sick myself and have not felt like this for a long time. *Not since Sandra, Alison, Barbara?* the cynic asks.' Was it my karmic preordained destiny to have multiple, simultaneous loves, as portended by my five-year-old adoration of three loves in Primary One? The judgement of the words from an opera we sang at school rang in my mind, 'Now your days of philandering are over and your straying from flower to flower. You'll no more as a faithless young rover, play Adonis with each pretty maid.' Was it not, I asked myself, poetic justice to have this reckoning?

My deep sense of desolation and loss determined me to attempt to repair the breach. Ina agreed to my visiting her in Copenhagen. Her mother, the epitome of calm and cosiness, welcomed me, and my protestations over a week persuaded Ina to resume our liaison. The frost thawed into Ina's natural sanguine and sunny disposition, and so we agreed to continue. We recovered the spark and fun, indeed so brightly that we decided to marry. And so, relieved and indeed exhilarated, like one released from prison to the fresh air of freedom, I returned to Buxtehude.

In my mailbox was a serendipitous excitement, a letter from James Doyle, my gruff and philosophical companion from Melville College days, informing me that there was a post in the English Department at the Royal High School in Edinburgh. Instantly I knew I would leave Germany, the Halepaghen Gymnasium and the mad Oberstudiendirektor, Dr Gütling and, with sadness, my friends, companions, comforters and lovers in Buxtehude. But I knew with total inner conviction and clarity, it was time to go.

I knew because the Head of English at the Royal High School was Hector MacIver, reputed to be the best teacher of English in Scotland. Only a few times previously had I met Hector. He was a friend of James Doyle, and I had got to know many of his ex-pupils who were English students in my year at university; all of them spoke of him as a god. Subsequently I learned that many of his ex-pupils were illustrious men of letters. On one occasion I saw him turn the air into icicles at a meeting of English teachers in Boroughmuir High School. The debate, on some matter of policy, had raged vociferously hither and thither. I recall that Hector had remained silent, listening to the arguments, and then, characteristically, in a well-chosen moment of pause, he arose from his seat and deliberately naming the three previous speakers and the schools they represented, he expressed the view that their opinions were not only erroneous but irrelevant, and announced that unless the company were to consider the point that he briefly outlined, we would all be better employed by adjourning to the nearest hostelry. The air was a chill of silence, and he sat down. He was elegant, incisive, a lover of words, and so as a young man I came to fall under his spell.

I wrote to apply for the post at the Royal High School and had a succinct telegram from Hector, which said, 'Too late. Apply Rector direct.' This I did with unaccustomed alacrity! The Oberstudiendirektor expressed himself, to my deaf ears, as devastated at the loss of such a valuable teacher.

As my time in Germany was coming to an end, my father's edict had been fulfilled, 'David, if you knew people's stories, you would not be able to judge them and you would understand them.' The inner promptings and questions about the nature of the German people had been answered; that answer had been provided by the stories of the people who had become my loves and friends. I realised fully that with people, or peoples, 'by their stories shall you know them'.

In Buxtehude, I had found firm playful friends, friends scarred by their history, courageous friends. I had formed a little poetry, guitar playing, music entourage in my little den and learned much from my intimacy with three remarkable women: the one whose company and fibrous story most profoundly taught me of our varied but common bond of humanity was that of Frauke who now, half a century later, is one of my lifetime friends and one for whom I had been a successful matchmaker.

From my journal in Buxtehude:

My first picture of Frauke, from the stories she has told me, will al-ways be as a long, thin sparsely-clad hollow but big-eyed kid of seven, holding in one hand a podgy three-year-old and I see her in a desolate place, ruined buildings, approach the gates of the British Army Camp in

Hamburg, the enemies. I see her laden with food from the soldiers given to her little sister, the infant Renata. And I see these children return, bewildered by the plenty to the house of her religious, simple good people, foster parents, And I hear the blood of fear singing in the ears of the old man and mingling the shame and crushed pride and wounds of a confused sort when voices of his childhood's education whisper to him along with the shouts of war, the groans of defeat and the bitterness. Now these two illegitimate wards, a skeleton and a baby, clutching to them skirts full of enemy chocolate was dynamite. The old man seizes and beats and beats the scarecrow child until his awful moments of drowning in shame and fear are pacified. In time, the child grew to understand his actions because she knew that in his fashion, he loved her. With him and his wife she was safer than anywhere else, safer certainly than with her mother, whose own confusion kindled vicious words or blows, for who came but to invade?

That will be my picture of Frauke, the vision of a lonely brave child with a fierce energy, a child who was, at 12, mothering a half-brother, who near the War's end had foraged amongst twigs for the edible scraps and learned to tutor for bread. I have then the picture of an adolescent living with a neurotic mother, a late-released from Siberia new step-father, simple, good-natured without a boyhood to remember, a man who went from childhood to war, to prison, to marriage and his wife's two daughters. This man was plagued by the neurosis of Frauke's mother and would beat her daughter till the blood came. And so, she ran and lied and learned to distrust and to fear. Her passport photo of that time depicts a sulky young woman, eyes heavy and watchfully dull, hair unglamorously cropped, for what reason was there to be glamorous?

I see that picture and yet she had an amazing fearlessness and determination. This made of her a wanderer, travelling continents alone, sleeping rough if necessary, and picking up acquaintances on the way. This picture changes. The picture then is of a girl in an office doing tasks too easy for her, finding the world foolish, retiring into the gloom of German philosophers because they knew, a sort of courageous superiority, but an isolation from people. Then the picture of days at work, nights at night school, the long hard study, sleep, monotony rarely broken and the will to go on snapped, save for the camaraderie of another in a similar plight, and a lover, a Jew, whose distrust and fear and uncertainty dwarfed hers and caught her in sympathy and guilt. This was the companionship of outsiders.

The woman I met in Edinburgh was the eager-beaver Frauke, take-me-as-you-find-me, mad about literature, fond of life, game for most things, the out-and-about film and theatre buff, dancing off to London for a day to see a play, back tomorrow, body worshipping, gurgling with laughter in bed Frauke, live life, love life.

Marvellously, an interview with the Edinburgh Corporation Education Department was arranged. This letter arrived on a day that Maria was visiting. When she learned its contents a pall fell on the day. And yet, as if taking a last farewell, Maria went out and returned with a bottle of champagne.

We lay together in the bed as night fell, lay almost motionless, and afterwards a silence of gold was broken by Maria's 'I have a bottle of champagne,' and that was popped, poured, pledged and put aside, and in a peaceful sleep the day melted away.

It was dark when I woke and Maria had gone. I recalled these lines from Willie Soutar's poem 'The Tryst':

> ...she smool'd saftly thru the mirk
> Afore the day wud daw.

When I left Buxtehude, it was with Maria that I travelled to Hamburg, en route to Denmark to see Ina, and thence home. Maria and I travelled over the Elbe bridges, and out of each other's lives. This aspect of our journey was so surgically clear and yet we talked in the usual commonplaces, then she said, 'I think when you return to Edinburgh you soon will marry.'

In the stillness of this farewell journey, I thought of my love for Maria, for Sylvia, for Frauke, each so different. Sylvia, a burst of adventure, confidence, drama, fairy tales, and a wildness in bed I had never known; Maria, thoughtful, brave, sad, with a legacy of childhood pain, slowly learning to trust, a Martha from the Bible; and Frauke, whose story I have told. These three women, above all, and my teacher friends, Rüdiger, Herr Düren, answered for me the questions that had taken me to Germany.

I wished my father had been alive to greet me on my return from Germany and hear the stories of the people I met.

When I look back, I wonder at how unbelievably feckless I was, an immediacy-monger with thought for neither past nor future; like Robert Burns's mouse, 'the present only toucheth thee.' For on the boat back to England, I fell in with an attractive Danish girl, Pia and spent three happy nights with her in a cupboard in the flat of my friend Ron in London. Fecklessness squared. I would be late for my interview with the Edinburgh City Education Committee!

13

A Kindling Spirit

WHEN I RETURNED to Edinburgh, I recall sitting down on the pavement in Princes Street, drunk with the very stones and the light, the Old Town buildings across the valley, the mighty presence of the castle. After the concrete of blitzed, rebuilt Germany, this was an intoxication. I was surprised to be overwhelmed by tears and the sense of, 'this is my own, my native land'.

My mother was alarmed and relieved, and in her economical Scottish way, joyful to have me stay with her in the house in St Ronan's Terrace, bought courtesy of Lord Bracken's endowment. She was alarmed at my gaunt, underfed appearance, which she at once set about rectifying. The photograph taken of me at my brother's wedding, podgier than ever before or since, is evidence of her temporary success.

Such was Hector's reputation that he managed to rearrange the time of my appointment that I had so irresponsibly missed. After his fashion, he arranged his own interview with me to be held in one of his favourite howffs, the public bar of the Café Royal. When I arrived, he was already occupying a seat in one of the half-moon recesses by the door, conservatively dressed in a suit, tie, white shirt, neat, tidy. He rose, greeted me and enquired,

'Whisky?'

Hector's compelling attraction was his unhurried pace, his economy in movement and in speech, precise and with the indelible island cadence. He seemed to glide to the bar and occupy the space.

'Two JG Smith's Glenlivets, please.'

These, the first of many in the evening, came with a little jug of water. He asked about the German school I'd come from, enquired when I could start.

'Immediately.'

At the conclusion of our meeting, he offered me one piece of advice.

'I don't think,' he said, 'the Education Committee would be impressed by your brown corduroy shirt.'

So began my time teaching in the Royal High School as a member of a glittering English staff. These were inspiring, happy days. It was sheer exuberance to teach with Hector. Exuberant and challenging. I recall one morning as we waited to go into assembly Hector saying to me, 'David, you seem to hold a high opinion of the so-called Beat poets?'

'Yes,' I agreed.

'Perhaps then, three weeks on Friday, you might care to address forms four, five and six and the English staff, in the hall, on your opinion of their work.'

Hector kept you on tiptoe with his challenges; the department was always a-buzz with ideas for what best to teach and to whom.

'What do you think of trying this Charles Causley poem with the third year?' And so on.

Hector's love of poetry and dedication to teaching infused his staff and pupils. He particularly loved Yeats and the Scottish ballads. He knew all the contemporary Scottish poets personally, as well as Louis MacNeice, Charles Causley and the theatre director Tyrone Guthrie. Dylan Thomas stayed with him during his visit to the Edinburgh Festival in 1948 to give readings in the Freemasons' Hall. A former pupil of Hector's told me this story:

It was nine o'clock on Monday morning, in room 3 – Hector's room, the first class of the morning after assembly, and Hector addressed his sixth form class, whom he always dignified with the appellation 'Gentlemen.'

'Gentlemen, we have been studying the beautiful poetry of the Welsh poet Dylan Thomas, particularly his great evocation of boyhood in the poem "Fern Hill": all we have lacked has been the voice of the poet himself.' At that moment, on this cue, the door flew open and a burly, tousle-haired figure burst into the room, incantating the very poem:

Now as I was young and easy under the apple boughs
About the lilting house and happy as the grass was green

Dylan Thomas, in full powerful voice and presence: an unforgettable moment, and, as teaching, sheer genius.

For Hector, words were a flame, and the flame filled the English Department with the same fire and enthusiasm. To me, that time was incandescent.

I remember Hector inviting Hugh MacDiarmid to give the Immortal Memory at the school Burns Supper for the staff and upper forms. With Hector, I met MacDiarmid before the event in the Café Royal for a pre-prandial dram. Not surprisingly, the hands of the clock spun and we hastened, late for the occasion, to the extreme irritation of the headmaster. But MacDiarmid's sheer courtesy and controversial, but electric, address redeemed the peccadillo and all was smiles and congratulations.

Living in such an atmosphere, in such company, the energy was contagious. Lessons needed to be original, inspiring, different. I recall teaching a wonderful class, the top class in the fourth and fifth years. In one way I was a tyrant; I learned from Hector's quietness, and from 'Spats' Westwood, my eccentric English teacher at George Heriot's, who surprised us by saying to the class, 'Now, five minutes to talk to your neighbour.' I would hide copies of texts under the desks, and when all was silent, would announce, 'Read what you'll find under your desk,' and then I'd say, 'Listen,' and I'd play a recording of Dylan Thomas, then perhaps of Richard Burton, with their readings of 'Fern Hill' and ask, 'Which did you like best?' Then I would read myself, and finally appoint a pupil or pupils to read verses in turn before discussing the poem. It was a love affair with the poem, and the class.

Even setting exams, one felt the questions had to be fresh, stimulating, aimed to kindle imagination. Tom Pow, one of the pupils in a talented class, won first prize in a *Scotsman* poetry competition, where it was adjudged that any one of his five entries would have won. Tom, who became a lifelong friend, also reminded me that one of the questions I'd set in the Higher prelim was: 'In what way do the names Lamb and Bacon reflect the style and content of their writing?' Crazy question! Tom also always remembered being much delighted by my saying to him about a short story he'd written, 'Well handled, Pow.'

The relationship the English Department staff had, particularly with senior pupils, was mature and easy, reflecting mutual respect as typified by Hector's addressing his upper formers as 'Gentlemen'. In those days, things were different. When Hector was producing *Othello*, over which he had conferred with the great director Tyrone Guthrie, he would, after rehearsals, take his two leading characters, Othello and Iago, to the Robin's Nest for a beer to reflect on the rehearsals and simply socialise. When I came to produce Jean Anouilh's play *Becket*, I was reminded 50 years later by Peter Hammond, one of the cast, that I invited some of the senior boys to my house for a jar and a chat. Nowadays, I would have been dismissed.

Among the boys who remained a friend after he left school was a precocious, mature boy called George Robertson. To his classmates, when he was only 14, he was known as 'The Prophet'. At that age, he used to pop into my classroom after school with his poems, and once surprised me and made me wonder how he had divined my extra-curricular wildnesses, by giving me a Chinese novel to read called *The Before Midnight Scholar*. Its protagonist was a charming and dedicated night visitor to ladies' boudoirs. George also presented me with a play he had written, casting in the main role the only black boy in the school. I produced that insightful play for the whole school in the wonderful oval-tiered school assembly hall designed by the famed architect Hamilton.

As a former pupil, George wrote a tender and imaginative script of *Alice in Wonderland* for the Festival Fringe performed in Fort Knox, of which more anon. We corresponded till the end of his life in 2018. I visited him several times in London, where he was involved in a spiritual organisation. In the end, he was completely paralysed by multiple sclerosis, spending his last years propelling himself by his chin in an electric chair, and lovingly looked after by his wife Anna, whom he had married at a mass ceremony by the Reverend Moon in whose church George would serve till he died.

His closest friend, David Mann, was a classmate in the Royal High School, and I recall they came together to my classroom at the end of a school day. They had a guitar and suggested they sing to me 'The Night Visiting Song', a ghost folk song, to present amongst others in a review I was devising. I still sing that song today.

Another of our favourite budding thespians was Brian Dunnigan, a lean, quirky and enterprising humourist. He decided that his Sixth Year Studies did not require his constant attendance at school, and so applied for a part-time job in the Edinburgh Parks Department. He was assigned the task of mowing the grass in the grounds of the Royal High School! One afternoon, a peaked cap low over his eyes, Brian was mowing the grass when the rector looked out of his room and thought, 'That looks like Brian Dunnigan, in Edinburgh Corporation working clothes. It is Brian Dunnigan!' We appreciated the liberality of the then rector, Baillie T Ruthven, that one of our favourite actors was not expelled.

These individualist, charismatic, creative pupils were nurtured by the ethos of mutual respect and creativity that Hector inspired – the legacy he was to leave to his successors and the English teaching staff. He died, aged 54, in 1966. Now, over 50 years later, I hear the lilt of his voice, see the clarity in his blue eyes, feel the frisson of his fearlessness, sense the measure of his speech, his walk, his presence. In memory, I sit opposite him in The Grubby, the canteen of the Edinburgh Royal High School in the elegant building it once occupied on Calton Hill, so nearly chosen as the site for the Scottish Parliament.

In flowing black gown he crosses the High School Yards at lunchtime, raises his hand to me as he moves by, and utters the one word, 'Grubby'. This means that we will drink tea together after the last bell rings at 3.30pm.

Mrs Hounslow, the dragon of 'The Grubby', is translated by Hector's island gentlemanly courtesy and respect into 'an administering angel'. She prepares a tray: china teapot, cups and saucers, milk jug, sugar bowl and a plate of biscuits. Hector, summer or winter, switches on all the lights in the long, low, barn-like building, and carries the tray to a table three-quarters of the way up the canteen, and we take our place opposite one another.

At these meetings, because of my huge admiration for Hector, I was always expecting him to utter some wise 'open sesame' aphorism that would suddenly open the door of deep understanding for me. Only later did I conclude, as Oscar Wilde did when he wrote to Bosie from prison, in 'De Profundis', there are no such things as great things and small things, they are all of equal importance. It was the stories and the whole friendship that was the gold.

Hector was a storyteller, a seannachie, and had fascinating stories to tell of his Lewis childhood, stories of the supernatural, and Edinburgh stories of the little comic incidents of his friendship with the roguish poet Sydney Goodsir Smith and the coterie of remarkable Scottish writers, artists and poets that at that time frequented the Rose Street pubs.

I even have a vivid recollection of a dream Hector told me he'd had: in his dream, he had reached the final round of a BBC *Mastermind* contest and sat before a blaring spotlight in an imprisoning chair.

The question master announced, 'This is your final question: what is the most beautiful thing in the world? You have 60 seconds, Mr MacIver.'

The big hands of a big clock ticked round as Hector flicked through the places his wide wartime naval travels had taken him, the machair of his native Lewis, the pyramids, Iceland.

In desperation, he looked to the crowd in the audience for help, but their faces were like blank sheets of white paper. The hand was sweeping toward the minute. He felt as if he were in the electric chair. He was shivering and sweating, then in the last moment he said, 'The most beautiful thing in the world is the human face.'

At that moment he heard an outburst of applause from the audience, and looking at them saw that they had all now smiling, happy, rapturous faces in place of the blank white paper of before. He had won *Mastermind*!

He also invited Ina and me to visit him at home with his wife Mary, in the East Lothian village of Temple. But time was running out: he had cancer.

Before morning service in the splendid oval school hall, the teachers congregated in the adjoining staff room. The English staff gathered around Hector and I recall he was clearly disguising the increasing distress of his condition.

I saw him in hospital where he had, in anticipation of my visit, worked out the actual number of lines of the characters in a Giles Cooper play I was producing.

The funeral service was at the church in Temple. John Melville, who was to play Becket in my production, read out Dylan Thomas's 'And Death Shall Have No Dominion'.

The effect on me of Hector's death was profound. My grief infused a determination in me to make a production of *Becket* by Jean Anouilh my tribute to this man I admired and loved. Hector had so elevated the importance of drama at the Royal High School that there was as much zeal to be in the cast of drama productions as to be chosen for the School's first rugby 15. The competition to be in *Becket* was keen and my choice after the auditions difficult. For the King, I chose David Robb, a dashing blond with a fine voice, and a taste for fame; for Becket, John Melville, a totally different young man, with an intent and punctilious desire to inhabit every moment. David became a well-known West End and TV performer; John a multi-talented clown, singer, filmmaker, actor, writer and street performer, hugely acclaimed across Europe, though hardly known in Scotland and the UK.

For six weeks I devoted myself to this task. I knew every syllable of the play. I worked with individuals in the cast. George Robertson was to play the Queen Mother. I studied the movement, the gestures, the carriage, the gait of women, with an intensity as never before. And so for each character. When David Robb got the headmaster's permission to grow a beard for his part, the responses of the staff went from lofty censure to hilarity.

Feelings ran high: Jock Dewar, a Classics Master, kidnapped one of my cast from a rehearsal to play cricket. I sent a taxi to the playing fields and snatched him back.

Ultimately the performances in the Churchill Theatre were brilliant, worthy of Hector, a kind of expiation of my grief. Shortly after this, we moved to the new building of the Royal High School at Barnton.

My Royal High days were brightened by another joyful and mutually stimulating meeting. Jim Goodall joined the Art Department; exuberant, contagious, iconoclastic, inventive and devoted to art and to communicating his love, enthusiasm, industry and dedication to his pupils. It was not long before he had a coterie of devotee pupils and not long till he and I fell into a zestful friendship with shared ideals. His disciples became, under his leadership, the designers and stage crew for our drama productions. Jim became a drinking companion, then a lifelong friend, with dramatic consequences for both of us.

It was Hector who kindled my love of Celtic stories and lore. His favourite story was of the legendary poet Ossian, an enchanted tale. These old Celtic tales were later to take a significant importance in my life when I became a professional storyteller and writer. They motivated me to write a book of Celtic tales, *Out of the Mouth of the Morning*. Amongst the favourable reviews, the one that most heartened and pleased me were the words of Karl Miller in his letter to me in January 2014, shortly before he died: 'I am greatly obliged to you for sending me a copy of your excellent stories.' He was one of Hector's most luminous pupils, becoming a highly regarded writer and literary critic. In his *Memoirs of a Modern Scotland*, he devoted a chapter to expressing the genius and inspiration of Hector and his huge affection and indebtedness to him as a teacher and friend.

I had arranged to visit Karl Miller to discuss his times with Hector, but in his letter postponing my visit, he announced he was 'Too low in the water' to receive me. Like Hector, he succumbed to cancer.

14

We Ran Our Heedless Ways

PERHAPS ONE OF the explanations for the extravagances that were to become my Edinburgh lifestyle when I returned from Germany was my sense that marriage would mean 'now your days of philandering are over'. Like all searches for reasons and explanations, this is completely inadequate and a stronger ingredient doubtless was my own born nature.

From the confines and comforts of home life, the enticements of the town and my friend Gordon Allan's invitation to share a flat in Portobello were too alluring to resist.

And so began months of a whirlwind helter-skelter carnival of hedonistic indulgences and equally devoted and energetic teaching at the Royal High School; stimulations of different sorts by night and day.

The experiment of living with Gordon had limited success and duration. My punctilious dedication to teaching and timekeeping didn't accord well with Gordon's leisurely morning ablutions, although he obligingly drove me to school at Calton Hill in his car. Moreover, our landlady's idea of seemly behaviour and reasonable hours was seriously at odds with ours, so that we were politely invited to terminate our stay.

This problem I approached by adopting a peripatetic lifestyle, billeting myself mostly on accommodating lady friends. This Jekyll and Hyde existence meant that I would be carrying the exercise books of my pupils and correcting them as and when I could. This I did with haphazard diligence since my devotion to teaching was equal to that of pleasure.

I had some lucky landings. One of these resting places was fortuitously a beautiful flat in Regent Terrace, adjacent to the Royal High School and with an open view of Arthur's Seat. This luxurious sanctuary came about in a dramatic way. At this time my most constant friend and drinking partner was Gordon. He was, and still is, a loquacious character given to express his opinion in a flamboyant and theatrical fashion with gestures more Italianate than Scottish. He and I, and an occasional girlfriend Rosie, together were at one of the 'cairry oot, cairry on' parties typical of Edinburgh when the pubs in the evening had a closing time of 10.00pm. This was a period when gatecrashers with an adequate 'cairry oot' of booze were generally welcome, so exactly whose party it was, or when it was, I don't particularly recall except that it was in a house, possibly in the Grange or Morningside – classy!

Gordon and I loved dancing and frequently at student hops, or parties such as this, partnered each other in free dancing in the absence of less theatrical partners or dancers. It didn't occur to us that this might draw conclusions about our sexual proclivities and, if it had, I doubt if it would have much concerned us.

Late into the night I was resting on a couch beside a lean, attractive American woman of about 40. After a short conversation, she turned to me and said, 'Why don't you give up your horsey girl and homosexual-type friend and come home with me?' There was little incentive to refuse. I bade my friends farewell and left.

Our transport was a shiny black long-nosed sleek Jaguar XK. We rocketed off down the empty street, my back pressed against the seat with something like g-force. The Regent Terrace houses are elegant, spacious; hers was leanly and tastefully appointed but generously supplied with drink.

Jean, my newfound friend and hostess, was doing a PhD in Theology at New College on the Mound. I chose a Glenfiddich as my preferred drink and in this she joined me. She had been married to a man she described as a kind, humane and rich oil executive. From her account of how they parted, I made a short story called 'The Eye of the Needle' for the BBC. Its essence was that one night she woke to find she had an empty bed and, descending the stairs, saw her husband at her desk in her study. His face was streaming with tears as he pored, uncomprehendingly, over the pages of one of her dense theological texts. He looked like a deaf man at an opera. Their interests had parted and so did they.

At the conclusion of this story, Jean laid down her empty glass and said in her slightly honeyed Southern voice, 'Now, you can sleep there in that nice cosy room by yourself or come to my room and have an orgy.'

Her bed was large, silky and soft. She roused me in the morning to tell me she had run my bath, which was commensurately large and resting on it a large glass of cool, fresh orange juice. Had I landed in paradise?

This was the beginning of a beautiful, educative, loving and passionate friendship. One of the things Jean loved was poetry, particularly to hear me recite or read it in my 'Scottish voice', and so she had my repertoire of Dylan Thomas, the Metaphysicals, Donne, Marvell and Herbert – these particularly suited her.

Jean was large-hearted, generous and demanded nothing. At the morning conclusion of my visits to her sumptuous flat and sumptuous company she'd part from me at the doorstep with the words, 'See you when I see you, sweetheart.'

From time to time she entertained a coterie of New College Theology students and invited me, I think, as an *enfant terrible*, particularly after an occasion when one of her earnest young fellow students was expostulating on the spiritual vapidity of being attached to material possessions. I caught a glimpse of his fine gold wrist watch and affected to be in need of such a timepiece. I asked him to bequeath it to me. This dispelled his theological equanimity and created an enlivening stir in the group, but I didn't get the watch, which I neither wanted nor needed.

Of an evening when I called round, Jean, knowing my limited purse, would say, 'Let's take a turn into town.' She would then press £10 or so into my hand and say, 'David, you pay,' and we'd set sail for a cruise to the Rose Street pubs or a meal.

This idyllic, sporadic, instructive and loving companionship had a sad conclusion. Jean made a visit to Germany and died in high-speed crash on the Autobahn.

Rose Street, in those days before ubiquitous canned music, television sets and jukeboxes, was the favoured drinking and socialising precinct for a variety of folk. The literary gang favoured the Abbotsford, Milne's Bar, the Café Royal; and the artists and their community of art students, Paddy Crossan's. There, the proprietor encouraged a catholic clientele, and along with artists such as John Bellany, Sandy Moffat and Jim Goodall would be a sprinkle of workers, shop assistants and, before the word was in use, a small gay clientele.

I was, one summer, having an early evening drink there with my friend Rosie. As I ordered a drink at the bar I glanced at my neighbour, a bronzed neat American whose dazzling, unusual eyes struck me. I remarked to him, 'Beautiful rainbow eyes.' Later this artist visitor called Mike joined us. Rosie and I conducted him on a walk along the Water of Leith and a tour of Dean Village, to him a bit of Brigadoon.

Mike thereafter became a 'time to time' fellow drinker with myself, Jim Goodall, and other like-minded pals in a corner of the Café Royal. One evening, as I relieved myself in the Gents urinal, Mike alongside was doing likewise when to my naive surprise he turned to me his beautiful eyes, and said, 'David, it doesn't seem that you and I are going to make love.' Blink. 'No Mike, my life is complicated enough as it is.'

One evening, drinking late and excessively in the heady social intoxication of the Traverse Bar, I was talking to Mike when I realised that I hadn't thought of a place to spend the night. 'You could come to my hotel,'he suggested. Seeing my hesitation, he added, 'there are two beds.' With this reassurance, I accepted his offer and we arrived in his hotel room with two beds. 'I'm going to shower,' said he, having donned a blue silk dressing gown. He handed me a book of short stories by Tennessee Williams.

'You might like to read "One Arm",' he said as he departed for a lengthy shower.

I read this story about a one-armed rent boy. It induced in me the uneasy feeling that this might be an overture and woke in me the sense of being a Victorian virgin in danger of losing her virtue. Mike returned, and to my relief sprang into his bed. We talked for a while, he telling me the story of discovering his sexuality and of his San Francisco upbringing. I was getting sleepy when he rose from his bed, came over to mine, leaned down and gave me a full deep kiss, then retired to his own bed leaving me considerably agitated. The frisson of the kiss left me confused, shaky and wide awake.

When I reflected on the physicalities involved in a homosexual relationship, in either role, I knew I could not in any way further complicate my already complex life or my emotional involvements.

In all my rushy life, I always kept time to visit my mother every Sunday. On one visit, she said to me, 'David, where are you and Ina going to live?' In my headlong hedonistic days and intoxication with teaching under Hector and his stimulating staff at the Royal High School, I had failed to address this. It was six months before the date of my wedding to Ina.

I found that Jenners department store had a property department, and on my first visit there was offered and accepted a mews flat for a rent of £20 per month, in Belgrave Crescent Lane, just across from the splendid Dean Bridge.

I was delighted with it. Ina's reception of the Victorian abode with its ancient furnishings, iron range for heating, and kitchen with room only to house a gas cooker and a sink, was to be less than ecstatic.

It was a measure of my mother's affection for her improvident son, her fondness for Ina and her dismay at the prospect of the bride arriving to this abode, that she set about at least improving matters. She enlisted the help of my brother and his wife and they spruced up, tidied and polished the place.

Ina's pre-wedding letter from Denmark was typically witty, outright funny and untypically punctiliously practical. I'd sent her Charles Causley's poem, 'Timothy Winters' with exam questions.

Thanks for your letter this morning with poem. The poem is ok, but the questions are useless. Some of them at least. Some I can't understand; some I can't read. [We planned for her to go to Edinburgh University, which she did]. I don't know the British mark system, so you'll need to write, 'Good. Very Good. Brilliant. Fantastic. Intelligent interpretation.' Or things like that.

   Have you noticed, my sweetheart, that the style of our letters has changed slightly since we decided to get married? The previously so tender and loving love letters have now been more or less replaced by firm and short orders, asking... this and that, cruel letters in bits, neither of us want to appear over eager on this idea of getting married. We play it dead cool. I tell you that I am very happy we are getting married. I tell you this too, I love you.

   Now, darling David, please answer this in your next letter. What is the address of the flat in Dean district? There are quite a few people

I want to give it to. I would be very grateful if you would remember! The wedding will be fun.

       Love as aye, Ina

PS: Love to your mother, Eric and Christine, ... Rhona, Gordon, Shirley, Bob, and Anne, and everybody.

All my friends and family delighted in Ina.

Our best man, the voluble and exuberant Gordon, and I set out to drive to Copenhagen at the end of July 1965. I would be 30 in a month. Indefatigable, we drove non-stop to London on roads more devious and slower than the concrete highways of today.

Our first destination, how surprising, was the flat of a girlfriend in Old Brompton Road. She and I had had a to-and-fro correspondence about whether I should make this a pre-wedding resting place, but she invited Gordon and me to stay overnight on our helter-skelter journey. Our relationship had been fond, sporadic and passionate. I surely loved her. I find it impossible, as this memoir clearly shows, not to love many women, and men, that come into my life, partly for their struggle and bravery, but also that indefinable mutual magnetism that dictates some meetings. Our meeting was such a one and so it was that we spent a fond night together after a congenial meal with Gordon. Years after I married, when she was living in the turmoil of western Beirut, our letters were still a mutual nourishment and refreshment.

The wedding. Gordon and I spruced, kilted, excited. Ina neat as you like, radiant in modest white, and glowing. My mother tasteful, immaculate, contained (beneath the surface) as ever, and Mor, Ina's tea-cosy mother, warm as a new-baked cake. So, congenially, in a little church, neither of us thirled to its beliefs but consecrated and comforted by ritual, we were married. Afterwards, Gordon's wordy flow climbed into an excessively lubricated peroration, so we were all happy and Ina and I set off to the coast for a brief honeymoon before Scotland and a beginning.

As we lay on the sunny beach, I concealed the tears that moistened my eyes. All the fear and horror of expectation that I imagined was the concomitant of conventional marriage, drowned me in this dystopic vision. The song 'Little Boxes' by Malvina Reynolds played in my ear. Illogical, unlikely, but these were the thoughts that invaded me. It seemed that the riotous days when 'the sizzling beds of the town cried, quick!' were over. It was not, of course, to turn out that way.

Despite Ina's initial astonishment at the 19th century, unheated, primitively accoutred mews flat, cold above an empty garage, once a carriage house, she began to enjoy the style, adventure and sociability with which we enlivened it. Afterwards, during her time studying for an MA, she even fondly, perhaps whimsically, described it as a 'Brigadoon, a dwelling in the valley of the forgotten.'

For sure, we had fun and were inventive. We established a weekly evening with my girlfriend-love from university days, Maureen, and her accountant husband, Alan.

In early winter 1965, shortly after our marriage, the visit of a stranger out of a cold, dark night expresses something of our modus vivendi. On his travels in Denmark, a friend had given Keith Chambers, an adventurous Australian, our address. An extract from Keith's journal of the time reads:

It was dark and cold, and I was wondering how I was going to ask a complete stranger whether they could put me up for the night. They lived in what seemed like a secret little cobbled lane. I tentatively knocked at the door. It was answered by a vivacious young woman who immediately said, 'Come in,' and took off upstairs. Not 'Who are you?' or anything. When I introduced myself, 'Would you like to stay the night?' It was my introduction to Ina, Danish-Scottish hospitality, and much more!

I was ushered into a bedroom where David was in bed with a cold. Two of their friends, Maureen and Alan Mellor, were there. They'd had a meal and I was immediately given a home-brew beer, and a part in the play they were reading.

Afterwards it was decided we improvise a play, and I recall that Alan was given the part of Scrotum Charlie and David assigned the role of a homosexual. I don't remember much else.

I stayed not just the night, but for two months, a momentous introduction to Edinburgh and Scottish friends, to wildly inventive evenings of play and poetry readings, and parties where performance, music, dance, games, were the norm.

On top of this came the introduction to my future wife. I joined David, Ina, his artist friend Jim Goodall, and some others in a favourite haunt, the Café Royal, one night. With them was Frauke, a friend of David's, on a nostalgic week-long return visit to Edinburgh.

Enough to say that we were mutually attracted, and by the end of her week-long stay, decided to get married. On a night when I had agreed to baby-sit for Jim Goodall and his wife Barbara's son, Adrian, Frauke, to my relief, offered to join me. I knew nothing about babies. During that baby-sitting evening, our son Phillip was conceived, and 49 happy years later I have to be eternally grateful for that life-changing meeting with David and Ina.

Life in these first years of marriage in Belgrave Crescent Lane was busy, sociable and fun. Weekends, particularly, were crowded and excessive, with crammed parties in our little flat, theatre visits and expeditions to explore Rose Street haunts.

A colourful addition to our entourage was Robin Harper, later MSP, leader of the Scottish Green Party, and ultimately MBE. I'd met Robin in Greyfriars Bobby's pub whilst I was declaiming from Allen Ginsberg's *Howl*. His entourage and mine joined up and, equipped with the traditionally accepted entrance ticket of a 'cairry oot', we were welcomed to gatecrash a party.

Subsequently he would visit our mews flat and either sleep in my unlocked Morris Minor, or very late in the evening when we were asleep, having ascended the drain pipe, literally 'drop in' through the window into the kitchen sink. In the morning, we would find him abed in the spare room, or, ever cheerful, on the cramped couch in the kitchen/living room.

Amidst this whirlwind, not surprisingly in the atmosphere of the time, or perhaps simply because of the characters involved, there were several diverse liaisons. In an email that Ina sent me in 2016, she economically expressed a feature of our own relationships: 'Well, you had your affairs, and I had mine.' I remember that before Jim met Ina, I had told him that my wife was Danish. I was well known as a trickster, and when he met her for the first time, her English was so good, he thought I was joking.

That apart, his animation and exuberance matched hers, and they found one another equally intriguing and attractive. My response to his artist wife Barbara was similar. We were a mutually stimulating and creative company. Barbara and Jim were painting, Ina was creating a fashion agency, and I was writing, teaching and producing school plays.

At this time, Jim and Barbara had a baby son, so that we would for convenience often adjourn to their flat above the Auld Hundred pub in Rose Street. Lines from Dylan Thomas for me express the sense of ease and freedom and excitement of these giddy Edinburgh days: 'Young and easy we ran our heedless ways.' Young and easy, and excited by and in one another's company, there was an unquestioning and tacit understanding about our relationships – Jim enjoyed Ina's talent and presence and company, as I enjoyed Barbara's.

For my part, I loved and learned from Barbara's painting, and from Jim's exuberant and lucid exposition on the work, method and style of different artists. Jim, painter-teacher; Barbara, the pure artist. She painted my portrait, but later, in a fit of pique when my fickle attractions moved, had two mutual friends kidnap it from my house and, Dorian Gray style, slashed it to ribbons.

My busy life was dramatically halted by two events in 1968. After a visit Ina and I made to her mother and family in Denmark, we returned to find the ceiling in our main kitchen/dining room had collapsed, drenching the place and furnishings. This sharpened Ina's resolve for us to find accommodation more attuned to that of her native Denmark.

The second life-changing event was that I contracted mumps. My mother had solicitously, but unwisely, quarantined me from my little brother Eric when we were children, so that now as an adult the assault of the disease was life-threatening.

The high fever, testicular swelling and accompanying pain persuaded our GP to have me rushed to hospital. There the cause for concern was that the condition would attack my nervous system and affect the brain.

During the six weeks of my anxious hospital stay, I was visited by my mother who irrelevantly, but nevertheless, felt responsible for this happening at this stage of my life. Jim and Ina were often enlivening company at visiting hours. When I was discharged, I was surprised to find how weak I was, able to walk only short distances. I was further surprised, but perhaps not totally so, to find Ina enthusiastic to make love. Later, the reason for this enthusiasm confirmed my intuition: she was pregnant.

This suspicion disturbed me less than the sharp pain in my left testicle that activity induced, with a resulting Pavlovian reluctance for further sexual involvement with Ina, or elsewhere. That testicle remained sensitive and tender for a long time.

The effect of the mumps was, as I was to learn much later, to render me sterile. This may, in the great wisdom of things, have been as much a boon as a bane. I came to the conclusion that somehow there is a congruence in the events of life – the influence and teaching of my father, the composure and creative practicality of my mother, my Buddhist phase, all adduced to a conviction that 'There is a divinity that shapes our ends.' And so the fact that became ever clearer, that the baby, Juliet, that Ina bore was Jim's, never really disturbed me. Years later in an email of July 2016, when Ina and I were reminiscing about these times, she said:

> When Julie was born at the Western General Hospital, I looked at
> the little princess and my first thought was that she was a miniature
> edition of the Mayor of Newburgh [Jim's father]. She still looks more
> like her dad than she looks like herself.

Juliet's birth in October 1968 furthered the impulse to find a more spacious and warm place to live. We had no money in the bank. Mortgages could only be had by putting down a deposit.

Ina found a flat in 33 Dundas Street. Our capacity to buy it was facilitated by serendipitously fortunate circumstances. One day I met an old school mate, Brendan Lynch, now a lawyer. He suggested we buy the mews property, owned by an old lady, and with his astonishing acumen finessed a price well below the valuation so that we got a 100 per cent mortgage loan. The surplus made it possible for us to buy the New Town flat in Dundas Street, sufficient left over to install gas fires and other furnishings mainly from the bidding adventure playground of the Lyon & Turnbull sales in Thistle Street Lane. There, for instance at the remarkable price even for these days, we bought a fine wooden desk for a shilling, a coffee table for 5 shillings. Now, that flat bought in 1967 for £4,200, is worth considerably more than half a million. Thank you, Mr Lynch.

The greater space in Dundas Street predicated an expansion of people and activities. I wallpapered the spacious back room with madly excessive zeal and colour: a tropical night ceiling with gold enamelled frieze, blue and maroon Indian-style wallpaper and low lighting. This was our moody dance area.

In the front room, equally large, we would have drama-style games, inventing human machines, the characters forming parts, making interlocking motions and appropriate sounds. 'Adverbs' or 'In the Manner of the Word' was a favourite game, and I took the part of a tyrannical orchestrator of the evening, a role which almost everyone heartily accepted. 'Now, dancing!' I'd say, and we'd all change rooms, and jive, rock 'n' roll and move freestyle to the records. Amongst the regular entourage at our parties were Brian Lang, later Dean of the University of St Andrews; his friend Roger Johnson, who sang wonderfully; Cyril and Maud Forest – Cyril a talented mime artist who would feature in our Fort Knox Festival Review; Alan Rowland, a vet, friend and squash partner; a surgeon, whose name I forget, whose theatre procedures I would have dreaded, considering the excess of alcohol he drank deep into the morning previous to attending his operations. Also close Royal High School friends: Sandy Neilson and sometimes his wife Beth; Mike Riddell, the Classics teacher; Billy Boog, History teacher. Various others, including folk from Milne's Bar and the Abbotsford, and assorted gatecrashers with their cairry-oot entrance ticket. Jim Goodall was a frequent and welcome guest. Jim and I both recall the heady drink-warmed eloquence of our arguments and discussion, and his appreciation of my evangelical poetry readings which fed his own love of words.

I look back with sympathy on the trials of our downstairs spinster neighbour, Miss Campbell, with whom we miraculously remained on good terms. Not so later with Mr and Mrs Field who succeeded our patient and accommodating Mary Campbell.

My enthusiasm for drama led me to attend a Shakespeare course at Stratford-upon-Avon. This course occasioned a significant meeting.

I bade Ina farewell and was settled on the bus crowded with teachers and Shakespeare enthusiasts. Beside me was one of the few vacant seats. A young teacher who was to influence the direction of my life took this seat. Leslie Hills and I made the journey to Stratford short by our immediate rapport, the sharing of socialist views, life stories and literary enthusiasms, unsurprisingly drama and poetry.

After this course when we returned to Edinburgh, our friendship and mutual passion for drama involved us in interesting and sometimes hilarious enterprises. Gerry Slevin, the Edinburgh Education Department Drama Advisor, appointed Leslie as teacher in charge of an adventurous new Theatre Arts Centre in a disused school in Davie Street.

Leslie prompted me to join the drama workshops Gerry ran for teachers. He was a skilled and inspiring workshop leader and my attendance at those courses so fired my interest that I suggested to Sandy Forsyth, Hector's successor as Head of the Royal High School English Department, that I should give up the English curriculum and teach drama. Sandy was a great encourager, and so my classroom was denuded of desks and became a drama studio.

About this time, the actor Sandy Neilson was also appointed to teach Drama at the Royal High School. Sandy was a 'relaxed' character, perhaps in part induced by tokes of cannabis. I think it was he who introduced me, and possibly Jim Goodall too, to that experience, although we were both less devoted to its use.

We three collaborated amiably and creatively in running the school drama club productions. Jim co-opted his pupil acolytes as set designers, builders and stage crew.

The Abbotsford Bar on Rose Street was, in those days, a great meeting-place for actors, poets, staff from Jenners and a variety of interesting barflies. There Leslie Hills one evening suggested to me that the premises in Grindlay Street opposite the Lyceum, the Heriot-Watt Social Centre, were vacant and would make an admirable Edinburgh Festival Fringe venue. Enthused by this suggestion, I proposed to Jim and Sandy that we hire the premises and offer something for the Fringe. Our ebullient threesome boldly devised Fort Knox, the name intended to turn the citadel of John Knox into a golden treasury arts fortress. Our unquestioning boldness followed Goethe's precept: 'Whatever you do, or dream you can, begin it. Boldness has genius, power and magic in it.'

Fort Knox was the first-ever multi-arts complex on the Fringe. Our only capital was enthusiasm. The concept was subsequently taken up to become the money and fame driven ventures of today. Oh, how innocent were we! At that time, 1970, the A5 Fringe brochure was 40 pages long and contained 42 companies. As I write, the Fringe brochure has over 3,000 performances and the Commercial 'Assembly Company' has a book with the dimensions of a telephone directory.

Here is our entry from the 1970 programme:

FORT KNOX. New Edinburgh Arts Complex at Heriot-Watt Social Centre, Grindlay Street. Refect or reflect, morning till evening. Coffee, tea and light meals – bar, refreshments and snacks. Walk around or witness: DOUBLE BILL: LANDSCAPE by Harold Pinter and IN CAMERA by Jean-Paul Sartre, theatre 'in depth' if you like, or... RELATIVELY SPEAKING by Alan Ayckbourn, theatre 'not in depth' if you prefer. DOUBLE LATE: choose between THE CLOTH BETWEEN, thematic sense and nonsense, PHASMATROPE, reflections on our environment projected by multi audio-visual systems. TRIPLE POESY – three themes presented in poetry and song – MacDiarmid, MacCaig, Garioch, Jackson, Morgan... TRIPLE OPTICS – James Goodall, Edinburgh College of Art, moves in new medium of constructions, closely thematically linked to previous prints and paintings of former festivals. Scottish prints. Photographs. FASHION SHOWS, presented in choreography and sound. MUSIC – folk group, jazz. Finally Fort Knox Golden Ball finishes the Festival.

In 1970, our Grindlay Street venue became for three exciting weeks our home from home. We three had not a penny of capital amongst us, and no business experience. We had, however, the wit to co-opt the accountant Alan Mellor, the husband of my adventurous sporadic girlfriend, Maureen. My resourceful wife Ina had established a fashion agency that was to form a colourful addition to our enterprise. So we were set.

We began our all-engrossing preparations while we were still teaching the summer term at the Royal High School. There we found a ready advertising force of pamphleteers. We shamelessly gathered a zestful band of schoolboys, who disseminated our flyers throughout the city so effectively that the remarkable Ricky Demarco, meeting me one day, asked how on earth we made that distribution. It also excited that perceptive entrepreneur to offer us artists for our subsequent Fort Knox production the following year.

The entry from the Fringe brochure gives a good idea of the breadth of our enterprise, but little notion of the magnetism with which we attracted helpers of all kinds. It became a launch pad for some actors and nestles in the memory of some participants as gold.

Val King, our tireless, resourceful and unpaid stage manager, wrote in a letter for my 80th birthday in 2015:

Working on the Fort Knox production was certainly the happiest time in my life. The calibre of artists and backstage staff was formidable! The energy generated then gave us all the opportunity to move forwards in whatever direction we chose, and if ever age catches up we can share the music, dance of true friendship.

The cunning distribution of flyers and posters by our fleet-footed team, and press releases, gathered good audiences; and that, with some generous donations, meant that our bold enterprise concluded with from £3,000 spent, a squeaky final residue of £40.

In the spirit of those early Fringe days, our actors, poets and artists took part for accommodation and expenses. Our auditions were attended by final year students drawn by the exposure and attraction of the Fringe. Several came to make a name in the profession.

Our press coverage was a boon. Allen Wright in *The Scotsman* expressing the spirit of our aims: 'Fort Knox is the kind of enterprise that makes the Edinburgh Festival Fringe worthwhile.' And the *Daily Express* had this to say about the fashion show Zip Zip: 'If there is a prize for the most attractive cast that appears during the Festival, Zip Zip must be considered the frontrunner.' The attractive models in Ina's zippy and novel fashion show – presented in movement, music and imaginative lighting sequences – certainly put a buzz amongst the young male actors and crew, and spawned at least one romance.

The champagne buzz and excitement needed cork-popping fizzy after-show parties with their inevitable friendships, liaisons, and who knows, who would tell what 'houghmagandies'? We concluded our Festival with a Golden Ball, an entrance ticket all of ten shillings! The excitement and hyperactive bustle, the intoxicating success of our bold Fort Knox enterprise, induced a heedless euphoria, along with a contented exhaustion. Perhaps that was the recipe that occasioned a final dramatic scene.

After the last performance and a dizzy party, I returned in the early hours to a silent Dundas Street household. Juliet was asleep in her little bedroom, Jo Summers – whom we'd enlisted as a helper – was asleep in the other front bedroom, and Ina, I assumed, was asleep in our back bedroom. I opened the door and at once saw that in the bed there were two figures: Jim and Ina.

Quietly, I left the room, closing the door behind me. I went into the kitchen to have a drink of water and consider. In our tacit arrangement, this was not in the equation.

Ina had wakened and came into the kitchen. Memory is a fickle friend, but my recollection is that she suggested it might be better for me to leave. What I do recall is that I quite readily acquiesced to this suggestion.

What was in my mind? Was it the consciousness that Jim, Ina and Juliet were a family? Was it that our tacit contract was broken? Impossible now to recapture what prompted me. But anyhow, I caught a lift with the accommodating driver of the early morning electric milk wagon up Dundas Street and thereafter, at five or six in the morning, walked down Victoria Street and rang at the door of an antique shop whose owner lived above the shop. With her I spent the short remainder of the night.

Next day was Sunday, a day when Ina, Juliet and I would visit my mother in her small Morningside flat for a splendidly cooked meal. I decided to visit her myself. For whatever its logic, my memory draws a curtain on what if anything I said to her of the events of the night.

Having left my mother, I had a problem. Where to stay? I was quite habituated to an itinerant existence, but next day was Monday, the first day of the winter term of the Royal High School.

During Fort Knox and at various folk song events, I had come in a casual way to know Lesley Stewart, an attractive sporty redhead who worked at Edinburgh University in the Physical Education Department. I knew that she rented out a room in her flat in Broughton Street. Speculatively, I phoned her. 'Had she a room?' 'Who would it be for?' 'For me.'

So, quietly enough, began a chapter of seismic events and meetings. I moved into the spare bedroom in Lesley's flat in Broughton Street that evening.

In that helter-skelter of the Fort Knox weeks, and the abrupt transition back to teaching in the autumn term, I don't think I had or took time to know what was going on in the David Campbell psyche. On the surface, I seemed remarkably unruffled. I certainly had no ill feelings towards Jim or Ina, and perhaps felt things to be only a new phase in my giddy lifestyle.

After a while, when Jim left Barbara and flitted to Dundas Street, I offered to drive him to school which was en route from Lesley's flat. Thereafter, we arrived at school each morning with the appearance that nothing had changed.

Jim remains a close friend, and Ina and I are on easy terms.

15

Into the Dark

NEITHER MY DIARIES nor my memory record how my mother or family responded to this dramatic shift, but my life continued without any apparent ripples. Lesley was a hospitable hostess, a genial and attractive companion, and so it was unsurprising that our friendship metamorphosed and I flitted from the spare bedroom comfortably to hers. Lesley had already come to know many of my friends through her interest in Fort Knox and the Heretics, and we shared an enthusiasm for dance, theatre and sport.

At about this time, the Royal High School moved from its historic building on Calton Hill, splendidly overlooking Arthur's Seat, to a modern site at Barnton. Sandy Forsyth was a worthy successor to Hector MacIver, whom he taught alongside in the old school. Sandy had lectured for a time at Moray House, where his disillusion prompted him to return to teaching.

He inherited and continued Hector's free-reined inspiring leadership. He, like Hector, encouraged the five colourful members of our English Department to teach what they loved, and so each taught to his greatest strength. The English Department staff room was a Prospero island of wonder and inspiration on which the sixth form pupils were guests, invited to explore the riches of drama, poetry, novels and heady discussions. Despite the daily companionship of this stimulating company, my love of literature, enjoying the pupils and teaching itself, something in my psyche shifted and a change from within dictated that I leave teaching.

I had no plan, but set the end of the school year as my time to go. My mother, not for the first time, was anxious that I should leave the security for such an aimless future. Blanche Dubois in *A Streetcar Named Desire* is often quoted as saying, 'I have always relied on the kindness of strangers.' I seem always to have relied on the kindness of destiny. Now was such a moment. I recall Lesley one morning at breakfast time spreading a copy of the *Times Educational Supplement* before me and pointing out an advertisement for a radio producer in BBC Scotland's Schools Department. I applied for the post and was invited to an interview at the BBC, Queen Margaret Drive in Glasgow – luckily on the afternoon of the last day of term, my last day at the Royal High School, my last day of school teaching.

School closed early on that day. The English Department had a tradition of lunching together before the summer break and, on this occasion, taking their farewell of me. We dined in the local inn with not inconsiderable accompaniments of toasts, reminiscences, drinks and good wishes.

When I set off from there to drive to Glasgow in my seasoned Morris

Minor, I was hardly sober; in these days, not an unusual practice. As I entered Glasgow, I realised that a gingery bristle announced that I was in need of a shave. I purchased some disposable razors, and in the toilet facilities of the BBC, commenced to shave with the green, slimy soap from the dispenser, hoping that the various besuited gentlemen who visited the convenience were not on the interviewing committee.

Five men sat behind a long table in the interview room when I entered at 4.00pm feeling extremely relaxed. I suppose they announced who they were, identities which I failed to register or immediately forgot.

I blessed Robin Aitchison, my very average third year Melville College pupil who with his poem had won a BBC radio prize and had his verses read, thus providing a useful credential. A surprising boon sprang from the past when one of the panel, who in fact was the Head of Educational Broadcasting, Sinclair Aitken, who was to become my boss and friend, asked me to explain something of my CV in my application.

'Ah,' said I. 'This is a tale that could occupy the margins of 20th century history, but a story in which I will not name the protagonist.' I thereafter gave what must have been a tantalising, yet brief, account of my role in the life of the fantasising Lord, whom I would not identify.

Fortuitously, I also asked the panel why Scottish literature didn't feature in the Scottish BBC educational radio output, unaware that a pet project of Sinclair Aitken was to appoint a producer for such a series.

Following this interview, the slow, grinding BBC Administrative Department forgot to inform me of their decision until I had in my frustration phoned weeks later to hear I'd been appointed as a producer in the then BBC Schools Department, working in Edinburgh. Sinclair later told me that at the end of a weary series of interviews on a hot afternoon, I was a fresh breeze, but even then he suspected that I would be a blend of imagination and trouble.

From the outset, working in that department was nothing short of a delight, with its new challenges, congenial staff, commissioning the best of Scottish writers, directing experienced actors, enjoying the cooperation of creative audio assistants – a brave new world for me.

Whilst living with Lesley, my social life took some new, dramatic and disturbing turns. Sandy Neilson had been part of our Fort Knox organising trio with Jim and myself. He was also a congenial part of the Abbotsford socialising coterie. He now plunged me into a nightmare world I never wished to repeat. He suggested we explore LSD, and so Lesley invited him and his wife Beth to dinner one evening. During the meal we each 'popped a pill' and were discussing how it seemed to have no effect when the floor began to move and our surroundings shift and brighten luminously. Beth conversed with a giant cat, and what had at first been a comical disorientation became a nightmarish and unstoppable sequence of hallucinatory images, frightening and endless. So alarmed was I at one stage that I phoned a good friend, John Bishop, and he kindly and swiftly came late at night and formed a stable place in the reeling world. Long the effects lasted and sleep was impossible. After John, Sandy and Beth had left in the dazzling light of the morning, a concomitant effect of the drug was a hyper-charged sexual electricity – no compensation for the demons of the night.

The dizzy days of Fort Knox past, I was also cheerfully, and mischievously, occupied teaching an Edinburgh University Extramural evening course in Public Speaking at Currie High School. I say mischievously as I began my first workshop / lecture by alarming the class with an appearance of nervous anxiety, heavily stuttering my introduction. They were trying to conceal their alarm when I announced, 'Boldness, boldness. Be bold. Now I have your attention.' After the class, I invited them to join me in the local pub where I spent as much money as I'd earned for the session and thereafter drove home with a few drams in my blood.

Life was full. Lesley introduced me to her brother-in-law, Alan Rowland, the beginning of a great friendship and a 20-year squash playing partnership.

A dangerously congenial R Barnaby Hawkes arrived to take my vacated bedroom. Barnaby, more English than the English, would have liked to be Oscar Wilde and did a fair job repeating his extravagances and despite, or perhaps, because of his mischievous but wittily playful 'jock' mockery, had the charm to engage folk of all kinds. From the first he was a consanguineous spirit sharing a love of words, drama and mischief. In the early days in Broughton Street we made excursions to various Rose Street howffs and the Traverse bar where I introduced the bold Barnaby, black sheep son of the deceased Bishop of Lindisfarne, to Mitzi, Lady Caroline Militza Maitland, maverick daughter of the Earl of Lauderdale, and thereby hangs many tangly tales, several involving my own life.

I was planning a second incarnation of Fort Knox. The rent for the Grindlay Street venue had risen so steeply that we abandoned that idea but hired Cathedral Halls, handy in Albany Street adjacent to Lesley's Broughton Street flat. My BBC office was a couple of hundred yards away in Abercromby Place. All cosy and convenient. In the spare time my early days with the Corporation afforded, my secretary, Carol, happily typed letters to the poets and performers who would take part in Fort Knox Mark Two. Life at work, and socially, was a busy and colourful merry-go-round, but 'A crack in the teacup opens a lane to the land of the dead'.

This line in Auden's poem, 'As I Walked Out One Evening', expresses for me the truth in the vessel from which I so unconsciously drank. A black hair in Lesley's bath was the immediate cause of my expulsion from 51 Broughton Street. It was evidence that I had entertained a dark-haired woman in her bath and, by correct implication, into our bed. Enough!

This precipitate exodus coincided with my developing a virulent flu and so I took refuge in the house of my ever loving, ever forgiving mother. For whatever reasons of her own, Lesley, aware of my enfeebled condition, invited me back, and much depleted and feverish, I took a taxi and arrived late afternoon to find Lesley setting an early dinner table for three. She informed me that she and a friend were going to the opera. In an uneasy meal, it was apparent that this was more than a friend and when they left, a feeling of devastation, desertion, weakness and panic enveloped me, as well as a blind anxious jealousy. Of course, there was neither reason nor justification in this response. Enfeebled and disoriented by flu, too weak to leave the house, I entered a chartless territory inhabited by demons, a labyrinth of bewilderment and the onset of a destructive obsession with dangerous, near fatal, consequences. The plummet continued.

For a time I remained at Lesley's while she made clandestine arrangements to holiday with her married lover: herein was the depth of my demented and ugly state. Prying, I found a letter detailing their planned Mediterranean rendezvous, photocopied this letter and sent it to his wife. Not till then had I viscerally understood Othello's rack.

In my mind was a tortured pleading dialogue, incessant and feverish. When her lover returned home from their holiday, in his rage he came into the flat and would have felled me had not a woman friend of Lesley's been present.

The nightmare was to worsen. A fierce nemesis. I had been running my heedless ways, giddy, without reflection and I had sought and found the welcoming arms and bed of a teacher who had performed a one-woman play in Fort Knox. She became aware that my relationship with Lesley had changed from lodger to lover.

One night, I was in a deeply dangerous cocktail of drink and pills. Whilst in this state of desperation, in a fit of jealousy, not unlike my own, she raged into the flat and with a long-bladed kitchen knife, attacked me. In my intoxicated state, I fled down the narrow hall, fell and plunged through the plate glass window in the door, splitting open my face and cascading blood on to the floor. The sight of this, and Lesley's appearance, deterred her murderous intentions.

An ambulance took me to the Infirmary where they could not administer an anaesthetic to stitch my wounded face because of the level of alcohol in my blood.

In the morning I was transferred to Bangor Hospital on the outskirts of Edinburgh and patched up. A semblance of sanity was that my main waking thought was not to worry my mother when she would see my ravaged and wounded appearance. Trauma draws a curtain over my memory of the next few days.

How did I subsequently survive in the BBC? Through the help of my secretary and friends. From my tormented state of mind with the frenzied dialogue of voices in my head and sleeplessness, I had found a solution. A feisty woman friend introduced me to a path of instant oblivion, the danger of which I was unaware of at the time; the prescription I adopted could have proved fatal. I would spend the evening in various bars with distracting company drinking and add a Mandrax tablet: instant oblivion.

In the studio I would be directing the actors from the control room when I would fall asleep, to be kicked under the desk by my solicitous secretary. In the traditional fairy tale, with which I was later to become more deeply acquainted, the protagonist, hero or heroine, has always reached the nadir of despair when a redemptive helper comes along. Such a place had I reached, believing myself to be without a future, unlovable and ugly. The flywheel of habit alone was propelling my days.

I was invited to a party at the house of Dolina MacLennan and in the early hours of the morning she and I were the only survivors. I can still hear her lilting Lewis accent, in sympathy to my derelict state, saying, 'Just sleep here David, and have breakfast with myself and the girls, Mary and Jane, in the morning.' Her kindness, the brightness of her daughters, was the fairy-tale elixir. At a future occasion, when Doli herself was in a dark place, I was fortunately cast in the fairy godmother role.

Another unlikely helper was Barnaby. Out of this pilgrim's mire of despondency, Barnaby induced me to drive him to Aberdeen to meet up with his 'friend' Patsy and her pal in the Kirkgate Bar. Recklessly supping whisky on the way, my spirits kept afloat by Barnaby's buoyant talk, we arrived at the Kirkgate Bar, an island of sweet forgetfulness. There, intoxicated by the novelty of the adventure, the company of two lively and attractive women, and the spice of Barnaby's wit, I passed an evening free of the haunting voices, living in the electricity of the present. From the boisterous Kirkgate, the mood of congenial exuberance demanded we continue the jollification, and so in obedience to the moral dictates of the time and the north-east of Scotland, where they still chained up swings in the play park on the Sabbath, we booked two rooms in the Gay Gordons Hotel as married couples. Barnaby's memory, not mine, records that we four shared a bed. My interpretation is that this was a reflection of Barnaby's fantasy, but nevertheless a euphoric holiday from my obsessed state haloes the evening and helped to bring me out of the dark.

Through a Glass Darkly

The crash of the door's glass
        breaking through his face
announced that he had scorned
            the Laws of Truth,
    to wake in the darkest
                        prison
        where hope shrank
            into the shadows.
Fear gathered his disciples
                in the night.
    Time, the warden,
                was a clock
between each tick and tock
            a thousand years.
The future shrivelled into
                    despair.
        Ugly
and unlovable he huddled there.
One day the warden slept,
        laughing morning children
                beckoned him
            silly cornflakes talked
to one another with such clownish
                            airs
            that he took up their tale.
The clocks began again
                to tick and tock
and put the pulse back in his days.
                (David Campbell)

16

Paradise Lost

AT THE TIME I joined the BBC, there was a freedom, an artistic completeness in the role of radio producer; the producer devised the programme (often from casual talk with writers), commissioned the script, edited the work, cast the actors, chose the sound and music in collaboration with expert studio audio assistants, directed the actors and edited the recorded tape. We were mothers from conception to birth, a beautiful and satisfying role, to be blighted and diminished in the not too distant future.

The ethos in the early '70s was generous, a generosity epitomised by the much-loved actor, that 'Parfit gentil knight' of radio, Bryden Murdoch, extolled for his gentle artistry, his adoration of radio and his nourishing of young actors, informing them often of the sensitive beauty of the listening ear of the microphone.

Once Bryden phoned me. 'David, I see from next week's script that I am cast as a Lewis man who has spent 20 years in Glasgow. Do you think there will still be a Gaelic echo in his pronunciation of *galore*?' What sweet professionalism and care!

Then again one day the phone rang. It was the late urbane maverick broadcaster and raconteur, Robin Richardson. I was a fledgling and hardly knew him. 'Hello David, Robin Richardson here. You free for lunch?' Lunch was an introduction to the writer, translator and poet Alistair Reid. Robin had us meet for no reason other than the sense that we would enjoy one another's company. No immediate utilitarian purpose, merely a bringing together of like souls which, however, blossomed into a friendship and future radio programmes. I admired Robin's spaciousness and generosity.

This ethos was exemplified by the Drama Department producers Gordon Emslie and Stewart Conn, who took the trouble to convey their pleasure in a programme I had made with writer John Herdman about the colourful poet, writer, founder of The Heretics, Stuart MacGregor:

This programme provided in my view a rare and rewarding listening experience in the best tradition of the radio feature. Its underlying concern for its subject and the way this came across, was deeply moving in human terms.

I strongly recommend that it be retained, with a view to a repeat broadcast, say some time this winter. The drama budget will happily cope.

Stewart Conn

I also had the opportunity of seeing Stewart directing a programme at first- hand, and witnessed there a care and concern, meticulous attention to detail and the taking of time in the interest of creating only the best that I learned is the necessary sunshine and nourishment of the creative process.

> Full many a gem of purest ray serene
> The dark unfathom'd caves of ocean bear:
> Full many a flower is born to blush unseen,
> And waste its sweetness on the desert air.
> ('An Elegy Written in a Country Churchyard', Thomas Gray)

In the BBC at that time were many unacknowledged and dedicated people whose work was unseen in creating the excellence of programmes: John Wilkie, the audio assistant, would sit behind the glass between ourselves and the actors and rub his hands in glee and delight at virtuosic sound effects blending with the artistry of the actors. Bill Milligan could, with the care of a brain surgeon, dissect and reconstitute tape to produce fluent sound and voices from awkward pauses and insecure performances.

But the benign leader of our little Education Department kingdom was Sinclair Aitken. He was a gardener of people who seamlessly blended the role of boss and friend. He won the affection and adoration of our staff. It was to be for me moving from two inspiring idealists and teachers to another, and making another lifelong friend.

With no need to read management manuals, he knew how creativity worked, the value of play and fun. Trusting his staff completely he gained our loyalty and affection. His department became a family. At coffee break, all of us trooped out to a nearby café so that secretaries, education officers, administrators and producers mingled with visiting notable Scottish poets, musicians, writers and colourful actors. These frequently extended breaks were the cauldron from which bubbled exuberant friendships and creative programming. He would be at his desk earlier than any of us with a single-minded dedication and yet he could walk out of the office and into civvies in a blink. He loved parties and frequently insisted on my own party piece, the song 'The Frozen Logger' by James Stevens. I relished singing this song about a feisty waitress who falls in love with a mighty logger whose hallmark is stirring coffee with his thumb.

His prediction that I might be an imaginative asset and a trouble proved accurate, illustrated by this feckless incident, but matched by the depth of his own understanding and generosity.

I was lying in bed at leisurely ease with an attractive lady friend when the phone rang by my bedside. 'Good morning David. It's Sinclair.'

'Ah, good morning,' I replied cheerfully.

A disturbing silence.

'Whatever you're doing, get yourself up here as quick as you like. You're due to outline to the Broadcasting Council Committee your proposals for next session's programmes.'

Down went the phone.

Oops.

Quicker than I liked and as fast as I could, I scrambled myself and my papers together and presented myself just after the coffee break, to which time Sinclair had reallocated my proposals on the agenda.

The meeting ended, lunchtime came. I had been congratulated on the freshness and imagination of my ideas. Sinclair drew me aside and we walked to the Abbotsford Bar, known to BBC folk as 'BBC Studio 4'. Sinclair ordered two large Glen Grant whiskies. 'Don't put me in that position again boy,' he said, 'Good proposals and your silver tongue.' And that was the end of it. Sinclair knew and appreciated that my enthusiasm was boundless and that to make the programmes as beautiful as possible I would, and often did, work for as long as it took.

Sinclair was quietly but powerfully driven by the high Reithian ideals of the BBC, particularly to serve the young people of Scotland with the best of their culture and to reconnect with what, often, was lost. In our department he was introducing the young people of Scotland to the neglected history and literature of the country.

When I was at school I had not even heard of the Highland Clearances, nor much of the pantheon of Scottish writers. Now I was producing a dynamic, dramatic adaptation of Neil Gunn's excoriating Clearance novel, *Butcher's Broom* and Iain Crichton Smith's novelette of lament, *Consider the Lilies*, missions or tasks close to my heart. I was also collaborating with inspiring demotic academics like Hamish Henderson, Derek Thompson and Douglas Gifford, later to become a mischievous and companionable lodger in my house.

The BBC, to the vociferous chagrin of the formidable and highly reputed folklorist Hamish Henderson, had shamefully neglected the Scottish folk song and story scene and now our department was introducing that world to our young people.

Sinclair also inaugurated and put me in charge of the series celebrating various voices of Scotland to scotch the widely prevalent belief, even among teachers that Scots was a debased English. I had several letters complaining that we were lowering the tone, broadcasting to pupils using gutter English.

I used the popular folk singer Alastair McDonald to present this programme. The audience loved him, plied him with letters and their own recordings. Alastair astonished me by the time, love and care he took to acknowledge these. I particularly mention his warmth, ease and communicability as presenter since this was at a future time to be the cause of a sad and destructive dispute.

Sinclair also championed the imperilled language and culture of Gaeldom, establishing the influential radio and TV *Can Seo* programmes. He put his money where his mouth was by attending Morag McLeod's Gaelic evening classes and encouraging me and Ishbel MacLean from our department to go along as well; so that three times a week for two hours, we found ourselves expressing what Mairi and Hamish did on the shore. Ultimately, we could conduct conversations in Gaelic on simple everyday matters. Alas, this quickly won facility was rapidly lost when I no longer had the opportunity to converse with Gaelic speaking friends.

Sinclair was inspired by the ideals of the BBC, but was not a Corporation man, a slave to the organisation, a yes-man. When the controllers and others of the Scottish BBC hierarchy proposed to cut the education and music output to save money, he formed and promoted an underground resistance. Many sympathisers, appalled by the cuts, including myself and members of our department, became secret agents gathering members of the press, academics, literary figures and cultural icons to the cause. Sinclair was the cunning and dextrous Che Guevara of the campaign. I remember when the hierarchy called a meeting in 5 Queen Street to outline their slashing proposals. I gave a spontaneous speech calling the three philistines by name, announcing, 'Chris Irwin, Pat Walker and Pat Chalmers, your legacy and memorial will be as the triumvirate who deprived Scottish schoolchildren and the Scottish audience of the nourishment of their own cultural inheritance of music and words.' This was greeted with a silence but afterwards Che Guevara quietly congratulated his lieutenant over a large whisky in the Abbotsford. With the galvanised public support the battle was won, temporarily at least.

At the heart of his work and innovative programme ideas was his love of Scotland. A nationalist, he believed a robust autonomy would give proper dignity, identity and pride to the Scottish people. His agenda was the resurgence of a proud Scottish nation led by the realisation of its own rich cultural heritage. He died in 2010. I would love to be conversing with him today about the state of our nation. He was for me, and for Scotland and broadcasting, 'a choice and master spirit of the age'; he was an ideal boss, but above all a great and much-loved friend.

One of Sinclair's most signal achievements as an astute politician was the creation of a ground-breaking radio programme called *Kilbreck*. At work in his office in the early morning, Sinclair had brainwaves. One of these was to create a radio series that, in the widest interpretation of its meaning, would address the health of the Scotland he loved. It would look at everything from bigotry to bulimia and to do so it would harness the ancient crafts of story and drama. Scotland's health record was the poorest in Europe. He needed allies and so formed a partnership with the Scottish Health Education Group to gain the additional means to finance a daily radio drama series. He had the further insight to emulate the tried and tested Rolls Royce logistics of *The Archers*. Giving *Kilbreck* 30 years of experience before it was born, he invited its producer, William Smethurst, to give the programme its first steps. Using this template, *Kilbreck* from its very beginning, could run. The team of producer, research assistant, secretaries, audio staff, writers and actors fell into coherent roles.

I recall an unusually earnest, and I thought apprehensive, Sinclair call me to his office and say that he would like me to produce the series, making it clear that this was an act of faith and trusting me with this large and complex enterprise by which my success or failure would be judged. It was a golden chalice and one that was to engage my total devotion, passion and abilities; it was to be a challenge, an inspiration, a multi-layered success and ultimately a sadness.

And so, in a sense, a town in the Central Belt of Scotland came into existence, a fully formed old town onto which a new one was grafted. A town with a memory, a history, alive in today's world. It soon gained an audience of 300,000 listeners every week. This town was brought vividly into homes throughout Scotland by the combined teamwork of the best of Scottish writers, actors, researchers and the production team of dedicated producer, research assistants, secretaries and skilled audio staff.

Over the period of its two and a half years' existence, it attracted the cream of Scottish writers, among them Alan Spence, Tom McGrath, Rona Munro, Carl McDougall, George Byatt, Johnny Bett, Caroline Lincoln, Catherine Lockerbie and Eddie Stiven.

Kilbreck in its storytelling way sought to make people more aware of one another. No one who got to know Dead Dora could look again with prejudiced eyes on a bright-haired punk not much older than a child.

It was hardly surprising that the series should offend some people: when a child was conceived out of wedlock people threw stones; when characters discussed contraception, some listeners were outraged. The Auxiliary Bishop in Glasgow was aroused to complain to the Controller of BBC Scotland. Letter dated 27 January 1981.

In a period of over a week I was bitterly disappointed to discover that hidden in all the innocence were rather furtive indoctrinations... lessons on extra-marital sex... If this sort of thing continues, I would be tempted to set fire to *Kilbreck* and return to Ambridge forever.

Our office also received many letters of appreciation. Margaret Torrance, a listener, wrote that '*Kilbreck* is the highlight of my day.'

The harmonious marriage with the Scottish Health Education Group, represented by Yvonne Bostock, was characterised by a spirit of enthusiastic cooperation and congeniality.

At our storyline conferences might be gathered, as well as our advisors and research assistants, Tom McGrath, who on occasion described his fellow scriptwriter Alan Spence as the 'brilliant miniaturist', or the youthful Rona Munro, now renowned amongst other things for the trilogy of James plays and who then, aged 22, wrote scripts admired by the others for their consummately fashioned and stunning insight. It was a stellar company making the conference's champagne bubbles of talk glisten with fun. Out of them, however, came stories, which replicated the experiences of the listeners and prefigured for me my later vocation as a world-roving storyteller. I saw the power of the ancient craft of story to enter the imagination and transform in a way that no exposition, analysis, argument or preaching can.

In June 1982, I wrote to David Player, the UK Head of the Scottish Health Education Group (SHEG), to apprise him of the gathering success of Kilbreck. By early November, Yvonne Bostock stated that the programme was a success beyond anything that SHEG could have hoped for and that her group were responsible for bringing 25 per cent of our 300,000 per week audience to the series.

Imagine the chagrin, astonishment and anger that impelled my letter to this same David Player in London, dated 16 November 1982:

Dear David,

There has been little pleasure in the abrupt and discourteous manner of the closure of *Kilbreck* since the production and writing team had diligently and enthusiastically researched and enhanced the quality and depth of the series on the assurances of Chris Irwin, Head of Radio Scotland, and yourself that together you had worked out a formula to ensure its continuation for another 14 months at least.

There was little care for the welfare of writers and actors to find the bold announcement of their redundancy in the morning newspapers. I cannot say that I took much delight in hearing from your representative Mr Much, when I was finally able to talk to him on the phone, that it was on your advice that the management committee acted in taking that decision. No one professionally involved in the series has doubted its success.

It was ironic that only in October 1982 had the Head of BBC Radio Scotland, Chris Irwin, awarded me a bonus 'in recognition of the way you have ensured the success of *Kilbreck*.' It was now my unwelcome role to send a letter to the cast of *Kilbreck* informing them of this premature abortion of the series.

In my dedication to the series it seemed to me that I had two lives – my own daily one and the other vicarious one with the characters and in the township of Kilbreck. Its abrupt demise, with its disastrous consequences for writers, actors and the production team, as if bombed out of existence from on high, so deeply disturbed me as to give me nightmarish dreams.

At that time I was making weekly visits to the elderly Austrian Mr Charles Kovacs whose appearance between that of Albert Einstein and Albert Schweitzer seemed an apt reflection of his wisdom. His insight I valued highly and I read to him an account of one of these dreams. His advice was brief and unequivocal, 'Go to the top David, the very top. The angel who looks after your dreams is a genius.' And so unbeknownst to anyone, that is what I did. I took a week's leave, travelled to London and on the Monday morning presented myself at the office of the Director General of the BBC, Alasdair Milne, seeking an impromptu audience with the high chief. Unfortunately, he had flu. From Monday to Friday I appeared there and waited but his health did not improve. So, I borrowed a secretary from my good friend Rita Udall in the London Schools Department and wrote a one-page letter, on 10 December, outlining the case for continuing the series.

Thereafter I returned by train to Edinburgh and considered my future. I had made the best case I could for the continuation of the series. Now a week later I was sitting somewhat disconsolately at my desk, having said farewell to *Kilbreck*.

Sinclair appeared. 'Come into my office, boy. A word.'

What sort of word?

'Sit down. David, I don't know what you've done or how you did it, but the Director General has been on the phone and promised contingency funds to finance another year of *Kilbreck*, so get your skates on. And by the way, no word to anyone about your visit down south. People just don't do that. The Abbotsford at lunch time?'

Wow. 22 December 1982. A letter from God:

BBC, London,
WIA IAA

Dear David,
I am sorry that I was unable to see you but I have since discussed the matter with Chris Irwin and I hope, subject to seeing some figures, to be able to hold out for another year at any rate.

Yours sincerely, Alasdair Milne

Well, we'd been forced to bundle up the series rapidly, and gathering the pieces and starting again was pushing a juggernaut uphill. However, we succeeded and the next year we went from strength to strength.

At this time, my little *Kilbreck* production family were cosily and congenially at home in our separate office in Thistle Street.

Sinclair Aitken, with a merry party and fond farewells, retired. In his place the BBC Board appointed a manager who had no experience of producing radio programmes, but who in their judgement was well qualified to implement the regime of prioritising economy and efficiency; this predictably had seismic repercussions for the department.

The first time James Boyle made his presence felt in our office, Paula, our secretary announced unequivocally, 'I don't like that man.'

His lack of experience did not prevent him from providing myself and the writing team with a 'hit-list' of topics our series should deal with. This military vocabulary is something I was to encounter painfully and more fully at a later date. When I showed this 'hit-list' to the writing team, Tom McGrath said, 'Put it in the bucket.' It was an early demonstration of a total divergence in our understanding of the creative process, undermining the collaboration with the Scottish Education group, and an intrusion resented by the writers and myself. We had successfully and organically incorporated Scotland's health concerns into the way our plot and character and storyline moved.

And so, meantime, we carried on, but could not be unaware of this new broom in the department. One of the first innovations was to sweep away the chairs round the coffee table, and then the coffee break itself. Thus, in that one gesture, a vital and vitalising occasion was abolished; an occasion when producers, secretaries, researchers, passing actors, visitors and writers would throw ideas in the air, hear about each other's lives, or just talk about the weather. Sweet, fallow times which any enlightened management manual would endorse fully. The motivation for the removal of the break was no doubt his conviction that it would improve efficiency, save time, avoid giving visitors or the BBC hierarchy the impression that the department was idling and not in the incessant pursuit of his notion of 'excellence'. Not surprising then that he chose not to join us in 'Studio 4', the Abbotsford Bar, where after work producers, writers, poets and actors habitually congregated and where he might have been party to the birth of many constructive and creative ideas in a congenial and friendly atmosphere. Now, in this new order, lunch could be gobbled down without interrupting work if you sent out to one of the growing number of fast food dispensers and ate it at your desk with no more inconvenience than a muffled telephone voice and a dessert of antacid pills. It was found in this so-called 'pursuit of excellence' that more programmes could be made by fewer producers with the implicit notion that the value of the department could be assessed by this arithmetic, just as audience ratings would be the single measure of programme success.

The vocabulary of Mr Boyle was much different from that of his predecessor, and favourite phrases were 'capture the market' or 'hit the level' and even the word 'disobedience' was heard. A curious vocabulary for an organisation, and particularly an Education Department which had enshrined the ideals of the BBC Charter. I was to experience at first hand this new order. I had, sensing that *Kilbreck* was again to face the axe, suggested that I garner the support of the press in opposing the finance-driven policy of a BBC hierarchy marching to the tune of business thinking and market economy. With Sinclair, an invitation to join him in the pub was invariably sociable and relaxed. With James Boyle it turned out to be quite other. His response to the idea that I would write an article about *Kilbreck* was, 'Do that, and your head will roll!' With that he abruptly left the premises. This ugly threat with reference to the guillotine chimed with another of his characteristic expressions, 'bite the bullet', from the practice of giving a soldier a bullet to bite so that he would not 'sing out' while enduring a flogging by the cat o' nine tails. These did little to endear James to me.

The Scottish Education Department commissioned a report from Stirling University to evaluate the impact of *Kilbreck*. A section of this report attributed much of the success of the series to the enthusiasm, drive, character and leadership of the producer – myself – and the co-operative cohesion of the whole creative process I oversaw.

This paragraph James Boyle demanded to be omitted, and so it was excised. His reason was the assertion that the BBC *supplied* a producer, an example of the mechanistic thinking that put pegs in holes. The Stirling writers of the report, Alec Main, Amy McAlpine and Dan Macleod, had been welcome to access all areas of our production and responded appreciatively with this acknowledgement:

> Most of all we wish to thank the citizens of *Kilbreck* who took us in
> and made us feel part of their community.

Despite the positive conclusions of the report, the temporary blood transfusion from the Director General was not renewed and the priorities of the new regime were not ours. Thus, the radio township of *Kilbreck* came to an end and the curtain finally fell on a brave and inspirational endeavour.

Amongst the many commiserations about the demise of *Kilbreck* was a telegram from our friend, the producer of *The Archers*, Bill Smethurst, who had been *Kilbreck*'s midwife:

> Deepest regrets – you were obviously too good to last.
> Have a good party anyway.

My overpowering feelings were of huge admiration and gratitude to the close-knit family whose diverse members had given their hearts, abilities and devotion to create this brilliant radio township and bring its vibrant reality to the people of Scotland. My greatest thanks was to my intimate little office team, my Boadicean Welsh secretary, Paula, my amiable Irish secretary, Heather, my punctilious English researcher, Jennifer, my assistant producer, Sandy Neilson, and our devoted advisor and contributor from SHEG, Yvonne Bostock. During the topsy-turvy vicissitudes of the series we had formed a warm family bond.

In response to their request I made a farewell speech which was both tearful and cheerful which concluded:

> You wrote their stories without compromising on the harsh realities. But the visions that you writers followed and the actors brought to life was to help those people to help themselves and, where possible, to find a rainbow of hope.

It was the sweet song of the heart. We drew the curtain on *Kilbreck* with a party. Our mischief began with a satirical song penned by Eddie Stiven, written after the pattern and to the tune used by Hamish Henderson for his World War II song, 'The 51st Division's Farewell to Sicily'.

Fareweel to Kilbreck

The Beeb has gone crazy – the heid yins won't pay
Ye'll no hear *Kilbreck* on your wireless in May,
The sky o'er Queen Street is gloomy and grey
And a' the Kilbreck folk are weary.

Chorus

So fare ye weel the snack bar and Rowan tree,
Fare ye weel Tam's minimart tae,
You played oot yon pairts in yon studio –
Still mind the times there, sae cheery.

Our cast performed a comical sketch:

TAM: Aye, So ye're keepin all right then, Jim?
JIM: Och no' really. I think I might be getting a dose o' the shingles. I've got a nasty wee rash roon ma belly.
TAM: Morag hasnae been washin yer Y-fronts in biological powder has she?
JIM: Oh right enough – it could be that. I'll have a word wi her

aboot it ... when she gets better.

TAM: Oh? Whit's the matter wi' her?

JIM: Och nothin' much. Jist Post-Natal Depression, a guilt complex aboot motherhood, high blood pressure, Valium addiction, nicotine withdrawal symptoms, a weight problem, sair nipples and a wee touch o' the flu.

And finally, more fun, music, songs, drink, chatter and fond goodnights. And our revels now were ended.

After the demise of *Kilbreck*, the BBC Education Radio Department continued to produce programmes for schools as well as, at James Boyle's instigation, starting a magazine programme, of which more anon.

My role in production brought me into headlong conflict with Mr Boyle. I was now producing programmes for the upper school forms five and six on topics of literary and cultural interest for the Higher English syllabus. To that end, I commissioned Catherine Lockerbie to put together a programme on BBC news output. Catherine, who had written for *Kilbreck*, was a talented writer and journalist.

A newsreader in Glasgow objected to the part of the programme questioning why BBC Scottish news should be delivered with an RP English accent. On this perceived attack on the sacred cow of the news, Mr Boyle confiscated the broadcast tape and refused me access to it. He was in a fury and did not, as doubtless Sinclair Aitken would have done, support the producer and investigate the matter fully. I was the heretic guilty of blaspheming against the sacred Corporation and deserved to be banished. This was a fate to be not long delayed.

In the midst of this news wrangle where clearly there was no love lost between James and myself, I was considering taking the matter to the union. I was planning to take the train to Glasgow for a School Broadcasting Council meeting when James offered me a lift, which I reluctantly accepted. During that journey he took care to inform me of his intention to reward his secretary with a salary increase and affected a deep care for her welfare which unfortunately had the desired effect of temporarily softening my resolve to seek a resolution of the matter with the union. In this Stewart Conn, Head of Radio Drama, had supported me. He had been irascibly told by James to mind his own business.

There was not just a personality clash but a deep aesthetic disagreement between myself, with 16 years' experience of producing radio programmes and working with scriptwriters and actors, and James Boyle, who had done neither.

The contrast in character between myself and James was almost complete. Pam, my sister producer, pointed out that I was fond of fun, mischief and jokes, which I pursued along with my equal love of radio.

During one meeting at the time when Sinclair was boss, a Russian dele-
gation was present and I had become soporifically bored to the extent that
an elf of mischief prompted me to stand up unexpectedly and to a stunned
but attentive silence sang the whole of Hamish Henderson's great anthem,
'Freedom Come All Ye'. This was greeted by a round of Russian applause,
and Sinclair's covert approval, later endorsed in the Abbotsford when he
said, 'Well done, boy.' I couldn't imagine this response in the new order.

It is fair to say that not everyone concurred in my view or experience of
James, although some were as fulsome in their dislike of the man and his
methods, including my fiery Welsh secretary:

> He was the complete opposite of the very close, caring group of
> colleagues in the Education Department.
>   Even those who made allowances were unanimous in agreeing that
> he was not a people person.

Jane Noakes was a good friend of mine. Sinclair Aitken, seeing her in-
telligence, industry, abilities, artistry and attention to detail, had promoted
her from being his secretary to producing education programmes, to which
she brought the above qualities. For one series, she was going to employ the
singer Alastair McDonald as presenter whose skill in that area was a byword.
She told me, unfortunately not at the time, that James had called her into
the office and told her categorically that she was not to use Alastair McDonald. When she remonstrated, quoting his known and accepted qualities, his
huge popularity with the audiences in programmes he had made for me and
others, James jabbed his finger at her chest and said, 'You will not use him.'

Jane told me she became so fraught and anxious that, in a job she had
loved, she would be sick and suffer from palpitations in the mornings before
she came to work.

I was in America, in Montana, after I'd left the BBC. From my journal at
the time, 31 August 1989:

> I phoned my old friend Alan Rowland today and he told me Jane Noakes
> and her partner Rod had died in a car crash.
>   I realise the loss of a sister. Seventeen years, many vicissitudes.
>   My tears took me for a walk across the Montana grasslands and I
> came to a deserted house where I sat on a chair on the stoop, gazing at
> the foothills of the Rockies.
>   A hummingbird came and sat in the air, not more than a foot from
> my ear, silent and motionless there it stayed, a strange, beautiful,
> consolatory companion as if a messenger from my dear friend.

For Jane

Only yesterday I was thinking of you,
Reading your careful hand
On the page.
And for reasons unconnected,
From Montana here
I lifted the phone
And like a dunt under my ribs
Heard you were dead
In Scotland and everywhere, dead.
I climbed a hill
And looked to the mountains
As I gazed
Beside me, suddenly,
A little perfect humming bird
Arrived and sat, pert
Upon the air, kept by
Invisible fluttering wings
Quite still, motionless
One needle eye
Poised in greeting.

In the new order, the freedom of the producer was eroded. A Big Brother role was now assumed by the manager; this elicited from me this spoof advertisement:

Applications are invited for the position in Radio Scotland's Education Department of a Yes-Person. The main qualification required is obedience, since no professional judgement is required for the post.

Acts of creative imagination are subject to the approval of the series editor but a capacity for high-speed assembly will be considered an advantage.

Personnel appointed by the Yes-Person to fulfil radio duties for the programme can at any time be dismissed by the series editor, which relieves the Yes-Person of the necessity of evaluating such matters as presentation, scripting style or a sense of commitment to any person so appointed.

Varied radio experience will be expected of the Yes-Person, although judgements based on this experience may be disregarded. This relieves the appointee of the often tedious necessity of learning from experience.

It is of additional advantage that the series editor does not participate in the programme production and this ensures the impartiality of his judgement. His decisions are taken with all due regard to the importance of gaining the whole-hearted approval of his superiors.

When I became so deeply disenchanted with the demanding and dispiriting imposition of this new ethos, I wrote a poem. This poem I took into James's office when the retiring head of the Education Department, Gordon Menzies, was present and read it as my brief assessment of how the role of the producer had been leeched:

> They asked her to paint a picture, divine Medicis,
> But when they told her what colours to use
> The heart left her painting.

Unfortunately, this gesture fell on heavily waxed ears. Gordon, I think, wanted an easy passage to his retirement and I cannot believe the poem had any meaning for James Boyle.

James suggested that I apply for a radio post in Africa with The Voice of Kenya on a new weekly drama series dealing with health and community issues. I applied for this post but failed to be appointed. At the time, I thought that James was putting an opportunity my way, but I soon suspected it was a strategy to get rid of me. The interviewing panel put a favourite question of the time, probably still current, 'Do you think you work well under stress?' My answer was that my aim was to create an atmosphere and modus operandi where stress was not a factor, but fun was. The worshippers of the new gods failed to acknowledge that stress is a concomitant cause of many illnesses.

After 16 joyful years in the employ of Auntie, I now saw people like mice on a treadmill trying to provide ever more with ever diminishing resources.

People became hurrying shadows, depleted of manners, depleted of courtesy, depleted of humanity, and ultimately depleted of creativity, imprisoned by speed. And lack of time to feel the beauty in things stains the productions of our imaginations.

For an animal to be a chameleon is a marvel… but to try to be all things to all men is to be nothing.

The final chapter in my BBC saga was in its own wry way ironically amusing, although perhaps predictable.

James gave me a gift.

He had meticulously worked out the deal I could get if I left the BBC, not only what lump sum and pension I would have, but the offer of possible freelance work for the department over a limited period. This, considering my disillusion with the ethos and practice of the department under his management, was music to my ears, an offer I wouldn't and couldn't and didn't refuse. I might have suspected him of an iota of altruism had a little subsequent incident not confirmed my suspicion that a different agenda was in place. Being a faithful Corporation disciple to the last, following the new gods, money was the ruling factor and part of the motive to dispense with David Campbell.

James was now the Head of Education Broadcasting Scotland and his replacement in the Radio Department was Alan Jack. Following the instructions of his leader, he diffidently approached asking me to sign my resignation agreement there and then.

'Why the haste?' I enquired.

With some hesitation and embarrassment he informed me that perhaps James wished me to sign it then to save the sacred Corporation a month's executive producer's salary.

I had to laugh, to save Auntie a morsel, this meagre spirited miserliness. But, after all this was the dawning of the age of accountancy. It reminded me of how overtly dismayed James had been when he discovered that as an executive producer I was paid more than the other producers in the department.

As another, and I am sure well-intentioned gift, James recommended me to a whizz kid investment expert in Glasgow. It was not his fault that this expert advised me to place a lump sum in futures, a sum which was soon lost in the gamble. And I swear Mr Boyle grew pale when I told him of this loss.

It would be ungrateful and churlish if I did not mention that it was at his suggestion I offered the stories I had written for the Scottish Religious Service to the St Andrew Press, who published them as *Tales to Tell*. The last story in that book is appropriately titled, 'Goodbye'.

17
Musical Chairs

AFTER JIM, INA and Julie left for Denmark, I came back to live in my flat in 33 Dundas Street which was occupied by friends as lodgers and continues to be so to this day.

The ephemeral dramatis personae of the residents provided a succession of dramas and liaisons in a better than fiction soap opera.

Memory's a fickle companion, and so the order of these episodes is determined, with a little help from my friends, by the random library of my recollections.

Dramatis Personae:

Barnaby Hawkes

Mitzi, Lady Caroline Militza Maitland, and Barnaby had become an item. Barnaby, who had moved out of Broughton Street, told me Mitzi was looking for a room and so she came to occupy the spacious back bedroom in my flat, with Barnaby as a frequent visitor.

One of Barnaby's money-making sidelines was to run a little team of go-go dancers with whom he supplied the evening's entertainment in one or two Edinburgh hostelries. His random management skills meant that not infrequently the demand outgrew the supply. Mitzi loved dancing and was a fine dancer, and so it would be: 'Mitzi, darling, I'm short of a dancer for tonight.' Hence, the scantily clad Lady Caroline would dance in a bamboo cage in Jess's Bar in the West Bow.

Their affair was going so well that they became engaged and went to London for Barnaby to be introduced to Mitzi's parents Lord and Lady Lauderdale.

All was sweetness and joy, but prior to their visit someone had leaked the news of Lady Caroline's evening occupation to the ears of her father.

Boldness is all. Barnaby made a preemptive strike. To Mitzi's astonishment, she saw her father standing by the fireside, sharing cigars and port, when she heard Barnaby announce, 'Oh yes, I persuaded Militza to give up that crazy go-go dancing thing.' 'Most grateful, most grateful.' And Barnaby had an approving prospective father-in-law.

The bliss was short-lived. For reasons that Mitzi kept private, she shortly afterwards terminated the engagement.

Unfortunately, this juicy piece did not escape the attention of the *Daily*

Mail gossip columnist William Hickey who, under his 'Parting of the Ways' headline, pointedly reported that Lady Caroline Militza Maitland, daughter of Lord Lauderdale, with an Honours Degree from London University, had broken her engagement to R Barnaby W Hawkes, youngest son of the deceased Bishop of Lindisfarne, who at 'the rather advanced age of 26 was studying for O Grades at Stevenson College of Further Education.'

Barnaby wrongly attributed this leak to Mitzi, and arriving in the flat one evening pursued her to her room, which she locked. In his rage, he attempted to break down the door leaving cracks evident to this day. For a time he was, in the flat at least, persona non grata.

Varrie Scott

Before Barnaby's exit from the flat, while he was at Stevenson College he had, in the role of Pandarus, said to me, 'There is a gal in my class you must meet!' Subsequently, one afternoon as I was hurriedly putting together the last pieces of a talk I was to give that evening to my Edinburgh University Extramural Modern Drama class on Bertolt Brecht, Barnaby appeared with this 'gal', Varrie.

Not one to miss a chance, I immediately commissioned her to put page markers in a couple of the plays I was going to illustrate. Her curiosity aroused, she expressed an interest in drama, and I invited her to come along.

Varrie was strikingly beautiful. She joined the class and, with most of the students, joined me in the pub after the lecture. She accompanied me home, and that was the first night of her residence in Dundas Street, and of our relationship which was to last a year to the day and conclude as dramatically as it began.

She was, as well as attractive, spirited. One evening, when my sojourn with congenial actors in the Abbotsford had rendered me forgetful of time, and I realised I had promised to take Varrie out for a meal, belatedly I phoned the house attempting to appease her by saying, 'We could go to the new Chinese restaurant in Hanover Street, the Sik Tek Fok.' She banged the phone down with the words, 'You can Sik Tek Fok off!' This was not the end, but presaged things to come.

Robin Harper

Robin Harper, who'd been a regular, often nocturnal visitor, to our flat in Belgrave Crescent Lane, now arrived to occupy a front bedroom in Dundas Street. At the time he was a flamboyant, popular and eccentric teacher of Modern Studies in Boroughmuir High School. In the evenings, he was the regular guitar-playing troubadour in Henderson's restaurant-bar in Hanover

Street, as well as leading the four-piece band, Fourth Estate.

Not surprisingly, Robin's pupils loved his eccentricity. His teaching was, by all accounts, relaxed. Neither did his bedroom bear any sign of rigour: nothing was by half. A three-foot high pile of newspapers, presumably for his Modern Studies, a suitcase with accumulated washing delivered to the launderette when it was crammed, and for no good reason that I could fathom, a lawnmower he had recovered waiting to be uplifted from the kerbside.

At that time, we all smoked and drank liberally. Robin had a unique ash disposal system: he would hold open the turn-ups, fashionable at that time in flannel trousers, and flick in his cigarette ash. Prophetic of his future Green environmental credentials?

He was nothing if not extreme. When Fourth Estate was doing a gig in Leeds, my bedside telephone wakened me at two in the morning – Robin, to inform me of the spectacular success of the band that night. 'We slayed them,' he announced, 'I have some of the audience to talk to you.' Three enthusiastic Africans – Ezekiel, Samuel and Timothy – passed on in succession, brightly informed me, 'Your friend Robin Harper and his band were wonderful.'

All Robin's friends are accustomed to his letting them know of his notable achievements. In anyone but Robin, this could be seen as unabashed egotism; it is anyhow his unabashed delight to tell his friends of his triumphs.

Robin was lavish, spontaneous, generous and credulous, the last characteristic mercilessly exploited by me. I recall seeing Robin as I drove along Bruntsfield on my motorbike. Still wearing my helmet, I stopped beside him by the kerb and in a muffled, disguised voice asked him for directions which with endless patience he repeatedly offered when I affected deafness and a dismal lack of comprehension.

When we arrived by chance simultaneously one evening at a school to give different talks, I asked him to accompany me back to my car as I had 'the shakes'. In the car, I seized a bottle of whisky and affected to glug plentifully, informing him I was now needing more than a bottle a day. Once more, he was not only totally believing, but showed heartfelt concern. Not very kind, David!

One morning, I was unaware that Robin was entertaining a young lady to breakfast in the kitchen when I wandered in naked. Aghast, to spare his guest embarrassment, he said, 'David, make yourself decent!' I departed and returned with only a kilt sock appended to and dangling from my genitals to Robin's horror and the titters of his companion.

When Varrie and I returned to the flat one evening, she feeling unwell, we entered the stairwell to hear the sound of revelry, a party. As we ascended the stair, it was clear that the sounds emanated from my flat. I opened the front door to be confronted by a small assertive figure with, 'Who the fuck are you?'

I informed him that I was the owner of the flat. This was the actor

Ronnie Letham, remembered amongst other things for his ingenious use of expletives. Once, in full-flow in The Abbotsford, he asserted, 'It's a fucking ill fucking wind that blows no fucker any good!'

Robin had, with his generous nature, unannounced to me, decided to throw a party for his sixth year school leavers, so that apart from being greeted thus by Ronnie Letham who became a good friend, I found my newly-laid hall carpet variously bespattered and stained.

Irene

Robin's generosity of spirit led to a new drama in the flat opera. One evening, while he was entertaining the clientele in Henderson's, I answered the front door bell to an attractive blonde young woman who informed me that if she was in any trouble, Robin Harper had told here to come here. Irene worked in the Scottish Department of Holmes MacDougall bookshop. What trouble had led her to our door, I didn't enquire. She had one suitcase and I showed her into Robin's room where, when Robin returned, she spent that and subsequent nights. After a few nights, however, Robin placed a bolster pillow down the middle of the bed.

Re-enter the bold R Barnaby W Hawkes, my erstwhile flatmate and companion in Broughton Street. He telephoned to ask if he could stay the night. 'No, Barnaby,' I answered. His violent assault on Mitzi's door was still fresh in my mind. 'David, I'm really stuck,' continued Barnaby, and my fondness for this congenial spirit persuaded me to relent.

Inevitably, one night led to several in which Barnaby occupied the double bed settee in the front room. One evening, Barnaby invited Irene to dine out. This had three consequences: Irene returned renamed Irené, which more fitted Barnaby's sense of suitability for a mate; she flitted from the bolstered bed shared with Robin to the bed settee of Barnaby, Robin indicating a half-hearted show of regret; and whether on that occasion or subsequently, Barnaby miraculously straightened Irené's blocked fallopian tubes which should have impeded conception. She became pregnant, a condition which 'necessitated' a wedding in Old St Paul's Episcopalian Church where Barnaby was a regular member.

On one side of the aisle was Barnaby's twinset and pearled ample and elegant mother flanked by his two blond brothers, who might have modelled as Aryan prototypes. In contrast were Irené's parents: her father a small man with a wig, a tradesman in the Barras Market in Glasgow, and her mother looking somewhat bewildered. The music for the entry of the bride was provided by Robin Harper, wearing a colourful tie and suit that might have been slept in, and an out-at-the-knees-jeans Barry Jones was the photographer. A more casual and laid-back character it would be hard to meet, but his black and white photography was imaginative and skilful. Irené, radiant in a white three-quarter length wedding dress entered to the strains of Robin on guitar playing Bach's 'Air on the G String'. 'Appropriate,' muttered Barnaby to me, his bridegroom companion in the front row, and then his wickedness had me having trouble to hold back my laughter when he whispered, 'Rather like being at the wedding of the Arch Dreg King!'

The scene for the reception was 33 Dundas Street where was gathered an assorted entourage of friends from our social circle to celebrate the King and his glowing bride. Thereafter, the pregnancy expedited the flitting of Barnaby and Irené to a house in East Lothian.

Barnaby and Varrie: reprise

Gerry Slevin, the Edinburgh Education Department Drama Advisor and actor in many of my radio features and short stories, put in my way the congenial task of adjudicating a one-act drama festival on Mull. There I had a room in the Mishnish Hotel, famous amongst other things for its association with the legendary accordion player Bobby MacLeod.

I was not long ensconced there when, to my surprise, jack-in-the-box Barnaby arrived to join me in an adjacent room. A dangerous cocktail.

As well as adjudicating the drama contest, I was taking the opportunity to record local notables for historical and folklore radio programmes. For this purpose, I carried a bundle of five-inch reels for the hefty but compact and high-quality German Uher recorder, courtesy of the BBC.

All went well until I discovered that I was short of a reel to record the local bank manager, Angus Macintyre, famous for his poem, amongst other things, on the sinking of a whisky-laden boat, the ss *Politician*, in Tobermory Bay. This event is celebrated in Compton Mackenzie's *Whisky Galore* and in a film based on his book.

Determined to record this, I borrowed a ten-inch reel, commissioned the willing assistance of Barnaby, and we called after breakfast on the kenspeckle bank manager.

We could not begin, insisted Angus Macintyre, without a warm-up whisky. He poured three large measures of Tobermory malt into our glasses, yarned a while, and generously replenished our glasses before he was ready to begin.

He could not record standing still, so with Barnaby balancing the ten-inch reel on a pencil end to feed the five-inch reel on the hefty Uher I carried, while I, microphone in hand, followed the mobile Angus about the room, as in high performance mode and fine Highland brogue, he began:

> 'Och, times are hard in Barra',
> You'd hear the bodachs cry.

'No food to feed a sparra,
And effry bottle dry.'
Old men once fresh and frisky
So full of ploy and play
Dropped dead for want of whisky
That blessed Usqua Bae.

And so exuberantly he narrated on, with me and Barnaby in train as he dramatically strode about the room. Afterwards it was necessary to replenish the glasses.

The whisky and company had accelerated the hands of the clock, and now we would need to race to catch the ferry. So, heedlessly, foolishly, tipsily, we careered down the windy road to Craignure, arriving in time to join the end of the queue to board the ferry. The dizzy drive meant that we headed for the bar to top up.

In Oban, we had one more drink before driving to Edinburgh. Our first port of call was the Abbotsford, where I met a friend, Maggie, who invited us to her birthday party. With Maggie, I spent the night, and at morning light, sobering reality drove me repentantly home to Dundas Street. There, in place of Varrie, was her room emptied of every sign that she had ever been there. A year to the day from her arrival, she was gone.

Too late I lamented. Later I discovered that Robin had heeded her plight and plea for help and had assisted her flitting to a room in the flat Mitzi now occupied in St Vincent Street. The guttering flame of reconciliation did not last long and we both moved on. As I write, time has long healed that breach and we are good friends, she happily married with a charming daughter.

Douglas Gifford

Sinclair Aitken, my boss at the BBC, suggested I get Douglas Gifford, lecturer and later Professor in Scottish Literature at Glasgow University, to write scripts for my radio series for upper schools, *Scottish Writing*.

Like Douglas himself, his scripts were lively, imaginative, entertaining and overflowing. I recall being as excited to read his scripts on Robert Louis Stevenson and James Hogg, his great enthusiasms, as I had been to meet him. Their one problem was to cut them to length. Not surprisingly, they received an enthusiastic reception from teachers and pupils, and synchronously were a main ingredient for one of my secretaries passing the Scottish Education Department Higher English paper.

Douglas's girlfriend was Barbara McLean, and soon they came to live in a bedroom in the flat, Douglas contributing to our frequent ceilidhs with his guitar accompanying rousing versions of Scottish ballads, particularly memorably his foot-stamping 'Baron of Brackley'. The stamping caused our patient downstairs neighbour to phone about the noise so that a cushion thereafter was placed under the offending foot.

Barbara was a congenial addition to the household. Being an Honours English graduate and English teacher, meant she and I shared interests and enthusiasms. She also became my confidante about the vicissitudes of my love life.

Companionably too, we spent hours planing and revarnishing a solid old low coffee table I had bought at a knock-down price at Lyon and Turnbull's lane sales.

Douglas was commuting to university, frequently attending meetings and conferences. It was Barbara's discovery that not all of Douglas's absences were occasioned by academic demands that led to their abrupt break-up.

Barbara's despondency, I learned, was not even so much at the deception but at the knock-out blow to her self-confidence that she had been so myopic, so unaware. So ended Douglas's stay in the flat.

18

The Course of True Love Never Did Run Smooth

Let me not to the marriage of true minds
Admit impediments. Love is not love
Which alters when it alteration finds,
Or bends with the remover to remove:
O no; it is an ever-fixed mark,
That looks on tempests, and is never shaken;
It is the star to every wandering bark,
Whose worth's unknown, although his height be taken,
Love's not time's fool, though rosy lips and cheeks
Within his bending sickle's compass come;
Love alters not with his brief hours and weeks,
But bears it out even to the edge of doom.
If this be error, and upon me prov'd,
I never writ, nor no man ever lov'd.

(Sonnet 116, William Shakespeare)

THIS SONNET FOR me became talismanic in expressing the meaning, nature and implications of the deepest human love and of what it is not. The course of my love for Barbara McLean took me some distance on that path of understanding. The mode of expressing that love has changed with the changes of our circumstances, but its essence endures.

After Douglas's departure from Dundas Street, Barbara and I continued as friends and it was I that now assumed the role of confidant. She continued to live in the flat whilst enthusiastically teaching at an experimental school.

One evening, after bidding goodnight to David Turpin, a BBC radio producer who was by now resident, I knocked on Barbara's door to see how she was and to say goodnight. I recall these moments vividly. I was kneeling on the floor in front of her bed when she took my face in her hands and, an electric current! Metamorphosis, a new relationship.

Life in the flat continued to have its dramas. On the occasion of my 40th birthday, Barbara, myself and another friend, Val Inglis, had adjourned to the Abbotsford. Among the usual habitués, Norman MacCaig, Seamus Heaney and David Hammond were ensconced in a corner seat where, at Norman's invitation, we joined them. As lunchtime closing hour approached, Val announced that it was my birthday and so as usual we bought a 'cairry-oot' to carry on at my flat at 33 Dundas Street where the craic was not diminished by the flow of drink or Norman's favourite malt that we purchased en route. Barbara recalls the witty congeniality of the afternoon:

> It went on in a wonderful glow with the closed-eye style of David Hammond's singing, talk of poems and poets, flyting and liberal libations of choice malt of which David seldom lacked a bottle. It was a fantastic spur-of-the-moment party. Unfortunately, at a certain point in the evening we had to absent ourselves because we had a table booked in a country house hotel on the outskirts of Edinburgh, but that didn't deter the company at all. They were merry and said, 'Off you go,' so, leaving them to it, off we went to the restaurant, where we had a perfectly nice meal but I do remember that David stood up and sang a song to the assembled diners because of course we must have been absolutely 'fleeing'. I remember I went to the loo and there was a big staircase in this big country house, faded, but with big Turkish carpets and the usual paraphernalia of a country house – chintzy furnishing and chairs. Coming back along the corridor from the loo I noticed on a shelf was this stuffed fox. On an impulse, I took this fox and concealed it under my coat. Later I was appalled that I'd done such a thing.
>
> When we returned, the party was still going on. They probably just blinked an eye and lo, we were back again. Of course we were delighted to see the party was still going because it had been quite sad to leave it, a brilliant party.

With a strange appropriateness the continuing jollifications when we returned offered a poetic comment on the fickle nature of memory: late in the evening, Seamus, his resonant tones rendered doubtless more sonorous by the whiskies, spoke in my ear Yeats's poem 'Memory' which seemed to be his talismanic poem of the moment:

> One had a lovely face,
> And two or three had charm,
> But charm and face were in vain
> Because the mountain grass
> Cannot but keep the form
> Where the mountain hare has lain.

To me that poem expresses how memory retains the feeling or impression of a time, an event, but not the details. My recollection of the abduction of the fox firmly places me as the culprit. Barbara is just as sure that her version is what happened, and maybe it is, but it is not what is stocked in the library of my memory.

Next morning, however, what is certain is that I presented the fox to Seamus as a gift. Barbara thinks he was happy to receive it. In retrospect I tend to think that he took it out of graciousness and courtesy to his host. It certainly carried to Ireland the memory of a night none of us forgot. Years later Seamus signed his collection *District and Circle*: 'For David, thinking of the fortieth,' but I didn't learn of the ultimate fate of the fox that flew back to Ireland until I had a note from Seamus on 8 September 2009:

Dear David,
    This is Hammond's film take. A TV camera is in the house for a 70th birthday documentary and I'm pretending to write a poem. Hammond would have loved it. Your note was a strong and sweet reminder of a great revel; I don't know if I told you that Hammond named his film company 'Flying Fox' and home was given to the D Campbell fortieth birthday fox trophy as an emblem for his office... It would be good to see you but I'm not going out much these days. In good enough nick, all the same.
                        Love from the dame as well, Seamus

David Hammond I knew had opened his own television studio but I hadn't heard that the fox was adopted as its emblem providing a neat rounding of 'the revel'.

When I heard of the death of Seamus in 2013, I wrote a poem commemorating that first unforgettable meeting. A mighty evening, 'easy as eggs', he might have said.

For Seamus Heaney

'Because the mountain grass
Cannot but keep the form
Where the mountain hare has lain.'
These, Seamus, are the words you whispered
In my ear again and again
On the night of my fortieth birthday.
They still reverberate there.
And now you are laid under the grass
The imprint of the hare of your poetry
Keeps the form of not just your words
But you.

For some months, Barbara stayed in Dundas Street and then bought a flat in East Broughton Street.

Together we made a bold trip to Ireland on my Suzuki single cylinder motorbike. A meeting on this trip supplied a new tenant for Barbara's vacated room. Unpractised as we were for this Irish jaunt, we set off top heavy with tent, sleeping bags, utensils and packed rucksacks, and careered pell-mell down the motorway to Liverpool, splattered by thundering lorries and nursing a suddenly hiccupping engine. In the motorbike camaraderie of the road a passing Samaritan stopped and temporarily fixed the distributor, so that we arrived safely for the ferry to Dublin. There, amiable Irish garage mechanics in awe of our load, fixed the bike.

Visits to Ireland, my favourite country outside Scotland, were always colourful and eventful. We now made a rendezvous with Seamus and Marie Heaney, where we enjoyed a couple of nights of Irish hospitality.

From my diary at the time:

We took the 44 bus and I saw one clock showing five minutes past twelve. One broken face of a tower clock said seventeen minutes past seven, another quarter to eleven, a third quarter to eight, and yet another clock declared five to six, and when we alighted and Barbara asked a woman in Grafton Street the time, she consulted her watch and announced that it had stopped. Ah well, Ireland.

By luck we were not too late to meet Seamus and Marie in Doheny & Nesbitt's Bar (Irish time and Highland time are Celtic twins) and we occupied a cosy snug along with Seamus and Marie and a loud-laughing elderly loquacious Professor Green, who expatiated on Gaelic and Celtic Ireland. Harden, daughter of the poet WR Rogers, joined us to drink Bloody Marys and to smoke. The chat was as ready and easy and varied as ever you'd expect from the legends of Dublin snugs.

Bearing my BBC tape recorder, I was interested to hear Seamus say, 'The tape recorder annihilates what it tries to preserve.'

Yeats and George Bernard Shaw and motorbikes and more or less 'ships and shoes and sealing wax' made the evening timeless.

Next morning, more flavours of the Irish soul's love of the word.

We walked with Seamus across an old wrought iron railway bridge which workmen were raising a metre by means of jacks to allow the new electric trains access.

'You see,' says the worker looking up at us from below, 'We will raise each of the jacks "simultaneously". Now isn't that a lovely word.'

'What will you do with the added metre at the foot?' I asked.

'What do you think?' he said.

'I'd try to replicate the pattern of the old bridge,' I said. 'And isn't 'replicate' a lovely word.'

y Douglas Campbell, the author's mother, born 1900.

David Liddell Campbell, the author's father, born 1887.

David Campbell, aged two.

Charmed by a lassie, aged three.

Up to mischief, aged four.

Schooldays in England, aged six.

On holiday with dad and brother Eric, Pitlochry, aged seven.

Brother John in RAF uniform, 1943.

High jump, Western Roll-style, 1953. (*The Scotsman*)

George Heriot's School Celebrities 1953–54.

Left: Living the fantasy. '16-year old schoolboy Mike' (actually 53-year-old former Cabinet Minister Viscount Bracken) and 18-year-old David, Barscobe, 1954
Right: Morning dictionary quiz prep at 'Mike's' boarding school, 1954.

Muckerach, Dulnain Bridge
Thursday

Dear Riccy
    Thank you very much for your Christmas card.
    I should have sent you one but the only shop in Dulnain Bridge stocked such a collection of horrors that even I could not bring myself to send you one of their "Home Sweet Home at Yuletide" products.

Sir is completely recovered. Colour is back in his face, his appetite is good and he takes us for far too much exercise.
    He is very cheerful and is also very gay and strict at the same time. Only Sir can pull this off.
    A very happy New year to you Riccy
                Yours aye
                    Mike

Letter to David's brother, Eric, from 'Mike' (Bracken), 1956.

July 27. 1955

Dear David

I waited until you finished
your University class work and
were about to return as Head boy
before sending you my comments on
the Report you sent me on your
last stay at Joymount.

If you have worked really
hard during your special Latin
tuition periods, you are likely to become
stale if you have to do more before
your examination this month. You
will, therefore, be let off Latin during
the six weeks you spend at Lochnaw.

With all good wishes
Yours sincerely
John McLeod

Letters from Viscount Bracken depicting two of his many guises – both letters are from 'Mike's' supposed guardian, and the lower letter is endorsed by 'Mike's uncle', R Bracken, 1956.

If I have said nothing of Mike's needs so far and shall say little now, it is because of my belief that though he regards David in his official capacity as being exacting and instinctively knowledgeable of his deviations from work and rules, Mike looks up to David and likes him more than anyone ever placed in authority over him. The departure of David at this time, would so unsettle Mike that he would not work for any other Tutor and would never pass his University entrance examination, not even want to do so. Just as Mike would not like to prejudice David's University prospects so too, I am sure, David would not like to be the unwilling instrument of Mike's giving up a prospect of going to the University which required much cultivation by his father, you and myself. If you agree to adopt David's alternative suggestion, he should tell Mike while at Muckerach to disregard the letter about future tutoring which may be reforwarded in the immediate future. The less unsettlement there is about Tutor and pupil arrangements the better for future relationships.

During the next five or six weeks the employment bureau for summer vacation jobs conducted by the S.R.C. of Edinburgh and St.Andrews will have a long list of names of applicants. If David will ask the Secretaries to give him names of students, preferably educated at boarding schools, who are reading arts or history and are keen on games and outdoor life, he should be able to pick a good young assistant.

With such a man and a couple of good prefects, scratch games, such as cricket or soccer, can be arranged. This makes life more cheerful for all concerned.

J. McL.

Dear David
Here are McLeod's "thoughts".
I shall be in London as
from March 28.
Yours sincerely,
R. Bracken

August 25th 1957

Dear Mr. Cambell,

This is just a brief note to wish you every success in your examination. I cannot remember what date you said that you were sitting it on, but I expect that you have taken it by now.

So far as Scalpay is concerned, I think that we can look upon it as a closed book now. It was an unfortunate experience, especially for you, but like all experience it was perhaps not without some value.

I do suggest, though, that you keep an eye on the papers, especially before the next summer vacation, and see if any 'queer' advertisements appear. I shall do the same. Somehow I have a feeling that it will not be necessary, but it is best to be on the safe side. Please give my regards to Mr Carrol when you see him next. I would welcome a letter from you some time, just to know how you are going on.

Sincere regards,

Michael .T. Green

Letter from Michael Green who exposed 'Mike's' boarding school fantasy, 1957.

- 4 -

As it has already been indicated, payment for the first six months of the allowance will be made when the Halifax Society approve the house you have chosen. It will probably be convenient for your family if future payments are paid monthly into your mother's bank. The Insurance Company will do this.

Yours sincerely, Bracken

Please send Xtian names as soon as you can.

Letter regarding the house purchased for David's family by Viscount Bracken, 1957.

Viscount Bracken, Churchill's Minister of Information during WW2, pictured c. 1947.
(Image reproduced under Creative Commons CC0 1.0 Universal Public Domain Dedication;
the original image is held by the Dutch National Archives, The Hague)

First big romance, with Sandra at inter-school athletics championships, aged 18.
(Photograph courtesy of DC Thomson & Co Ltd)

Student days in Edinburgh.

21st birthday celebrations at home with girlfriend Barbara, dad, Eric, mum,
Bob (Anne's husband) and sister Anne.

Wedding to Ina, Copenhagen 1965.

David with baby Juliet, 1969.

As a young teacher, Royal High School, 1969. (Photograph by Robin Gillanders)

Fort Knox, 1970.
Back row, L–R: Neil Seager, Vivien Small,
the author.
Front row, L–R: Val King, Robin Harper.
(Photograph by Robin Gillanders)

Ina (left) with Fort Knox fashion models from her
agency, Status, George Square, Edinburgh, 1970.
(Photograph by Hamish Campsey)

Girlfriend Barbara with Ivor Cutler, Gayfield Square, Edinburgh, 1970s.

Barnaby and Irené's wedding reception, 33 Dundas Street, Edinburgh, 1974.
(Photograph by Barry Jones)

Society outing at James Hogg memorial, June 1983.

breck production team, David, Jennifer, Paula and Heather,
tside BBC Scotland, Queen Street, Edinburgh, early 1980s.

David addressing the haggis at The Heretics Burns supper, Norman MacCaig seated.
The Calton Studios, Edinburgh, 24 January 1979. (Photograph by Gordon Wright)

Lucky guest, vagrant Bert at Barbara and John's wedding reception, February 1986.

Below: The master appraises the apprentice. Telling stories with Duncan, 1988.

With wife, Linda Bandelier, 1992. (Photograph courtesy of Edinburgh City Libraries)

On the high tops with Catriona, Buachaille Etive Mòr, 2001. (Photograph by David Bathgate)

'A lovely word,' he agreed.

And that exchange to me expresses something of the enchantment of Ireland and the Irish.

We progressed to the wonder of the Great Newgrange Chamber, climbed Mount Brandon with 19-year-old Neil, son of a family who had spoiled us with their lavish hospitality, camped on the Dingle Peninsula in the rain, where we met a man who knew everything about mushrooms and introduced us to his American wife, Eris, who later came to stay in my flat. We luxuriated in the world of folk song in County Clare, and in a little village had two sad encounters.

In a bar, Barbara, in her motorcycle gear, went to order a pint and half of Guinness. The barman ignored her, but served male customers as they arrived. To Barbara's understandable chagrin, I had to get our order.

Walking along the street, a small woman approached me and said, 'I wonder if you could help me? I'm looking for my son. I haven't heard from him since he went to England.' I said that, as I worked in the BBC, I'd see if I could get in touch with local Liverpool radio. She gave me a piece of paper with his name. A little later, she ran after us and said, 'Don't do it. Give me that paper back. I don't want my daughter to know I'm hurting.'

My journeys with Barbara – geographical, emotional and spiritual – were educations of the heart.

In 1979, Barbara had temporarily stopped teaching, and we made an extensive three-month tour of the United States.

Our arrival on 11 September 1979 was neither auspicious nor cheerful. Barbara, like a rabbit before a weasel, was grilled by a chilly lady Customs inquisitor who paralysed her memory, tied her tongue and, after an hour, made her feel like boarding the first return flight to Scotland.

We had intended to fly on to Madison, Wisconsin at the invitation of Barbara's friends, the Elmendorfs, and our mutual friend Marilyn Reizbaum. Then the whizz-bang of America. I phoned my ex-girlfriend Karen who with her partner Len persuaded us to stay in Boston. Len, with explosive energy and bewildering speed, changed our flights, introduced us to his millionaire hardware store boss and took us to a dinner of giant lobsters. Eager as a child with playmates, he took us proudly on a whistle-stop exploration of the city; everything being the biggest, highest, richest and by implication, best in the world. From 900 feet aloft in the Prudential Insurance Center, we beheld a dazzling kaleidoscope of city lights and enjoyed dining extravagances, which Barbara announced to be the most delicious gastronomic moments of her life. We were given the seaside mansion of Len's boss and his wife, the Cazeaults. This was another stunning introduction to a new world, a house full of frogs of every material and size with every imaginable function and Eleanor Cazeaults herself a great frog leap of boundless hospitality. She showed us a photograph of her son Jordan, a vast young man well over 20 stone, occupying most of a couch, but when we met him he was slim, athletic and charming; he had dieted from 370 pounds down to 170, the excess flesh having been stitched together by plastic surgery.

Overwhelmed by these impressions and the generosity of our hosts, Barbara and I closed our bedroom door and laughed out loud with sheer pleasure as we took to our four-poster bed under a portrait of Admiral Benbow and surrounded by frogs.

We now turned our thoughts to our mission to gather interviews for a radio programme, *Impressions of America*. Our plan was to travel from east to west, south and back north to New York while I took up en route invitations to offer lectures which I titled 'Scotland Small', culled from MacDiarmid's ironic poem of that name. My lectures at the invitation of various universities and eccentrics were anecdotal talks on contemporary Scottish poets and writers I knew.

En route to Philadelphia we flew to Chicago, an impression of which I wrote in my journal:

Chicago airport, the entrance and first chamber of Hell, a matrix of humid labyrinths, sterile and endless, through which wander with blank faces what look like the lost and anonymous souls of a dead planet. Giant metal birds unload carrion cargo and transport legions to unknown and unknowable destinations. Waitresses with petrified faces and knives for voices sell frozen beer for evilly high prices in joyless dark bar rooms filled with purgatorial muzak. The round of activity, day and night never stops as if it had known no beginning and will last automatically forever.

Barbara and I were daunted by several experiences that brought us face to face with our naivety about the attitudes we encountered in sections of the American population. Visiting our friend Sally at the time of the crisis in Iran, we attended a meeting addressed by professors at Lehigh University in Hellertown, near Philadelphia, city of brotherly love! I was moved to rise and offer a speech. A university economist caustically berated Iran for failing to appreciate the bounty of America for conferring upon them the boon of the motor scooter, and others had made it clear that the sane and final solution to the crisis was the buck or the bomb. I cited the cultural legacies of the western world of Greek, Roman and Hebrew traditions, compared to the boast of a motor scooter! To my surprise, these sentiments were enthusiastically applauded by a small section of the audience, some of whom joined Barbara and I for a congenial drink afterwards.

In Philadelphia we continued our interviews for the programme.

It was a disappointment to me that I was too ill to go to an interview I had arranged with the Dalai Lama who was visiting Philadelphia.

By stunning contrast to his message, we attended the lavish pre-match ritual razzmatazz of an American football game, interviewed the coach Dave McLain and recorded his philosophy on the Game of Life:

> Football is like a religion here; we learned a lot from football. You block, you run with the football, you gotta cut, you work, you try to do better than your opponent. Work hard; if you are willing to work hard and overcome adversities, you learn all that in the game of football.

Not two miles from the football park, the Native American Floyd Westerman gave a talk, which Barbara and I attended. Afterwards, we interviewed him:

> We seek our vision in front of the tree. There's power there that the White Man doesn't know about that we realised for thousands of winters. The White Man has only been here 200 winters and his way of life is on a downhill run to nowhere. We should be thinking about leaving urban areas. We're going to be forced to leave because of mass pollution.

How well Greta Thunberg, David Attenborough and their like would have applauded that lecture.

In Scotland, Barbara and I loved our camping and hillwalking times in the Highlands; here, in America the mountains gave us one of our most precious memories, a golden afternoon in the Rockies on White Diamond Peak, a vast, Moby Dick rock which at over 12,000 feet would dwarf Ben Nevis. We gazed down on the western planes of Colorado stretching endlessly eastwards. Somehow, after this struggling, exhilarating ascent, we made the most perfect beautiful descent I ever made on any mountain. Walking with a loved companion in such a place at such a time seemed indeed the summit of human happiness on earth.

Our next port of call was Nebraska. Here, at the university in Wayne, I gave a talk on Scottish writers. We were boarded in Bowan Hall guest quarters and the insane jukebox began its loud rantings at 8.20am and woke the day to Bedlam. It is curious how American students seem to regard silence as a sinister enemy in any waking moment as if it would lurk in a corner and face them with some monstrous presence.

The story told by our driver to my lecture, where I was to receive a fee of $50, made me chuckle in a sour way. It became clear from his story that many in the medical profession there were more interested in the stock market than the Hippocratic Oath and she told us of yacht, ranch, private jet, mansion, shooting lodge, multi-millionaire doctors, and one whose daily surgeries taking in $2,000 were frequently interrupted by calls from his New York stockbroker who had a more insistent claim on his time than the maladies of his patients. Apparently, people spend years repaying debts and some pay with their life by fearing to attend a surgery because of the cost.

Moving on in our breakneck travel, I gave a talk to a small, pleasant group at Denver University. Dr Priest, who had arranged the event, was a gracious, scholarly gentleman. Fifty dollars for the talk. Unfortunately, afterwards, we had to drive full tilt over the speed limit to arrive and give the same talk on Contemporary Scottish Literature to the University of Colorado in Denver, a large and appreciative audience. Fifty dollars again. Then with Barbara and Bob Gale, John Herdman's brother-in-law, to a very pleasant reception party for me at which Bob, Barbara and I sang vibrantly and cheerily. Bob and I then drank and talked at home till 3.30am. Up at 7.00am, driven painlessly to the airport we caught a plane, and with a heavy hangover landed in Los Angeles. I wrote in my journal:

Sunday 28 October 1979
Today we were bathing in the Pacific Ocean just after the fog horn ceased to boom and the mist that gave everything a strangely *Death in Venice* surreality had magically lifted. We rushed amongst huge breakers in the sunshine. The beach was full of fat joggers, dainty, sprinting thin-legged seabirds playing 'What's-the-time-Mr-Wolf?' with the incoming ocean; sunglassed loafers; predatory beachcombing beggars wanting a quarter for the bus fare; frisky freaks; peacocking beach boys and languid ladies, sand-castling urchins; a tear-stained Mexican 'mama' shrieker; football aspirants; roller skate gliders; solitary old men pondering the waves; couples locked by their glands or love; fat ponderous gulls; tall thin palm trees like clusters of up-ended feather dusters stuck in the sand; laughing, wobbly black women daring the big breakers with their big bosoms; camera addicts with long-nosed, inquisitive lenses; another lovely fat girl; a shiny black athlete fighting the ocean with his thighs; a beach comedian Canute style trying to sweep the ocean back with a broom that the tide had delivered; a hovering helicopter; dozens of yachts; a silver kite with a long tail swimming above the beach like a tadpole, and Barbara and me.

The last weeks of our tour continued to bring dizzy contrasts: the sultry haze of New Orleans, the jazz, Black energy, time-warp evocations of Tom Sawyer's Old Man River Mississippi; in Pennsylvania, countryside millionaire self-made protestant work ethic entrepreneurs; San Francisco's multiracial melting pot where we were lavishly entertained by friends of Barbara in the gay community and lastly, before home, the Big Apple. More black and white contrasts. In a bus we approached New York through a tattered New Jersey, sad black men sitting around the fire on a street corner, dilapidated buildings, flaking hoardings and rubbish-strewn gutters; thence to the city: The Players' Club wood-panels smacking of another age, brandy, cigars, and the quiet purring of contented men under portraits of stage giants. In the Museum of Modern Art Chagall exhibition, we had a surprise meeting with Liz Lochhead, who later joined us to hear Irish music near where we were staying in the 'artist haven' of Greenwich Village.

So, a companion Scot to see us on our journey back home to Scotland.

Dizzily in Edinburgh, Barbara and I completed our radio programme, *Impressions of America*, for the BBC. It was a congenial and satisfying recollection of our three-month pilgrimage.

Glen Etive

There was no more grounding and refreshing way to return home than a jaunt to camp in this most beautiful of glens under the shadow of Buachaille Etive Mòr, the Hill of the Great Shepherd, the mountain at the entrance of Glencoe. By a natural swimming pool we put up our tent. In that historic glen we established a midsummer tradition welcoming many friends in years to come and exponentially, friends of friends.

On this, our first sortie, we lay on a day of incessant rain, reading in our tent, when we saw, making her way along the winding single track road, a bedraggled young woman. Hailing her, we discovered she was intending to find, at the end of the glen, the bower of Deirdre of the Sorrows of Irish legend. She had come on a pilgrimage from San Francisco because, aged nine, her teacher had told her of that Irish heroine and of her glittering beauty. It was a beauty so great that stealing a glimpse of it through a crack in the door of her exile bower, the messenger was blinded in one eye and yet reported that for another such glimpse he would gladly lose the sight of the other.

This story so impressed our young pilgrim that 12 years later she made this journey, alighted from the bus at the glen's end and walked.

Her name was Derby Brown. I informed her that the legendary bower was a 14-mile walk to the head of the glen. We drove her there, where there was a nine-pupil school taught by a Miss Campbell who had sent contributions from her pupils to my schools radio programme, *Scottish Magazine*.

She welcomed our visit and informed us that this was the very day she was taking her pupils to see Deirdre's bower. The rain fortuitously cleared and Derby, along with ourselves, was conducted to the few stones and foundations of the bower. This event was for me a prophetic foretaste of my future career as a storyteller with a deep interest in tales of Irish and Scottish

Celtic mythology and lore. Derby was dancing with delight.

One of the great love stories of the Celtic pantheon, this legend compelled me as much as it had the young Derby, making it a favourite of my repertoire.

Having dramatically closed the door on Presbyterian Christianity, I had discovered Buddhism, and through Barbara, the wise counsellor, Mr Kovacs. His interpretation of my dream it was that had propelled me to go and directly approach the Director General of the BBC, and thus to save, albeit temporarily, my radio series *Kilbreck*.

At this time, Barbara and I, along with our friend Mitzi, became regular followers of Tibetan Buddhist practice led by Edie Irwin – meditation, visualisations, teachings and massage. The sheer practicalities of this form of Buddhist practice took me back to a sense of the wholeness and interconnectedness of all things.

As my relationship with Barbara in many ways became closer through our journeys of many kinds, we decided to dispense with contraception and hopefully conceive a child. As this through time showed no sign of happening, I had fertility tests at the Western General Hospital. The letter from the consultant demonstrated clinical efficiency and little tactful empathy, stating uncompromisingly that 'In your sample we find no trace of sperm.'

So that was that, except that he suggested I could have an operation that might free any blockage in the seminal vesicle hair-thin sperm-bearing channels. This I arranged and it turned out to be unexpectedly traumatic for Barbara and my mother, and disquieting for me.

Disquieting it was for me given that the night before the operation an intern informed me that they had lost all my notes and began to take my history again. In the morning, my pubic hairs were shorn. The operation was several hours delayed and afterwards, unconscious, I was moved to another ward. When Barbara visiting me there heard my intendedly light-hearted but groggy account of these events, she fainted, fell, knocked herself out and was taken off on a stretcher to be treated. My mother, arriving to find the usual bed in the ward empty of me, with a strange instinct, asking no one directions, made her way to where I was in the new ward, not the only instance of her maternal intuition.

The subsequent letter from the consultant confirmed the first. The operation had not opened the tubes. For me, enough was enough, and I decided to interfere no further with what fate had ordained. In a way, I had had a premonition of this infertility: I was talking one evening to my American friend Marilyn Reizbaum about how fortunate I was to have wonderful parents when unaccountably I had burst into tears and when she asked me the cause I told her I was suddenly overwhelmed by the feeling that I could never be a father. And so, when I had the doctor's verdict I had already experienced the distress that this news carried. I said to Barbara, that should she meet someone with whom she could have a child, she should do that. That was not something that at that time she entertained, but the future held a different beckoning.

My exuberant first wife Ina had said to me, 'Well, David, you had your affairs, and I had mine.' The relationship with Barbara was signally different. With Ina, our extra-marital relationships were tacit. With Barbara, they were known, expressed and shared.

At one time, Barbara fell into a gloom because a close lover was not communicating, phoning, or getting in touch with her. She was clearly miserable. I decided to go to see him, which I did, expressing to him that this neglect was causing her much distress. Would he at least communicate? As I left his flat after an amiable meeting, I was aware that in a strange way, I was playing the part of Pandarus, trying to bring two lovers together.

Barbara often surprised me. One Easter, we made a wild, cold motorbike journey to Orkney, arriving in Scrabster in time to see the ferry leaving the harbour. Freezing and dispirited, we sought solace and a dram in a local hostelry where we fell in with an amiable local Samaritan; Sam, his wife being on holiday, invited us to his home. There warmed by a hot bath, a meal and a dram, we recovered and set out exploring Sam's world of childhood adventures in Thurso, and attended a live-band dance in the British Legion, visited pals, drank excessively and sailed home late to Sam's. Another dram, prelude to the surprise: Barbara announced she was off to bed, and invited us to join her.

Equally bewildered by this invitation, we confided that this was outwith our experience but accepted the gift. I could see how this was Barbara's best way of expressing her gratitude for the hospitality and generosity of our host. It was another step into my deepening understanding of the many faces and expressions of love. It would be false to pretend that the echoes of habitual, taught and accepted attitudes did not have their voices, but the journey proved to be sanguine and bright.

The onward exploration of Orkney, and visit to George Mackay Brown, had their own pleasure of friendship and discoveries.

John Donne has a poem with these lines:

> On a huge hill,
> Cragged and steep, Truth stands, and he that will
> Reach her, about must and about must go,
> And what the hills, suddenness resist, win so.

For 'truth', I can readily substitute 'love' to be standing on that hill, for at no other time of my life did the first lines of Shakespeare's sonnet 116 so directly question the character of my own search:

Let me not to the marriage of true minds
Admit impediments. Love is not love
Which alters when it alteration finds...

In our journey were many vicissitudes, connections and questions to the heart.

When we returned to Edinburgh we had been invited to a party in Calton Studios, but an attack of flu prevented my going. Barbara, now living in her flat in Broughton Place, came to see me before she set off and said she might pop in afterwards.

It was well known in our family that my mother had premonitions, not something I inherited, but that evening I had a clear sense that Barbara would make a significant meeting. This proved to be true. When she came round next evening, she said she'd met someone she'd like me to meet – John MacInnes.

This was a fulcrum meeting for all of us, one to temper and test the heart. I immediately liked John, and he liked me, but during the ensuing period when Barbara was our shared lover, we found it in different ways challenging.

One autumn evening, Barbara and I were out strolling in the New Town and Barbara suggested we call in to see John, who lived in a nearby flat. He was already in bed, but invited us in. We talked a while, and I sensed his apprehension about our departure and said, 'John, you don't want Barbara to leave, do you?' 'No,' he said.

I knew as I walked along Albany Street, in the late autumn fading light, that this was the tilting point. Hard to recall my emotions as I clearly knew they would be in bed, making love. I had no regrets for my decision, but as my relationship with Barbara subsequently changed, the sexual withdrawal was like getting used to an amputated limb. I have never lost my love for her, nor, I am sure, has she lost her love for me.

In my house at the time lived Eris, whom Barbara and I had made friends with in Dingle on our Irish trip. Eris was in her 50s, ample in every way, a Buddhist and my house companion confidante. It was a comfort that night to have her compassionate and understanding ear as we shared a goodnight dram, a farewell libation to one mode of my love for Barbara.

I was delighted to be the only non-family guest at Barbara and John's modest marriage lunch party in a small Danish restaurant, Es Danes, in Thistle Street. Apart from the general conviviality, I have one indelible memory from that occasion. My friend, Bert the Tramp, who clearly had an arrangement with the manager to have a cup of tea, appeared and was immediately welcomed. He ensconced himself eventually beside John's unmarried Edinburgh solicitor aunt, Hope, a gracious church-going, middle-aged lady. Instantly it seemed they were deep in conversation about what it is hard to imagine, but this anomalous couple, quite comic to behold, clearly enjoyed one another's company. The newlyweds considered this stranger at the wedding a good luck totem. Certainly their lasting marriage and family has been creative, warm and hospitable.

In the years when a bundle of pals made a midsummer encampment, like a nomad's village, in Glen Etive, John and I would often be the last survivors as we sat talking in the sunrise by the river. Barbara and John are my closest friends, our companionship formed by many experiences. To this day, John and I share very Scottish nonsense and flyting conversations, his wit and fun bring me to bubbles of laughter. Now, in my 80s, he, in an unobtrusive, solicitous way, helps me, particularly in tricky tasks in my caravan at Glenuig. He is a craftsman, artist and perfectionist.

As well as chronicling our American jaunt with the radio programme *Impressions of America*, Barbara and I together compiled a radio portrait of our mutual friend, Orcadian poet George Mackay Brown. We also assembled a cast for a stage adaptation of the book Barbara published on the precocious child genius Marjory Fleming. Among her many admirers, Mark Twain hailed the child as 'The World's Wonder'. Our stage presentation of the life of the Scottish-Yukon poet Robert Service revealed Barbara to have been a closet thespian.

My concluding poem 'Selchies' is a celebration of my sense of having an avuncular role in the MacInnes family.

Selchies

Two boys,
companions,
not a moment of the day unlived
poised like seabirds on a rock,
above the waiting sea,
and one,
two,
three,
the first boy plunges,
a flat smooth dive,
breaks surface sea-foamed,
squealing bird-like,
gasps of unhuman delight
a merchild
glistening
pulls himself onto the rocks.
The second boy,

silkily arcs
and becomes a white flash
in the sea,
and sleek as a seal
breaks surface silently,
wonder
and freshness
shaking from his face,
a smooth and immaculate
immersion
and emergence,
old as ever
and new as never,
and the two companions
of this heedless baptism
in the ordinariness
of being brothers
scan the rocks for the next beckoning
moment,
and I, on the isolated island,
of adulthood
bless them for this thoughtless
contagion of innocence
and throw myself
momentarily with them
into the water
and emerge,
just a little retrieved
by seadrops of glory.

19

The Heretics

In the Right Corner

Stuart MacGregor Esquire Doctor
Poet Playwright And Patriot

Flyter unflinchable
Tale teller titanic

ROUND I

with the mind at cocky stance
nods to clear the air or hair
flashes a glance
turns a taunt
jabs a jibe
circles in argument
short cuts the comment
flustering reason with fistfuls of thought

ROUND II

with as neat a telling as will
sway you to painshot
hug you to tears
he'll dainty foot you through a tale

ROUND III

with an enemy audience sullenly crouched
his dancing tongue
curls from the corner
lilts like fire
darts and sways
with surprises
tantalises
and wins the quarrel-wreath with smiles

PROMPTED BY THE knowledge that he was in the university boxing team, I wrote this poem as a contribution to a farewell book for Stuart MacGregor when he was leaving Scotland for Jamaica in 1972.

Who was he? A pugilist stepping into the ring of life, up for the tussle whatever, and ready to get in his retaliation first. A feisty charmer with a preacher roaring in the pulpit of his head and a bull in his balls. A devoted Christian soap-box orator on the Mound, his strident voice punching the air with evangelical fervour. A sincere charmer who loved the ladies, and one the ladies fell for. A Scottish nationalist who realised that the cause has to be won in the poetry, song and music that fosters an awareness of pride in our cultural distinctiveness and identity.

To this end, he formed The Heretics with aims that coincided with the work and inspiration of his Sandy Bell's Bar drinking pal, Hamish Henderson, who was bringing folk song out of the tents, fields and islands on to the centre stage of popular notice.

I'd known Stuart since schooldays where we were contemporaries at George Heriot's School and he, along with a lad called Tommy Mayo, 'converted' me to go along to the highly evangelical Bristo Baptist Chapel in Rose Street.

In my student days in the late '50s, unpredictably Stuart appeared as a travelling troubadour, guitar strung over his shoulder, at a party we were having in a barn while we worked as kitchen assistants at Cultybraggan Camp for army cadets. That was the first time I realised that Stuart was a compelling singer.

One evening in 1970, by chance I met him in Milne's Bar with an Ancient Mariner glitter in his eye. He was direct, 'David, I want you to come to a meeting of this new group and read a Scottish text.' It was he who suggested 'Scottish Noel' by Fionn MacColla. The meetings were to be on one Sunday of the month in the West End Hotel. The aim was to have established poets, singers and musicians to perform along with lesser-known aspirants. So it was that such luminous writers as MacDiarmid, Sorley MacLean, Norman MacCaig, Robert Garioch, Eddie Morgan, Hamish Henderson read along with such fledglings of the time as Donald Campbell, Liz Lochhead, Bernard MacLaverty, Rory Watson, Tom Pow and others.

These riches were equalled by a stellar cast of singers and musicians: the beautiful Gaelic singers Ishbel MacAskill and Flora MacNeil, Doli MacLennan; folk singers Archie Fisher, Jean Redpath, Bobby Eaglesham and the versatile Adam McNaughtan; musicians such as Aly Bain, John and Phil Cunningham, members of Jock Tamson's Bairns and Billy Connolly, whom we paid the grand sum of £10 at one of our special concerts.

It was at The Heretics that I first got to know Sorley and met his daughter Ishbel, a meeting that began our relationship. She had her father's love of mountains and song, enthusiasms we now shared together.

Stuart's ideals are encapsulated by reflections of the now well-known poet and writer, Tom Pow:

> The core Heretics lived in Edinburgh. David was frequently MC. I recall Donald Campbell, who read with a vigorous awareness of the spoken word that made his move into drama less of a surprise than it might have been; John Herdman, who had a wit and irony towards his characters, that made his readings amusing and barbed; Dolina MacLennan, whose Gaelic songs were the first I had ever heard – plaintive and beautiful. Stuart MacGregor and William Neill had read at the first meeting to which I contributed. Stuart, a doctor, was about to depart to Jamaica where he would soon die in a road accident; Willie was about to move to Crossmichael, near Castle Douglas, where I would see a fair bit of him and enjoy his energetic flytings. At some point in the early '70s, I was the first recipient of the 'Stuart MacGregor Memorial Award for an Unpublished Scottish Poet'. There were several more years when I could have been a justified contender! Every so often, the Heretics held a kind of gala occasion, like the reading in which Billy Connolly topped the bill. I remember we both got paid with half a dozen cans of Export. The most commanding guest of The Heretics was Norman MacCaig. You could see him, up close, in a lounge bar in New Town Edinburgh; hear the poems before they came out in book form – and hear them in quantities – slipping down one after the other. I was close enough once to hear him, thinking he was out of earshot, say to someone, 'People think it's easy, but it's the result of hard work.' I never ever heard a like comment from him all the rest of the years I knew him.
>
> The post-Heretics ceilidh was often at 33 Dundas Street, David's large New Town flat, their favoured watering hole either Milne's bar or The Abbotsford. In the latter, I saw audience members I only knew by sight and I first met Joy Hendry with her satchel of *Chapman* magazines. I also had several lively meetings with David and Norman.

In these heady early Heretic days, Stuart was a vibrant and energising presence. To the meetings in the West End Hotel, he imparted a sense of drama and urgency, a sense that history was in the making, as Donald Campbell, the poet and playwright, observed. Donald's birth and development as a poet and playwright were engendered and fostered by The Heretics, and as he observed, 'At every reading, Stuart made you feel as if it was a historic occasion.' And so, when he decided to go to Jamaica in 1972, taking up a post as Lecturer in Social and Preventative Medicine, there had to be a farewell party. Members of The Heretics composed a book of poems and presented it as a farewell gift, little dreaming that it was to be a final farewell to Stuart.

This poem by George Brown gives a notion of Stuart's character, his endless and outrageous energy:

> If you should ever chance to meet
> A quiet man with laugh discreet
> It's not MacGregor!
>
> If you should see in leafy bowers
> A figure inside drinking hours
> It's not MacGregor!
>
> And if in bed you wake in fright
> With doorbell clang at dead of night
> It is MacGregor!

It was these qualities of character – his ebullience and sense of fun married to his utter commitment to Scotland, its literature, culture and destiny – that moved me and deeply influenced my own politics. I had been brought up by my father's strong sense of socialism, with stories of John Maclean, the idealism of the post-war Labour Government, the daily reading of *The Herald*, the only left-wing national at that time.

Stuart's compassion and cultural nationalism, and my involvement with the poets and writers in Scotland at that time, convinced me that our country with its in-built inheritance of hospitality and sense of egalitarianism should look after itself, that its cultural and social welfare could not otherwise be properly nourished. Contemporary Scottish poets evoked a powerful sense of this cultural richness, identity and variety of Scotland epitomised in MacDiarmid's incandescent poem, 'Scotland Small?' The poem originated as an angry outburst at a Sassenach who dismissively described Scotland as 'insignificantly small'. It is a fine MacDiarmid rant.

Even Norman MacCaig, who eschewed any party politics, told me when I interviewed him over a customary dram of malt whisky, 'I can't stand party politics. I vote Scottish Nationalist because over so many years, I've seen Parliament and what Douglas Young used to call "the adjacent Kingdom of England" passing laws that you would think are aimed at destroying Scotland.' Sorley MacLean, with his deep sense of history, was a champion of socialism and of Gaelic culture and identity. Stuart was a great friend of Hamish Henderson whose 'Freedom Come All Ye' is the quintessential voice of international socialism, echoing the sentiment of Robert Burns' 'A Man's a Man For A' That'. Burns and Henderson would have made a meeting of consanguineous spirits:

Then let us pray that come it may
As come it will for a' that
That man to man the warld o'er
Shall brithers be for a' that.
(Robert Burns)

Black an white ane-til-ither mairriet
Mak the vile barracks o thair maisters bare
(Hamish Henderson)

I remember singing Hamish Henderson's 'Freedom Come All Ye' in a Palestinian restaurant in Jerusalem during the intifada, the strike. Despite the strong Scots language, the owner came forward, embraced me and said, 'I know what this song says. It says "you are my brother."' What had prompted me to sing it was just that sentiment of solidarity and brotherhood with the Palestinians when I had witnessed, at first hand, some of the brutalising treatment of these folk at the hands of the Israeli military and extremists.

When Stuart left for Jamaica, The Heretics continued with an energetic committee meeting regularly in the home of Dolina MacLennan and her husband George Brown, joined by myself, John Herdman, Jimmy and Morag Dunbar and Stanley Roger Green.

Cultural changes are complex and difficult to measure, but in gathering and giving a forum and exposure to the public of the best writers, poets, musicians, folk singers in Scotland for the decade of the '70s, The Heretics contributed vigorously and imaginatively to a significant shift. Being a part of this company significantly altered my own thinking and attitudes. Synchronously, taking up the post in 1971 as a radio producer in the BBC Education Department, looking after literary series for schools, gave another opportunity to contribute to that shift.

It was saddening and alarming to have certain teachers respond to programmes I produced for schools using local dialects with letters describing these forms of Scots as 'gutter English'. This attitude and the general neglect and undervaluing of Scottish writers meant that I was excited and delighted when I was given the remit to start a radio series to be called *Scottish Writing*.

I found myself in two exhilarating environments, places to which I could contribute – one as part of The Heretics planning committee, and the other in commissioning Scottish writers to make programmes for Scottish pupils in the upper school and in the primary school.

Stuart's aims and ambitions, as Sinclair's, in their different realms were identical in their promotion of Scottish writing and desire to give a sense of political confidence. In this both celebrated the past and cherished the contemporary. Sadly Stuart did not live to see the creative effervescence of the next decades.

On 25 January 1973, I was giving an Immortal Memory address at Edinburgh College of Art, commemorating the birth of Robert Burns, when John Herdman appeared to inform me that Stuart was dead.

The shock that Stuart, with his flamboyance, zest and endless vitality, was gone was impossible to comprehend. We learned that he, the great Scottish patriot, had died on the birthday of Robert Burns, at 37, the same age as the poet. After visiting a Scottish friend in Jamaica, his car had left the road and he was found dead, with no apparent sign of injury.

Stuart's spirit of cultural nationalism, central to his convictions, was energetically carried forward after his death by The Heretics Committee which organised many ambitious and significant events. Alongside and replacing the original committee were young enthusiasts who included Catherine Lockerbie, Mary McGookin, Hugh and Aileen Daly – fresh blood.

The Heretics held concerts in the Charlotte Rooms – in 1971–73 – during the Edinburgh International Festival. In 1973, their themes on three successive weeks were Sweetness, Light and Evil. Adduced to these themes were Scots and Gaelic writers and musicians: Robert Garioch, Derick Thomson, Billy Connolly, Hamish Henderson, Aly Bain and other younger writers, poets and musicians.

In the '70s, The Heretics, with a various cast travelled throughout Scotland – to Kirkintilloch, Cumbernauld, Aberdeen Art Centre at the invitation of the colourful Annie Inglis, to Prestwick, and even south of the border to Stockton-on-Tees, a singularly unsuccessful visit where we were not paid and several Heretics rather over-heavily imbibed, with consequent extravagant behaviour.

One recalls the daft occasions, and I remember such a one when we were guests of Sir Willie Murray at Auchtertyre. He had forgotten to advertise and no one turned up, and so we took up Doli's suggestion to retire to the local hostelry where we were informed that an elderly local, Jock, was a good singer. When we invited him to sing he replied, 'Aye, I'll gie ye a sang, but first I'll tell ye a wee tale o' the time I bade in a bothy and walked oot wi' a quine ca'd Maggie.'

'Ane nicht the lads in the bothy said, "Jocky, fit road div ye gang oot wi' Maggie? Ye ken ither loons in the bothy hae pit a leg o'er Maggie. Fit road d'ye play second fiddle?"'

'So next time I saw Maggie, I says till her, "Maggie, I'm no' gaun to play second fiddle ony mair." She says, "Jocky, wi' an instrument like yours, ye're lucky to be in the band at a'." So, I'll gie ye a wee ballad.' And so he did.

Drink, especially whisky, affects people in different ways. Me, it always made more loquacious, affable, affectionate, but it had two other effects: one was to waken a dangerous tendency to climb, such as scaffolding, walls, chimney stacks, pillar boxes, whatever presented itself. The other less hazardous, at least to my own person, was to strip off and streak. I think I was a streaker before the term was invented. On the occasion of another visit to Sir Willie's at Auchtertyre, after a performance and many drinks, this urge overtook me. I was sharing a room with John Herdman and threw off my garments, descended the stairs and flitted un-nymph-like through the hall, past the guests enjoying a post-performance drink and giving my naked presence hardly so much as a glance. Adam McNaughtan, however, locked his bedroom door, fearing perhaps, but inaccurately, a solicitous visit. John Herdman was more amused by Adam's precautions than by my exhibition, but then, he'd seen it all before.

Much fun and nonsense, but The Heretics were deeply earnest in promoting and enlarging the interest and knowledge and awareness of our Scottish cultural heritage. Several events highlight the growing confidence and exposure of the public to this rich resurgence.

In 1977, John Herdman and I assembled a commemorative radio portrait of Stuart from the recollections of his friends. The variety of contributions, from foremost Scottish singers and writers, as well as the fond memories of cleaning and canteen ladies, patients and assorted barflies reflect the vitality, charisma, humanity and at times outrageousness of Stuart. The programme elicited warm responses, carrying the legacy of Stuart's vigorous personality:

> Dear Sir, I've been listening to Radio Scotland since its existence, and want to tell you that your feature on Stuart MacGregor was the most moving thing I ever heard on radio.
> Major FAC Boothby

In May 1980, The Heretics held a tenth anniversary celebration in George Square Theatre. We were looking back to a time when scarcely a poem of Scotland's greatest contemporary Gaelic poet, Sorley MacLean, was known; the works of Neil Gunn were hard to come by; a library of worthwhile Scottish books was out of print, and it was almost impossible for young Scottish writers to find a publisher. The climate was November-ish when Stuart MacGregor was averring with passionate intensity that the powers of the Establishment had no inkling where the cultural pulse of Scotland beat: the BBC virtually ignored the folk tradition and seemed unaware of the rich repository of lore in the School of Scottish Studies, and either seemed astonishingly ignorant of, or had a deliberate policy to ignore, Hamish Henderson. Even more sinisterly, there is much evidence to prove that he was barred because of his political sympathies. Yet this was a man known worldwide and sought after by such as Alan Lomax, Pete Seeger and cognoscenti of that ilk, as the greatest collector and authority in the Scottish and European folk heritage. The Heretics, in that decade, conversely, had through regular monthly gatherings, festival concerts and venues throughout Scotland, given exposure to established and burgeoning young poets, singers, and musicians. Stuart had, in getting Gordon Wright to publish *Four Points of a Saltire*, brought to sudden light the poems of Sorley MacLean, George Campbell Hay, Willie Neill and his own. And in *Memo For Spring*, Gordon published Liz Lochhead's first volume of poetry. She became, after Eddie Morgan, Scotland's Makar, gained wide acclaim as a poet and playwright and became a huge inspiration to developing writers, particularly women.

Donald Campbell's fine play, *The Jesuit*, had been twice rejected by the Lyceum and every other Scottish repertory theatre. It was symptomatic of the lack of confidence or discernment that all of these established Scottish theatres rejected the play, later to be generally recognised as one of the key modern Scottish plays. It was ultimately through The Heretics that it was successfully staged and acclaimed.

I remember well one night in the Abbotsford meeting Donald who had told me he had written a play which he subsequently gave me to read. I was immediately impressed and suggested a few amendments which he took up. Once more in the Abbotsford I met my friend the actor Sandy Nielson and told him how good I thought Donald's play. Sandy was sceptical, but when I persuaded him to read it he shared my enthusiasm. When I drew The Heretics Committee's attention to the play, they so enthusiastically endorsed our opinion of it that we formed an ad hoc theatre company, approached the Traverse and there on 4 May 1976 it had its first production received with popular and critical acclaim.

I was glad of my part in helping to make this possible, a fact Donald graciously acknowledged in these words corroborating my account for this memoir:

27 February 2017
    Your recollection with regard to *The Jesuit* is exactly right. Just in case you have any doubts on the matter, I have always been grateful to you, not only for your sponsorship of my play but also for giving me my first break in radio writing.
        Best Wishes, Donald

Subsequent to this successful production, The Heretics applied to the Scottish Arts Council for funding to tour the play. The SAC were dragging their heels. How things were different in these heady days. To waken a response from the sleeping body, several of us – Dolina MacLennan, George Brown and myself – staged a stubborn sit-in on the steps as a little encouragement. This impetus resulted magically in funding for the tour. A consequence impossible to imagine in the impersonal bureaucratic paralysis of today.

The Heretics modus vivendi, through their widespread readings, brought the words of poets and novelists off the page on to the stage of public readings. All this imparted a new confidence which was effulgently expressed on 10 May 1980 by the gathered assembly of Scottish literary and musical talent. This concert lasted all afternoon and evening, and subsequently into the night. Jean Redpath, in a remark symptomatic of that heartening influence, told me that it was from Stuart MacGregor that she learned the amazing truth – that you did not need clasped hands, a trained voice, and a drawing room piano to stand up and sing, which she did at that George Square celebration.

The work of The Heretics had been one strand in a fascinating decade which began to see more Scottish novels in shops, a vibrant folk festival in Edinburgh itself and more native drama. I myself became an avid follower of the mushrooming Edinburgh folk scene. At the Howff in the High Street I first heard Archie Fisher; the Corries were frequent guests. In the upstairs room of the Waverley Bar, Dolina MacLennan sang Gaelic and Scots song, and famously Sandy Bell's was a little mecca. The Edinburgh University Folk Club had started with Stuart MacGregor and Hamish Henderson as leading luminaries.

Folk clubs and folk festivals were breeding and gave generous exposure to emergent talents. These places were marvellously egalitarian. Women and men, old and young, performer and audience, academics and 'the people' comfortably, cosily, side by side, homogenised. All this adduced to Stuart's not entirely hidden agenda to jolt awake what he saw as a sleeping Scottish cultural and political consciousness. It was a move towards national independence. This was one way of popularising, making poetry and song more a thing of, and for, the people.

In this New Wave, the folk world and the literary world came together. Whilst Sandy Bell's Bar and the Howff were burning with folk music and song, up the road at the top of the High Street, the Traverse Theatre was home to energetic Scottish drama by such as Stanley Eveling, CP Taylor, Donald Campbell, Hector MacMillan and others. It also gave a stage to Britain's Beat poets, who were following in the steps of the iconoclastic Woody Guthrie, Ginsberg, Kerouac and Corso. These poets were also read in Jim Haynes's paperback bookshop in Edinburgh's then undesecrated George Square. There seemed to be a fizz in the air, the bubbles coming up from below.

The poetry was intrinsically demotic. I recall the excitement of attending the readings by Roger McGough, Brian Patten, Pete Morgan, Adrian Henri and Alan Jackson at the Traverse. They were hugely popular and spoke with a voice Woody Guthrie would have celebrated when he said, 'I do not want to sound like dew dripping off the pebbles of the morning violet. But rather like the ash cans of early morning… like the longshoremen yelling.'

Sad that there was still a legion in the Establishment whose fingers did not touch that strong pulse.

But now, over 40 years later, a resurrected Heretics, with young poets, singers and musicians, has given Stuart's ideals new life.

In August 2015, this new incarnation of devotees invited surviving original Heretics to offer an evening in the original format of music, readings and song at the Saltire Society. That merry gathering of oldies – Donald Campbell, Adam McNaughtan, John Herdman, Dolina MacLennan, myself and Liz Lochhead – acknowledged the galvanizing effect of Stuart's innovation and encouragement. Liz succinctly expressed this by saying that the invitation to these early readings with the cream of Scottish poets was, along with the publication by Gordon Wright of *Memo for Spring*, a confidence-inspiring and fair wind at the beginning of her literary journey.

And so the spirit moves on. Stuart's fine love song, 'Coshieville', is still sung in the folk world, as is his mischievous song of young love betrayed, 'The Sandy Bell's Man'. A copy of that song, along with his debonair photo, still adorns the wall of Edinburgh's original folk pub, Sandy Bell's.

I would like to conclude this section, with a poem of Stuart's written whilst he was in Jamaica. This poem expresses to me Stuart's capacity to relate deeply and compassionately to everyone he met.

Prayer of the Country Whore-Lady

Dear Jesus Lawd, they say you die on cross
To save my soul. But that can never be.
What's good is something different from me.
I know this now inside my body's loss
Of all the things it promised I would be.

You know I come here homesick and alone
And oh my God this Kingston's wild and mean,
But you heard Mummy spit her blood and moan
And when she die her child become a stone,
So what's it matter if I filth or clean?

This city night, she's black and hot and sweet,
Cicadas sing, the tree-frog croaks and cries;
Dutch sailor hurt my pussy, bruise my feet
And bled my neck, but still I did not bleat:
He never saw the hatred in my eyes.

The Falmouth man had gentle hands and voice
He wanted love I nearly give him free;
But if you want to live you have no choice
I got to give my ten percent to Joyce
And she cares less for love than even me.

I said I was a stone, but that's a lie,
For paint and night can't hide these tears I shed,
My lonely heart feels worse than bein' dead;
Then show yourself in answer to this cry –
Oh, Jesus baby, please come in my bed.

20

Tinker and Saint: George Mackay Brown

How refreshing again, again to breathe in Orkney and to walk over
the magical rocks of Rackwick (Letter to GMB, 12 April 1982)

ONE OF MY favourite places in the world is Rackwick Bay on the island of
Hoy. To walk from the pier at Hoy up the road and through the glen between
the Ward Hill and St Johns and come across the sight of Rackwick is like a blink
of ecstasy. The drug is the glittering Atlantic, the cliffs on either side, the little
stream running down the valley and the round boulders in the sea bay. I am sure
they are enchanted for when I first visited them in my elastic days, I bounded
and bounced from one to the other as if they were beautiful rubber balls.

From Rackwick it is but a short step to climb the slopes and find yourself
gazing in wonder down the craggy improbable stack of the Old Man of
Hoy. I recall lying with Barbara, close as possible to the cliff edge, dizzy
with vertigo and delight, watching the wheeling, screeching seabirds air-
pirouetting round the rock, and see far below the sun-flashed crash and
tumble of the white sea foam against the base. On the way we had to duck
from the dive-bombing bonxies, great skuas, anxious for their nests on the
ground, swooping at our heads.

Rackwick had been love at first sight, and I was delighted to hear that
George was going to be there in 1976 when Barbara and I were planning a visit:

I've plans to come to Orkney in the summer and look forward to
splitting a bottle, sharing a jar, and cracking the air with a bit of music
as well as determining the weighty matter of the worthiest protagonist
for 1976's Scottish Bore of the Year. (Letter to GMB, 23 March 1976)

Be nice to see you in the north in high summer. Peter and Betty Grant
are coming in July. We can have, as of yore, a drink and a sing-song,
and a round of merriment. It's time to shortlist for the Scottish Bore of
the Year 1976. There's a great wealth of talent but I think I still know
who's way out ahead. (Letter from GMB, 27 March 1976)

And so Barbara and I, bearing sleeping gear, provisions and a bottle
of Highland Park, arrived at Sylvia Wishart's cottage in Rackwick, where
George was staying. We were welcomed by Peter, Betty and George's familiar
greeting, 'And did you have a good crossing, Barbara?' He had the engaging
habit of often appending your name to the end of his enquiries.

It wasn't long before libations of George's homebrew beer, and a dram or two, lubricated the conversation and fun. Many people had told me of George's talent as a mimic, and on this occasion we had his rendition of Harry Lauder-style singing, 'Keep Right on to the End of the Road' and 'Stop Your Tickling Jock', and I offered an over-the-top cod Highland teuchterish 'Way up in Clachan with Dougal McCrachan'. There was no talk of art or literature, just banter and fun, and George's ever solicitous enquiries about how we were and what we were up to.

At one stage of the discussion, late in the evening, I was standing outside the cottage with George puffing on his pipe, when he said, 'Well, David, I think I'll just take a turn down the valley to visit one of the ladies of the night.'

The idea of there being a brothel in the now-deserted cottages of Rackwick Bay was hilarious. Shortly before this time, the last family had left after the tragic drowning of their little daughter in the stream and, apart from that, only the composer Peter Maxwell Davies sporadically occupied Bunerton, a house on the hillside above the Bay.

A little drink or two in familiar company brought the otherwise reticent George into song and mischief. He instigated an earnest conversation as to who should be Scottish 'Bore of the Year'. Betty and Peter Grant offered a poet as a candidate, a wordy, pedantic creature, and they ruefully recalled, that on the occasion of his visit, George had disappeared and left them to entertain this candidate. He afterwards remarked, 'Well, Betty, I was tired of him; I just couldn't take any more.'

It was through my friendship with George that I got to know and love Orkney, a friendship and love that was shared by Barbara. Her considerable interest in astrology also engaged George who enquired in a letter to me, 'How is Barbara? Has she worked out my horoscope yet? I'll be thinking about her on 17 October.' That was their shared birthday. I'd invited George who was making a rare visit to Edinburgh to come to a surprise birthday party I'd planned for Barbara, but one of his not unusual chesty complaints unfortunately prevented it.

On a subsequent visit to Orkney in 1982 I made some recordings for my companion producer in the BBC, Jane Noakes. And following the mischievous tenor of much of our correspondence, I wrote to George:

Jane Noakes was very pleased with the tapes although I had the distinct impression that she disapproved of these flamboyant and scatological monologues towards the end of the interview, and particularly that hilariously bawdy peroration you so vividly declaimed before you passed out. I'm sure she doesn't intend to use it, which is a pity, throwing as it does a clear light on your adolescent and middle-aged obsessions. I enclose two of my recent poems for

your enjoyment and am sending you four of my shorter novels for
your critical assessment as a prelude to letting you read my longer
work in 13 volumes, at the moment only in manuscript. In a sense it is
a study of human consciousness since the emergence of language, and
yet in another way it is merely a tragi-comic assessment of the nature
of mankind. I am sure you will enjoy it and look forward very much
to your remarks about it. I'm fairly busy at the moment so would
appreciate it if you could confine these to 30 or 40 succinct pages. I very
much enjoyed the gin and conversation on our last night in Orkney. I
was dog-sick on the way over. (Letter to GMB, 12 March 1982)

George's response to this nonsense was to send me a typically kind and
considered and helpful response to the one serious poem I had sent him:

Dear David,
    Many thanks for sending the poem which I thought beautiful and
moving: especially the single lines halfway through and the end. I
confess lines like, 'And the imagination / Of time's erosion' I find a bit
confusing – the abstract words? Be true to bare 'imagism'...
    Don't let my subjective first impression upset you. The poem has a
quality of pureness.
    The contrast of 'Virgins of leaves'... with 'Old woman in black
with kindled eyes' is very moving.
    Greetings from the north on a noontide of sun and rain,
            Love to Barbara,
                George

While I was working in the BBC, George wrote several stories for my
schools radio programme. Two of these – 'The Sabistons' and 'Betty
Corrigall' – later were published, and when I asked George if I might tell
them as part of my storytelling repertoire, he graciously agreed. These are
two of my best-loved stories to tell, and are amongst the only ones in which
I necessarily, for their consummate art, inhabit word for word. For me, they
express George's ever-present sense of the rich inheritance of the past, roots
and his deep sense of compassion.
    They are part of a performance celebration of George that the dynamic
Orcadian musicians, Hazel and Jennifer Wrigley and I gave in the Edinburgh
Book Festival's Spiegeltent in 2000, and subsequently performed in several
storytelling festivals in England, Wales and Orkney. We also produced it as
a CD, *Orkney After Sunset*.
    In 1990 I visited George for the launch of his light-hearted book, *Letters
to Gypsy*. Gypsy was a silky black cat.

A cosy fire is burning in George's council house in Mayburn Court. He is recovering from a major operation to treat cancer, but I am welcomed by his sudden, surprising smile. Having exchanged greetings, I produce the BBC tape recorder: 'Don't ask me any difficult questions, David. You know I am no good at answering them.' So, we travel back 40 years to our university days, and I suggest the lines he wrote then are really his personal poetic talisman – a celebration of Orkney, Scotland, poet, tinker, saint, and the beauty of nature.

He agrees, 'Yes, I suppose that's what I've written about,' and he reiterates his convictions that, around him in Orkney, is a richness in story that is inexhaustible.

His recent operation brings us to his candid contemplation of death, which lifelong precarious health has made omnipresent: 'It could have come any time in the last 50 years, but I'm not scared of it.'

My visit concludes with a fun little gathering at the house of Gunnie Moberg and Tam MacPhail celebrating the hero of his book, Gypsy the cat. George is the king of nonsense, but is tiring and takes his leave, perhaps discussing ancestral voices with Gypsy.

With his customary courtesy, George sent me a letter thanking me for my 'beautifully written essay' and ruefully concludes:

Ten years ago, we would have made last Thursday a night to remember, with whisky and wanton choruses and excursions into fantasy. Now-o-nights, I retire early into my geriatric fastness.

I conclude with my elegy for George that Hazel and Jennifer Wrigley and I featured in our performance and CD, *Orkney After Sunset*:

Elegy

For now your saint and tinker songs are sung
And yet they are not gone
For sweet and sharp they tang the air.
As long as tales are told and songs are sung
Then by the fire your tinker croons
Pier-head gossips crane and caw
The cleft saint chants his benison
Fishermen trawl stories from the sea
The vagrant combs the beach for lucky tides
And from her still and wind-blown grave on Hoy
Young Betty Corrigall wakens us to love

21

In Chase of Beauty: Sorley MacLean

For Somhairle Macgill-Eain
on his 75th birthday

Ten years ago your feet, broken in war
Were nimble enough to climb, through
Uncertain mist, the long Fionn Choire
And stand enshrouded on the summit
of Bruach na Frithe;
But for a great Bard of the Gaels
At that moment the clouds opened
To show ridge, ravine and pinnacle
Of your beloved Cuillins;
Fire leapt on the mountain
Echoed by the leap and fall of your voice
Like a song, enumerating the passages
Of these ancient places,
Familiar friends to the days
of your youth.
From the lofty sgurr
You danced the memories of fond places;
Dizzily, sure of foot, down the broken scree,
You skipped the rocky path of
Allt Dearg,
Down easily to Sligachan and on
to Peinchorran, home.
And now may your mind, unbroken
By the decades, for long scale
The white corries of Poetry
Ascending to surprises of splendid
illumination
Along delicate narrow ridges of
argument
To dazzling flashes of lyrical
peaks
Summits of physical and intellectual
beauty

High pitches of mischief and fun,
And bring from the ancient perspectives
Of your language and heritage
Wide visions of compassion and clarity
To the peoples of our
strugglesome times.

I was happy to receive Sorley's approval in a letter: 'I like the poem immensely.' I so well remember that day. Sorley's wife, Renee, had been dubious of the wisdom of Sorley, aged 65, attempting to climb the sister hill of Ben Sligachan, Bruach na Frìthe. He had not climbed for 20 years. Blown up, his feet had been injured in the Western Desert Campaign in World War II.

But the lure of the Cuillin put that twinkle and glitter in Sorley's eye. With his daughter Ishbel, we set off. A disquieting scatter of cloud hung over the summit, but we took our route up the Fionn Choire. Some way up the steep ascent, to the amusement of Ishbel and myself, Sorley announced, 'I don't remember the Fionn Choire being so long.' And Sorley's unique extension of the 'o' vowel in 'long', accompanied by his half-closed eyes, vividly expressed his heartfelt sentiment. It didn't seem to occur to him that his age might account for the extended length of the Corrie.

We continued upwards through mists, and suddenly as we neared the summit, the mist broke. 'It opens,' sang Sorley as the gullies, crags and pinnacles dramatically revealed themselves in sunshine. Sorley sprang into flames of words, enumerating the names of the Cuillin peaks he had climbed so many years before. He ran along the summit like a goat, and on our urgent descent, skated perilously down the scree slope.

Whenever Sorley read his poems, I seemed to hear him like a Celtic bard, the high peaks and plunging ravines of his voice as if orchestrated by his beloved Cuillin. His voice fascinated me since in its breathy pauses, its huge shifts of pitch, and lingerings in unexpected places, it replicated the craggy age-weathered drama of the Cuillin Mountains. I'm pretty good at emulating his voice, though John Herdman thinks he's better. I'd been talking to my girlfriend of the time, Alison Millen, telling her about Sorley, when we met him and Renee in the Botanic Gardens. In his enthusiastic way he greeted me, 'Ah, the Campbell, out and about. How are you, then?' Alison disappeared behind a bush. She had not believed my imitation was as extreme as this vivid reality. Not only was Sorley's voice and expression unique, but he fashioned his speech like a complex literary sentence: 'When Stuart MacGregor asked me to come in with him on *Four Points of a Saltire*, I thought of what Stuart MacGregor was for my brother Calum in the last four years of Calum's life, and realised I could refuse Stuart MacGregor... [pause, breath]... nothing.'

I was working with a new well-intentioned BBC Sound Engineer on an interview I'd made with Sorley. 'If I cut the breaths,' he suggested, 'we could save a lot of time.' 'And,' I said, 'we would lose Sorley.'

What repeatedly struck me about Sorley was his capacity to listen. He gave everyone his absolute intent attention. He listened with the stillness of a cat hunting its prey, watching and alert. My good friend, Alan Rowland, a big animal pathologist in Edinburgh Veterinary College, dropped in to see me. Sorley and I had been discussing a piece for radio. By the time I'd returned with a pot of tea, I was surprised to find them deep in discussion about the qualities of different breeds of bull, about which Sorley seemed extremely knowledgeable. When I was travelling to Skye with Duncan Williamson in my camper van to tell stories in schools there, I suggested we take the chance to visit Sorley and Renee in Braes. To put us in the mood, and introduce Duncan to Sorley, I decided to play a tape of Sorley reading his poetry which I loved. My companion didn't share my enthusiasm: 'Put that stuff off! Classical shit,' said Duncan.

But when we sat in Sorley's house in Braes, these two were instant companions, bound by their mutual interest in, and knowledge of, family history. Sorley somehow knew much of the genealogy of the Williamson Travellers.

On an occasion when Sorley's daughter Ishbel and I were going out together, and celebrating Hogmanay in Braes with the family, I decided, warmed by whisky, to bring in the New Year by streaking through the snow. Sorley recounted this incident to Duncan, in whom it inspired this bit of fun:

The Streaker from the Braes

Come lissen to my story and I'll tell you by and by
About an Edinburgh streaker on the Isle of Skye
The people will remember all their lasting days
When they saw the streaker running through the Braes.

The people gazed in wonder as he ran down the street
As naked as he was born from his head down to his feet
'Ha, Ha,' old Sorley cried, 'in all my living days
I have never seen a streaker a running through the Braes.

Old Angus Mckay was drunk that night
As he staggered on his feet
When he saw that streaker coming down the street
For he gazed in wonder and gave a drunken sigh
That's the biggest snowflake I have ever seen on the Isle of Skye.
Then old Kate McClean she ran out from her wee bit but and ben

Saying, 'I will never get a chance to see a thing like that again'
For she gazed in wonder the way that he would go
For she fell in love with that streaker in the snow.

Old Jean McNeil she gave a cry as he went running by
Saying, 'I would rather have him in bed with me than all the gold in Skye'
But on and on the streaker went as fast as he could go
Even though his willie was frozen with the snow.

But it still remains a mystery only Sorley knows
Who went a streaking in his birthday clothes
But people will remember as years and years go by
The day the Edinburgh streaker came to the Isle of Skye.

Sorley's response to my idiosyncratic desire to divest and caper through the snow was no more than an interested curiosity about what motivated 'the Campbell's behaviour" John Herdman subsequently reported Sorley's remark to him: 'I wonder what it is that makes David Campbell... (long pause, breath)... a streaker?'

Whoever visited, and whatever the topic got Sorley's full engagement; talking about the tides around Raasay with a neighbour, discussing some historical event as if it was yesterday: 'He was injured at Corunna and afterwards swam with one arm!', the Clearances, Macpherson's *Ossian*, cathedrals, the Gaelic Beginners Course, of which he was the proud innovator, his huge love and discerning knowledge of Gaelic song. He regretted that he could not hold a tune, but boasted, justifiably, that his discernment of time, weight and rhythm was impeccable. He told me that his exposure to great Gaelic singers was the deep source and impulsion of his poetry:

I think the first great artistic impact on me was my father's mother's singing some of the great Gaelic songs, but my father was better at the 'Cro of Kintail' than his mother was. My father's voice was good, and in some songs his timing and weight was such that I now find it difficult to listen to those songs from anyone else. My father also had a great interest in language for its own sake. I was much influenced by both of these.

Sorley's memory and knowledge were deep and wide, balanced by a distinct vagueness. The MacLean family had an amused tolerance of Sorley's material impracticality. Ishbel said his driving was so erratic that he was only allowed to drive in second gear until they got out of Skye, and then one of the family members took over. David Ross, later married to Mary, told me one or two amusing incidents of his lack of involvement with this world. This was before the day of mobile phones, and Sorley had phoned David's landline. When David answered, Sorley's first remark was, 'Are you at home?' Where else? Apparently also, Renee and Sorley were once in a hotel, and Sorley remarked to his unsurprised wife, 'Renee, I can't seem to get this phone to work.' 'You won't Sorley. It's the hairdryer.' For all Sorley's apparent unworldliness – Renee used to warn him at readings to take his watch off and put it on the lectern – he connected warmly and intimately with audiences and with people of every sort, and engaged universal affection.

I was sitting with Norman MacCaig and Dolina MacLennan at one of Sorley's readings in George Square Theatre. That Renee had cautioned him to be organised did not prevent him shuffling his papers at length before beginning, to which sotto voce Norman remarked, 'We knew Sorley was going to read, but we thought he was going to read out loud'. Finally Sorley found the poem he was going to read and prefaced it by saying 'The word Clachan appears in this poem and it designates not any village but one with the Church... (pause)... oh God! The word Clachan does not appear in this poem,' and then moving on to the next poem he announced, 'In this poem, the word Clachan does appear!'

Characteristic of Sorley's Celtic love of physical beauty and beauty of poetry and mind is this story Norman told me of Sorley: 'Norman, did I fall asleep at the ceilidh?' 'I don't think so.' 'Well,' said Sorley, 'after a certain amount of drink these days I would fall asleep if I had, on the one hand Helen of Troy, and on the other... Voltaire.'

Sorley expresses these twin passions in what he calls the automatic poem 'Dogs and wolves', where he sees the 'mild mad dogs' of his poetry, 'wolves in chase of beauty, beauty of soul and face... a hunt without halt, without respite.'

Knowing Sorley, hearing his conversation and readings, kindled in me a lifelong love of Gaelic poetry albeit in translation, and the Gaelic / Celtic inheritance. This in turn was to prompt my Celtic-inspired stories, *Out of the Mouth of the Morning*.

Now I can't look at the Scottish mountains without hearing the wonderful rise and fall of Sorley's voice, nor bringing to mind as, applicable to him, words with which he described his friend and admirer Stuart MacGregor: 'He was a man of great vividness and great warmth.'

22

The Beginning of a New Song: Iain Crichton Smith

I FIRST MET Iain Crichton Smith in the bar of the Traverse Theatre in the Grassmarket after a production of *The Caretaker*. He didn't look particularly well shaved nor sartorially elegant, rather a bit crumpled in dress, and tie not particularly well adjusted. There was, however, nothing that was anything but sharp about his conversation and intensity of interest.

With no prelude he simply asked, 'What do you think of Pinter?'

'I find him arresting,' I said.

'I think he's a genius,' said Iain. When I got to know Iain better, this remark didn't surprise me.

Iain always had this directness, almost naivety. Sorley MacLean, talking about him, would say, 'Oh, the blessed Iain of the purest spirit.' (A shame not to be able to replicate in print the glitter in Sorley's eyes or the breathy, almost straggly clarity of his enunciation.) We might add to Sorley's description, Iain's naked candour and honesty. No euphemism, I remember, in his telling me about his complete nervous breakdown: 'David, when I was mad and in hospital, I believed that all the doctors and nurses were actors, and that was totally confirmed when I heard them speaking about going to the theatre.' He also thought that Donalda, his wife, was part of the charade and then, to my surprise, he concluded by saying, 'Do you know, I think I really planned my madness myself.'

But that he had a serious total breakdown was in no doubt and his recovery was long and slow. When I visited him and Donalda in Taynuilt when he came out of hospital, he could concentrate neither to read nor write. Sad to see the wordmonger so diminished, but he recovered fully, and he speculated on 'the unknown darkness that lurks like rodents in the cupboard of the subconscious waiting to be loosed.' This frightening idea of rodents 'waiting to be loosed' prompted me to write this poem:

From the Dark
for Iain

Where is the rat hidden
In what corner or cushion?
Where are his white teeth waiting?
His burning eyes, where do they watch from?
When will the jaws snap shut?
Which vital part will they fasten to

Heart or eye or ear?
A hundred pairs of twin black spots
Gaze into my brain. They carry fever,
Black, slow death: They wait silent
Hunting out my fears and drive me to the black rat
Inside who leaps under the guard of my skull
And nibbles down to the black edge of fatigue,
And then, unpitied in the cave
I wait and idly watch the creatures there
Pacing their restless miseries
For I am soundless, without word,
Watching merely chanceless things.
The rat ghoul shrinks, retreats and I can talk again,
Register the sun's turning and shed another kind of tear.
I hear the river laughing under the trees.

Before his transformative marriage to Donalda, I remember in the '70s visiting Iain in his flat at 42 Combie Street in Oban. I was a great admirer of Iain's writings, his poetry, his celebrated novella, *Consider the Lilies*, his novels, short stories, and his sense of design and pure artistry. I was consequently much surprised at the décor in his Oban bachelor flat. The carpet was a synthetic swirly gaudy abstract. But what tickled me was that he had pasted sections of it to the panels of his inside door. And Iain himself, pre-Donalda days, wore garments that looked as if they hadn't seen an iron. When, on a visit to Edinburgh on a drizzly day he came through the door of the Abbotsford with a loose-fitting old fawn-coloured Burberry raincoat, he could easily have been mistaken for a flasher. But all that belied his wide-ranging intellect, his sharp wit, enticingly oblique thinking and often deeply earnest conversations.

I loved the brilliance of Iain's butterfly mind and the juxtaposing playful absurdities rejoicing in nonsense and mischief. He was the funniest of men, and of all the people I've ever met, the one who elicited the funniest response in me, tapped a source of unleashed fantasy I didn't know I possessed, mischief-maker as I was and am. Iain laughed readily and recklessly, sometimes needing to hold on to his false teeth during his unrestrained paroxysms.

While I was with Iain in the Combie Street flat, our conversation turned to theology, a subject which fascinated him and on which he had much to say. I decided to throw open the window, lean out and to deliver a thunderous sermon to the passing townsfolk of Oban on their Sodom and Gomorrah iniquities, of the dire catalogue of their sins and on the limitless pains of Hell they were to suffer for the multiple evils of their lives. As my sermon progressed, so did the hysteria of Iain's laughter at this wild denunciation, until at the peroration, he was lying contorted on the floor. The excesses of his wild glee, of course, encouraging the excesses of my oratory.

I suppose Iain's deep-dyed Lewis experience of oppressive, sin-laden Presbyterianism, and years of his mother's disapproval, lit the fuse of his glee at the sacrilege of my mocking homily.

Anyway, we celebrated with the communion cup of a healthy dram of Glenfiddich that I'd brought. Doubtless the whisky was lent an added flavour since, when Iain lived with his mother, whisky was a clandestine indulgence.

Two of Iain's visits to Edinburgh I recall for their extravagance and comedy. Robert Garioch lived near me in Nelson Street and I joined Iain, Donalda and Robert there for a drink. Robert was a cosy-looking small man, tweedy in an unaffected way and he had a droll, pan-faced sense of absurdity. He began to expound one of his ideas, an idea the fulfilment of which later that night was to occasion a brush with the law and a sonnet after the fashion of Petrarch. 'So, Iain,' Robert began, 'I've invented a Why? sticker. You see, you get these little sticky cards with a word clearly printed on it, the word "Why?" and when you come across a piece of bureaucracy or something you object to, well you just stick this "Why?" sticker on it.'

I had been invited to a party that night that Sorley's daughter Ishbel was giving. And so, after a few drinks, my suggestion that we should all adjourn there was readily accepted. Ishbel, of course, was well acquainted with that gleesome threesome, and we were all welcomed in.

In the course of the evening, Iain, whether from a bout of his famously unrestrained laughter or a severe anti-peristaltic spasm occasioned by excessive alcohol, projected his false teeth down the toilet. For whatever reason, he pulled the plug and they vanished forever. Time to go home.

Robert was well known for his reluctance to put his hand in his pocket and so the gleesome threesome decided to dispense with a taxi and walk home. This proved an occasion for the 'Why?' sticker.

Robert needed to relieve his bladder, and at Tollcross there was the prospect of relief – a public toilet. Alas, it was locked and in gathering discomfort, he applied the 'Why?' sticker, betook himself round the corner off the main road and proceeded to relieve himself when he was tapped on the shoulder by a lady police officer who'd had the courtesy to await the conclusion of the flood. Art has strange origins and Robert couldn't resist the pun:

A Fair Cop

Castalian Scots, nou may ye cry, Allace!
sen your True Rhymer, Garioch, met a leddy
polis, maist unexpeckit, in a shady

neuk near Tollcross, and nou he's in disgrace.
She met him, rather, but in onie case
it maks nae odds; she got her notebuik ready,
licket her keelivine, and jeez! She said he
wes 'urinating in a public place'.

Her very words, a richt wee caution! Pray
forgie me thon expression in nine letters,
a terrible expense: seevin wad dae.

Fendin us aa frae muggers and sic craiturs,
the Polis are maist eydent, I daursay,
but fancy fashin wi sic piddlin matters!

One evening Robert, Iain, Donalda, Barbara McLean and some others
were gathered in my house. Robert was well embarked on one of his fanciful
protracted monologues when Donalda, whose sense of fun and mischief,
particularly after a drink or two, was not to be denied, came behind the
unwitting Robert's chair but in full sight of the rest of us, removed her false
teeth and proceeded to agitate them about his head in her hands, in rhythm with
and emulating his chat, chat, chatter. We meantime, to maintain our composure,
fastened looks of renewed intense concentration on Robert's utterances.

One night when we, with Donalda, were in the local inn at Taynuilt,
Donalda unleashed an eloquent tirade of Scottish nationalist fervour on a
visiting Englishman who held the idea of a separate Scotland as an irrelevance.
The Valkyries could have learned their fury from Donalda. Iain first hid and
then scarpered home, leaving Donalda's onslaught on the startled visitor.

Amidst the serious conversations I had with Iain, on his visits to Edinburgh
and mine to Taynuilt, I loved the fun, the banter, the flyting. This nonsense
continued in our correspondence.

When I was working as a producer in the BBC, I commissioned Iain to
write a script for the *Scottish Writers* series aimed at school pupils. My mode
of commissioning Iain was in the ethos of our mutual love of fun, words
and absurdity, echoes of Pinter:

March 1981

Dear Iain,

To further obfuscate our dialogue of the second day of the last
quarter of the moon of the vernal equinox, a few muddled thoughts
for your ill consideration.

What you should aim at achieving for a 15, 16-year-old audience
is some dim idea of the miracle of what our words conceal from each

other, the deception and downright lies they carry with such apparent sweetness, the self-delusions and tortuous pretensions passing in the name of communication. In short, some vague idea of Auld Clootie, the Father of Lies, and the brilliance of his chameleon nature garbed in the sweet innocence of simple syllables.

Whether or not you have a Japanese protagonist (old or young) or use the form of prose or drama are questions completely immaterial to me, but the full moon of the vernal equinox, 5 April, is emphatically the date by which the work is to be complete.

I enclose with my best wishes to Donalda and yourself this invaluable book on listening which may encourage you to write. Also a philosophy of the official section which this programme is intended to address.

Regards, David

This crackpot letter of mine elicited from Iain by return of post a brilliant script somewhere between Saki and Pinter in mood and mode, an account of a late-night visitor who claims to be a former pupil of a schoolmaster who is rehearsing a self-satisfied retirement speech to his wife. Pinter fashion, the disquieting interrogation of the visit leaves the schoolmaster's complacency shattered. The script was the genesis of a play Iain later wrote.

Simultaneously with receiving the script from Iain, I had sent him a short play I had written. Our epistolary flyting and downright insults were part of the nonsense and joy these occasioned:

Dear David

I've spent a considerable amount of time looking at this play, staring at it in fact. I find great difficulty in understanding it and why it was written, and why the pages are numbered as they are. When I read it, plays like *Macbeth*, *King Lear*, and *Campbell of Kilmhor* come vaguely to mind, though I find this impossible to explain except to close relatives. The plot seems to be lifted from a newspaper but fails to achieve a catharsis (not to put too fine a point on it). Why did you not call it 'Sexes and Sevens'? I see it is called 'A Play for Two'. Do the two refer to the audience or to the dramatis personae? Donalda thinks this is a good play but as she's doing the Open University this opinion has no weight whatsoever. Why is there nothing in this tense drama about the Highland Clearances, not to say peat? And why is there a blank page at the beginning? Is this for Readers' Comments? And how long did it take you to type it? I have a strong feeling that this play will empty theatres all over Scotland, and that the people of Ardnamurchan will not take to it. Where is the profundity, the criticism of life, which no one has come to expect from you? Where is the tragic element? And why has page four got more words that page six? Is this favouritism?

... Donalda remains faithful to your typing to the bitter end, but I am afraid that I am not prejudiced in your favour. I know you for what you are – a fraud and a member of the BBC. If you care to answer this letter please do so. I shall be in a thatched house far from here. Embittered, envious, jealous, and overcome with bile as I am, I can still recognise this for what it is, the puerile ravings of an enigmatic egomania. Remember me to all who remember me. May God forgive you. Donalda says the same, though in less grammatical language.
                    Yours sincerely, Iain Crichton Smith

                                                    27 April 1981
Dear Iain,
     The dismay I felt reading your short story for the radio series *Talking Points* rapidly turned to incredulity. If you look into your heart can you possibly believe that anyone could listen beyond the first sentence, or phrase? Even the first syllable had a deeply soporific effect and my secretary fell asleep trying to type it. Have you the faintest idea of what it weighs? On the scales here at the BBC, which I admit still use the imperial measure, your story failed even to cause the faintest movement. You might glean some slim idea of what that means when I tell you that these scales are capable of weighing a 12p postage stamp. That same postage stamp similarly is crammed with content and meaning compared with the rigorous vacuity of what you alone clearly define as a story. Have you never read any books?
     I have no desire to discuss in detail the shortcomings of your story 'The First Day' apart from the predictable and overweening egomania, megalomania and delusions of grandeur evident in the very title. Don't you think you would be better to live in a place where there are more people? Oban seems only to aggravate the more vicious strains in your character. Doesn't Donalda talk to you? She seems to have both her feet on the ground. I thought her remarks about my play had a perception amounting to genius.
     ... As an old friend, could I advise you for your own good, to consider changing the title? I suggest 'God Knows' would be better. I could discuss this whole question of the title at much greater length and give my objections in greater detail but perhaps we can let it rest by saying that the title was the part of your story I enjoyed most.
                    Yours sincerely, David

PS Barbara enjoyed your story. She said it reminded her of James Joyce. I don't think she has been at all well recently.

Of course, our correspondence also had mutual serious appreciation and suggestions:

24 April 1981

Dear David,
    Seriously, I like this very much. I like the dialogue. It seems very lifelike. I like the changes of mood and scene and the use of the music. I don't think I like some of the inserts, especially the one facing page 14. I think it makes everything too explicit. I think the information should emerge in a non-explicit way. [...] I hope they put this on, as you've obviously put a lot of thought and work into it. It seems to me to work as a drama, and to have a lot of variety of tone, mood and everything else.

Most beguiling to me about Iain was his quirky imagination, innocence and lack of ego. His friend, the poet George Bruce, told him that he had been in America giving a lecture on Coleridge to some college students when one of the students raised his hand and said, 'Mr Bruce, I know what Coleridge was saying in *Kubla Khan*.'
'Yes,' said George, interested to hear this interpretation.
'He was saying "Wow!"' announced the student.
In glee, Iain reckoned he could publish a new slim volume of literary criticism, *Chaucer to Seamus Heaney*, in monosyllabic assessments from growls to whispers and chuckles –
'Ah!' 'Aha!' 'Mmmh.' 'Yep!' Pocket-sized.
I had to laugh at his insouciant unworldliness when Donalda told me that after Iain and she had been to a Gaelic play, Iain had said:
'That was one of the funniest plays I've seen!'
'You wrote it,' said Donalda.
Iain had completely forgotten.
Memory is a fickle rogue; I don't recall the specific occasion, but I remember asking Iain to write a poem for the impending Scottish Parliament. It was read in 1999 at the opening of the Scottish Parliament, its title echoing Fletcher of Saltoun's famous speech lamenting the demise of the Scottish Parliament in 1707, 'The end of an Auld Sang.'
Along with the poem came Iain's letter, introduced by the typical quirky fun and fantasy that characterised our correspondence. I received this letter in June 1998; four months later, Iain died. His poem was read at the opening of the Scottish Parliament:

Dear David,

Herewith the poem I said I would send. I am sure it will bring tears to your eyes, of frustration, rage, and involuntary catharsis. I hope all goes well with you in all the lands you visit and your simple unstructured stories enthral the camels, llamas, wallabies, etc. that you happen to meet.

All the best, Iain

The Beginning of a New Song

Let our three-voiced country
sing in a new world
joining the other rivers without dogma,
but with friendliness to all around her.

Let her new river shine on a day
that is fresh and glittering and contemporary;

Let it be true to itself and to its origins
inventive, original, philosophical;
If its institutions mirror its beauty,
then without shame we can esteem ourselves.

23

In Search of Simplicity': Norman MacCaig

For Norman
10 Years On

'Norman,' two men dying gave
Your name their final breath
And this sun setting night where
Grey stones glow
Sedately gay as you would know,
I wished to visit you,
To ring your bell
And wait to shout my name
Out clear and loud as an affront
A flyting in your ear.
Then hear the pause
Between the time you lift the entry phone
The careful silence that you time so perfectly
A small suspense
Before the mock so weary
Oh so reluctant
Mono syllables
'Come up.'

So up I spring cheeky as a daisy
And you stand gravely hospitable
Barely concealing the twinkle
'Come in.'
Later days, you shuffle through the hall
Before me, enter the front room, turn.
'I suppose you'll want a dram?'
Leaning on the 'ose' of suppose
Like a featherlight heavyweight.
'Have you a decent malt?'
So mild,
'Can I invite you to leave?'
(No wonder you didn't like theatre, you were the living art)
'I brought you an interesting bottle.'
'Uh-huh.'

You walk over to the little cabinet
By the window, sun flashing its edges.
'Will this do?'
Raising an Islay Malt
'Not my favourite.'
'Too bad.'
'I'll get the water.'

We sit
You pour a whisky that
Is not very small for its age
'Plenty water boy!' I oblige.
You settle beside Bach and Pibroch
And smoke like everything else you do,
Elegantly.
I am as happy as I have ever been
While like the unimaginable colours
Of this night's Edinburgh sky
The conversation technicolours
Into mischief, arcs of argument
The shortest jokes in the world
And you laugh when you tell one
Because when you tell it
You are caught by surprise
As if you have heard it for the very first time.

Is it you or the whisky that takes time out of time
And into your graceful stride
Along reminiscences of
The company you've kept
The best minds of our generation
Chris, Sydney, Sorley, Iain, Seamus?

Anecdotes of arguments
Fond strong pictures,
And underneath such fun, such celebration.
And while the night grows dark
The distillations of your mind and the barley
Keep me warm.

What more to say than you have already said
A better way when one you loved was dead:

'A branch from the tallest tree'
Held up by so many memories.

And yet the dying sun still splashes
The Craigleith stone
Its luminous reds as if
Nothing had changed.

My first memory of Norman MacCaig is not of his wit, his deftly chosen words, his voice or his poetry readings, but in the Abbotsford Bar watching the shifting drama of the expressions on his face, eyes twinkle, gaze, flash, mouth pout, purse smile, a burst of sun.

Later, visiting him in his flat in Leamington Place, I became familiar with, but always fascinated by, these changing weathers that accompanied his conversation. In this way he reminded me of my mother, a vivid storyteller, and you could see on her face how she was watching the film of her story unwind, and so you would know, 'this is going to be amusing, or serious, or sad', like a trailer. Similarly, on the stage of Norman's face, I enjoyed the anticipation when I saw the tell-tale creases that presaged his amusement in telling something funny.

Norman loved jokes, the shorter it seemed, the better since he was a disciple of the adage that 'brevity is the soul of wit'. I can see him in his chair, books and classical records around him, whisky and cigarette in hand as he told me a joke that particularly tickled him:

A surgeon visits his patient after an operation and solicitously enquires, 'Comfy?'

'Govan,' replies the patient, and Norman laughs anew, as if he is laughing in spite of himself, as if he could do nothing to stop it.

His jokes also told something about where his affections lay. He loved Lochinver, loved the local characters and their unique personalities. He told me that the proprietor had told a local man he'd had enough to drink, but could wait inside the pub, out of the rain, because the bus was not due for another half hour. To this the local replied,

'I'll go now. It won't take me long to wait for half an hour.'

This delighted Norman. I think it pleased him because like many jokes it held an embedded truth.

Apart from the ranging, and often serious conversations, a visit to Norman was simply joyful, warmed by his favourite malt or a bottle I had brought, as well as his wife Isobel's hospitality, occasional presence, conversation, and sandwiches before she would disappear to get on with her own magnus opus, compiling a dictionary of colloquial usage. It took me a while to realise the huge mutual respect and love they had for one another. Like everything, it was expressed economically and not for public consumption.

As well as my social and fun visits to Norman, on several occasions I made sound recordings for the BBC, on one of which my friend and ex-pupil, the fine photographer Robin Gillanders, accompanied me. Norman had forgotten he was coming to take some photos but, of course, welcomed him handsomely; someone new to be interested in. Norman protested, 'I can't cook!' the usual brevity, but he had put two eggs in a pan of boiling water. For Robin, I added another egg which ignited a furious flyting about my cooking ineptitude – submitting a cold egg to boiling water! 'The water should start cold!' So the tone is set; we are at once at ease in the familiar mode of flyting, and to his dramatic chagrin, my egg turns out perfectly! Galling for the champion of perfection.

It reminds me of one of our exchanges in a subsequent interview in which Robin was the voyeur photographer. I had said, 'You don't play the fiddle anymore.'

'No, because I got friendly with people who could play far better.' And Norman laughed.

'So, you are an elitist!'

'Definitely.'

'You sound proud of that.'

'Of course. I see nothing wrong with preferring the best of everything, even if it's poached eggs.'

'I take that as a compliment.'

'You would!'

As the level in the bottle lowered, he'd invite me to pour a dram and add, 'Plenty water, boy.' Remembering a tasty little anecdote of Norman's, I also always made sure there was also plenty of whisky in his glass. Whether apocryphal or not, he told me of a ghillie invited into the big house by the laird after a particularly successful hunting-shooting-fishing season.

'Try the malt, Hamish,' says the laird, pouring a dram. '20 years old.'

'Not very big for its age,' observes Hamish and Norman chuckles happily. Like his poems, the joke is deceptively simple and succinctly expresses something of the relationship between the Highland folk and the gentry, and delivered with an actor's timing and skill.

I used to tease Norman about his dislike of theatre. He said he never found it convincing. 'Of course not,' I'd say, 'when you are so histrionic yourself.' For answer, a slow elevation of the head, a widening of the eyes and mock contemptuous monosyllables, 'Pah! Not me!' delivered down the whole length of his fine nose, exquisite timing. Pure theatre.

I think of Norman as a man of laughter. As the evening passed, eased by the drams and many cigarettes, the conversation would range wildly, mainly over the things he celebrated and loved, everything from people to jokes, music, frogs and toads. 'Toad, stop looking like a purse.' Even in his conversation, often epigrammatic and precise, you felt he enjoyed and valued carefully selected words, his or yours, if they were neat and considered. He couldn't abide aimless rambling, or pretentious point scoring, which he could encounter at the Edinburgh University 'stiff club', as he called it, where he said, 'David, after ten minutes of these academic point scorers, I feel like calling a taxi.' You would never dare take a flatterer or a bore to visit Norman. He'd often say, 'I'm a merciful man,' but not where any variety of bore was concerned.

Conversely, he leapt alive in his favourite companies, which is why I suppose he extolled and loved the company of the iconoclastic and ever-combative Chris Grieve (Hugh MacDiarmid). I could see the mutual warmth and respect they had for one another when I drove Norman and Sean Murphy down to MacDiarmid's cottage. Sean was recording MacDiarmid's poems for an LP. Norman was prompting him. The hospitable, fiery Valda, MacDiarmid's wife, who could be a Valkyrie, was angelically welcoming. The birds twittered outside; a subliminal background orchestra is one of the charms of the recording. I was a grateful audience.

Shortly after this, I met Sean in the Abbotsford, and towards closing time we were engaged in a fierce argument about some matter of which I have no recollection. However, so locked were we in whatever it was, that when we were thrown out at closing time, we continued our argument as we made our way down St David's Street to Princes Street. There we arrived at Sir Walter Scott's monument and I, attempting to gain the upper hand, ascended and sat on top of Sir Walter's head to pursue my position, while Sean was relegated to his knees. Then along came two Edinburgh bobbies and vigorously told us to descend, which we did, reluctant to surrender our positions in the argument. The policemen, gentlemanly folk in these days, admonished us to be on our way, which we wisely did.

It happened that the next day I wanted to get a book of MacDiarmid's poems signed for my friend Marilyn Reizbaum who was returning to America. I phoned Norman to see if he could arrange this for me. 'I'm visiting Chris in Chalmers Hospital this afternoon,' said Norman, 'come with me.' I met Norman in Bennett's Bar in Tollcross and we had a dram before walking up to the hospital. MacDiarmid, despite having had a bowel operation that morning, was perky and wakeful, welcoming us warmly. Norman at one stage said, 'David and Sean Murphy were engaged in an argument last night, David conducting his point of view from the top of Sir Walter Scott's head.' With no hesitation, MacDiarmid observed, in his dry tones, 'Possibly the best use to which it could have been put.' Acquiescent chuckles all round.

Not so long after this visit, George Brown drove me to MacDiarmid's funeral in Langholm, the weather growing bleaker and wetter on the switch back road, and my stomach, never a good traveller, compelled us to stop the journey on several occasions and so I arrived in Langholm pale shaky and nauseous.

'Brandy and port,' George prescribed, as we entered a local pub.

'George, I am ill.'

'Trust me.'

I did, and two brandy and ports (mixed) later I was cured, a remedy I thoroughly recommend.

A few days later I sent a letter to Marilyn Reizbaum, the recent recipient of the book of MacDiarmid's poems he had signed for her.

Edinburgh
19 September 1978

Well Marilyn,

On Saturday the ninth of September the great man died. On Wednesday last, the 13th, George Brown and I drove down to Langholm to see him buried where he had been born... We adjourned to the nearest hostelry where were gathered such contradictory friends as you would expect at the great Grieve's going-out party. Poets and artists, MPs of the SNP cheek-by-jowl with the high heid yins of the Communist Party, Trade Unionists, friends and admirers.

At 2.30pm we all gathered in the cemetery outside Langholm around MacDiarmid's open grave. It was a dreich day with fine Scotch rain slanting in the wind up the slope of the green graveyard. The round Border hills stretched behind. We were three or four hundred mourners and made a wide circle about the grave.

Michael Grieve – the poet's eldest – spoke in a firm clear voice of his father's aims in creating a Scotland with dignity, of his fight for the country's independence and of how far these great aims had advanced. Alex Clark (member of the Communist Party) spoke of MacDiarmid, the contradictory politician leaving the Party as it thrived, rejoining when everyone else was leaving. Finally, Norman MacCaig gave a fine and fluent speech, his face set against the wind towards the grave, his grey hair swept by the wind, and his eyes challenging the air. He spoke truculently of those who saw MacDiarmid as a man of abstraction and announced how at the farthest extension of abstract thought, MacDiarmid would always be back relating it to the concrete.

He spoke of him as the most courteous, generous, most hospitable of men and then he said how people often fail to note one of the most notable of all things in the poet – his vivid sense of humour. The Government should, he said, as an appropriate tribute to the wild genius of his mind and the courteous generosity of his life, decree two minutes' pandemonium.

Norman then recalled how often they had sat together in front of a good fire with a bottle of whisky. Norman, awed by Grieve's capacity to chase an idea while he hung on behind, said he felt as if his mind was a dark city and Grieve, the lamp lighter... no, the torch procession of one... illuminating the grubby corners.

Then the coffin bearers were called forward and as each man was called, each took a cord: his son Mike Grieve, his grandson, the poet Alex Scott, Norman MacCaig, and so on, eight in all, they lowered the coffin into the earth. Just then Valda stepped forward and one by one threw roses into the grave saying, 'I know these aren't yours Chris, but they're the best I could get,' and as she threw the last, 'Goodbye Chris.'

Alex Clark had already quoted that fine MacDiarmid poem, 'The Little White Rose' which so succinctly in four lines characterises the poet's love of Scotland.

As we stood in the slanting rain after Valda had thrown the last rose into the grave, I looked across and saw Norman, standing like a stricken tree.

'He could do with a dram,' I said to my friend Craig Sharp. By wonderful foresight, Craig poured a large Glenfiddich from his flask and handed it to me. This I took to Norman, who said only:

'A sense of the concrete. Thank you.'

Most of the funeral party then retired to the hotel and got well drunk.

On the drive home much later, I was not sick. I hope you are well. Thank you for your letters. I will reply soon.

Much love, David

Norman was easefully at home in the world of MacDiarmid and the robust company and conversation of the illustrious coterie of poets who met in the Abbotsford and Café Royal. MacDiarmid would hold court in the so-called 'Kremlin' of Milne's Bar, where in these relaxed days, you could order food and drink and Eddie the Polish barman would bring the drinks and Scottish menu to the company. Amongst the disciples of the great man would be a remarkable group of Scottish poets of the time: Sorley MacLean, Iain Crichton Smith, George Mackay Brown, Eddie Morgan, Sidney Goodsir Smith and Norman MacCaig who would observe nostalgically, 'David, in those days, you could go down to a Rose Street pub any evening of the week and find good company.'

Good company was Norman's elixir, and in his other favourite place, Lochinver, he found it richly, when he abandoned Edinburgh for six weeks during the summer holidays. His favourite folk there were the head gamekeeper and the poacher who were friends, a pact of Highland camaraderie. Of his friend Angus, the gamekeeper, who like Norman was a devoted fisherman, he said, 'We would spend the day fishing the loch and in a tacit impulse we both rose simultaneously to go down the road.' Norman would tell me as if it came upon him as a revelation, 'I realised I loved these two men.' Like so many Scots of my generation, he was doubtless unaccustomed to use the word 'love' for something he already knew. Neither my mother nor my father ever told us they loved us, but they expressed it in their absolute care of us. Neither would have thrown the word about like loose coinage.

I recorded Norman in his late '70s for a radio portrait, talking about the folk in Lochinver:

'I got to know the people, loved a quarter of them, was bored by another quarter, and hated the other half. I began to see what was going on in local politics which is homicidal. I have to see things small. I got political things in a locality. I knew what was going on and I knew what the owner of that area was doing. It makes me sick to mention his name. The way he treated the locals increased my vestigial interest in politics.'

'Increased? What started that interest?'

'My visits to Scalpay when I was 12 to 15. These holidays were most important to me, made me realise I belonged to a race of people, had Celtic corpuscles belting through my veins, and that started an interest in politics.'

'I didn't think you were interested in politics.'

'I can't stand party politics.'

'What kind of politics then?'

'I vote Scottish Nationalist because over so many years I've seen Parliament in what Douglas Young used to call "the adjacent Kingdom of England" passing laws that you would think were aimed to destroy Scotland in their treatment of faraway places, like Scalpay and Lochinver.'

In a dramatic way, an ugly incident during the visit my girlfriend Barbara and I made to Norman and Isobel at their house in Inverkirkaig in 1978 corroborated Norman's detestation of some of the folk in Lochinver. Barbara and I were camped in the garden of Norman's cottage on our visit and in the evening Norman, Barbara and I walked the two and a half miles down to the Culag Hotel Bar in Lochinver which at the time was owned by the Vesteys, whose name Norman refused to utter.

With the usual accompaniment of malt whiskies and enjoyable conversation, time sped by until eventually Norman and Barbara decided to walk back home. I, however, was enjoying the company and decided, unwisely as it turned out, to stay. Ultimately, I had so much to drink that the resolve, or perhaps capacity, to walk back left me, and I woke up to find I'd fallen asleep behind a sofa in the hotel lounge.

No awakening could have been more alarming. I found myself helplessly frogmarched by four hefty young men, one on each arm and one on each leg, out of the hotel and down to the pier where they threw me into the harbour.

By the time I swam to the slipway, shaking and shaken, and looked around, my captors were nowhere to be seen. Propelled by this adrenalin shock, dripping wet, I ran the two and a half miles back to the house, and arrived at about seven in the morning to a momentarily relieved Barbara, until she learned the story. Norman was at first incredulous and then furious at the perpetrators of this violent and dangerous treatment. He surmised the thugs were obsequious employees of the hated hotel owner.

The hospitality of Isobel and Norman, until we left next day to climb Suilven, Norman's favourite mountain, was a honey contrast to the sour trauma of my unwelcome immersion. Norman's words express for me the startling surprise of that sugarloaf mountain.

> I listen with my eyes and see through that
> Mellifluous din of shapes my masterpiece
> Of masterpieces:
> One sandstone chord that holds up time and space –
> Sforzando Suilven reared on his ground bass.

Since Norman saw music as an art and a pleasure exceeding poetry, it is no surprise that he translates Suilven into a term for musical emphasis.

A single regret I have of my many visits to Norman was that I did not record the extraordinary way he whistled a pibroch one afternoon in his house in Edinburgh. He closed his lips until they had one tiny aperture in their midst through which came the pure, thin, subtle variations of the big bagpipe music.

When two of Norman's friends and admirers, Alan Taylor, writer and journalist, and Brian McCabe, poet and short story writer, decided that the occasion of the poet's 75th birthday merited a celebration, I was delighted to be invited to be the compère. The celebration was held on 18 November 1985, in the packed Queen's Hall in Edinburgh.

No better birthday present could have been devised than to gather this effulgent company of wordmongers, but above all friends of Norman, and I the privileged one to unwrap all the presents by introducing them, a cosmic event gave me the perfect introduction to the evening:

> Ladies and Gentlemen, welcome; from the far reaches of our galaxy we are visited every 75 years by Halley's Comet, an event that luckily coincides with the 75th birthday celebration of our friend and creator of shooting stars of words, Norman MacCaig.

So this is a once-in-a-lifetime occasion and befittingly are gathered a constellation of poetic luminaries.

My BBC work, membership of The Heretics and personal friendships with all of the celebrants gave me an easeful and enjoyable task. What a glittering cast: Seamus Heaney, Sorley MacLean, Eddie Morgan, Liz Lochhead, Alex Scott, Adam MacNaughtan, Iain Crichton Smith and Ishbel MacAskill.

Perhaps what gladdened Norman's heart most of all was that the presentation and toast was not alone for himself but for the other author from their flat on 7 Leamington Place, his wife Isobel. Isobel had recently published a work of 700 pages, huge scholarship, diligence and service to the English-speaking world, a dictionary of current idiomatic English, received with lavish critical acclaim. Of this Norman was hugely proud. Many in that company had been welcome at the generous door of their hospitality and rose in appreciation to the toast for Isobel and Norman.

You always left Norman feeling bright, vivified and delighted, which was the same compliment he paid to the company of his great friends AK and MacDiarmid. In this state of euphoria after one such evening, after many golden malts, Norman aged 80 accompanied me downstairs and whilst waiting for the taxi we had called, I stumbled and fell ignominiously into the gutter, from which my octogenarian friend elevated me and saw me safely aboard.

After Norman died I would often of an evening think, 'I must go and visit him,' and then remember he was no longer there. People do not die the instant their breath stops, but as Norman himself put it:

> The beneficent lights dim
> but don't vanish. The razory edges
> dull, but still cut. He's gone but you can see
> his tracks still, in the snows of the world.
> (from 'Praise of a Man')

24

Embro to the Ploy: Robert Garioch

DURING THE 1962 Edinburgh International Festival I wrote a poem prompted by seeing two well-intentioned Festival visitors, thinking to be helpful, raising an old Edinburgh drunk from the pavement and propping him against a wall.

I dropped into Robert Garioch's flat in Nelson Street to ask his advice about the appropriateness of a word in the poem I'd written in Lallans, which seemed the proper language to describe the slow progress of an inebriated down-and-out along the pavement of the Cowgate. Robert supplied tea and scones and the word I needed.

Foreign Aid

His een fixed forrit, schauchlin on his dowp,
I saw an auld man in the Cougate,
Legless fou and happit in a lang, black coat,
Guid wool, weel tucked ablow his stern
As he gaed, fit first, backside neist
And oarin up the causey wi his airms.
Wi muckle care he pit his stick afore,
A compass, in the high seas o his mind,
An like Columbus, kept his course aye til the 'Trades'
Whaur he wid win the treisure of a bed.

Black nicht it wis; the wind stuid fair for hame
When by cam twa Samaritans,
Braw, dapper chiels wha howked him
By the oxters up agin a waa
Syne gaed on, weel content,
But left our ancient loon
Bamboozled, beached;
Nae stick tae navigate,
Nae bum tae oar ashore,
Wi tempests screichin in his heid
Cliff taps frae hame abune the gurly grun.

Robert suggested I change one word but liked the poem, which subsequently, to my delight, was placed second in a poetry competition judged by Eddie Morgan and Joy Hendry, editor of the influential *Chapman* magazine.

The subject of my poem got Robert reflecting on the still pervasive Calvinism of the town that infected even such places as Milne's Bar. He then described for me the incident that occasioned his wry sonnet, 'Whit Wad Verdi Say?'

Robert had been in conversation with Adrian Secchi, Musical Director of the Lyceum. Both were of small stature, and in quiet conversation were discussing a theatre piece they were working on together, and sotto voce Robert hummed part of a tune. Whereupon the barman bawled at them, 'Nae singin' at the bar.' This Presbyterian-style censure appealed to Robert's sense of the ridiculous and elicited a sonnet entitled 'What did Verdi say?'

Today, many bars are full of live song and music. How times have changed. Willie Ross was the Hebridean manager of the Oxford Bar in Thistle Street, more recently notable as the haunt of Rebus, the detective of Ian Rankin's novels, and of the author himself. In these stern days in douce Edinburgh of the '50s and '60s when the zeitgeist was flower power, Auld Reekie was still in the shadow of John Knox, no more fervent disciple than Willie Ross. Famously, he was known to have closed his bar and taken a holiday during the frivolity of the Edinburgh Festival Fringe. On one occasion, two unsuspecting visitors to the austere environment of his bar asked for lager and crisps. He sold neither and invited them outside, and pointing at the pub sign, said, 'Do you see anything about this being a restaurant?'

My friend John Herdman, write and member of The Heretics, and I were one evening sitting together in the back room of the bar, no one else being there, and recalling some of our flyting correspondence and mischievous notions, one of which was to inaugurate a prize for the Scottish Bore of the Year. To name our list would be inadvisable, but a few were amongst the bar flies in the Rose Street pubs. I recalled for John that the sportsmanlike Professor Alan Thomson told me he had been invited to a reception where a young reporter had approached him. The Professor asked him who he was looking for to which the unwitting cub replied, 'I've come to interview a boring old fart called Alan Thomson.' 'You're speaking to him,' said the delighted Professor.

In the course of our chatter, something caused us to laugh uproariously, whereupon Willie Ross appeared at the doorway and fixed upon us a look of glowering disapproval before slowly receding to the bar, but a further guffaw from us invited his sombre reappearance to admonish us for the noise. Willie was a character, and whether or not this was part of his pose was hard to tell, but like children we resigned to restrained giggles.

It was told of Willie that trying to insert the large key to lock the outside door one night he was interrupted by a police car drawing up outside. The policeman wound down the window and remarked, 'Aye, pissed again Willie!' to which Willie replied, 'Aye, so am I!'

The 1962 Writers Conference was incandescent. Inaugurated by the creative catalyst Jim Haynes, the daring publisher John Calder and Sonia Brownell (widow of George Orwell), it ignited ferocious argument. It shook the Establishment with its stellar gathering of avant-garde and iconoclastic writers and its overt explosions, expounding and discussion of controversial and hitherto taboo topics.

In a letter to Hannah Arendt, Mary McCarthy expressed something of the dramatic impact:

> People jumping up to confess they were homosexuals; a registered heroin addict [Alexander Trocchi] leading the young Scottish opposition to the literary tyranny of the communist Hugh MacDiarmid... An English woman novelist describing her communications with her dead daughter, a Dutch homosexual, former male nurse, now a Catholic convert, seeking someone to baptize him; a bearded Sikh with hair down to his waist declaring on the platform that homosexuals were incapable of love, just as (he said) hermaphrodites were incapable of orgasm (Stephen Spender, in the chair, murmured that he should have thought they could have two)...
>
> ('1962 International Writers Conference, Edinburgh: An edited history' by Drs Angela Bartie and Eleanor Bell, University of Strathclyde.)

The robust flyting between the Scottish gay exile Alexander Trocchi and the Scottish nationalist/communist Hugh MacDiarmid put fire in the air. Trocchi asserted he was right to leave a turgid, petty, provincial stale porridge Scotland describing MacDiarmid as an 'old fossil'. Naturally this awoke a volcano: 'Mister Trocchi' – retorted MacDiarmid,

> seems to imagine that the burning questions in the world today are lesbianism, homosexuality and matters of that kind. I don't think so at all. I ask Mr Trocchi where in any of the literature they are referring to... are the crucial burning questions of the day being dealt with, as they have been dealt with in Scottish literature, if you knew about it!

In the slowly changing zeitgeist, Robert Garioch's poem 'Embro to the Ploy' is a fun-filled account of douce, respectable Edinburgh transformed by the Festival. Robert gleefully describes the outwardly respectable, East windy, West-Endy, fur-coat, nae-knickers Edinburgh residents. One incident particularly highlights the prim outrage of the unco guid of the city and hit the headline in the *Edinburgh Evening News*. A young woman was wheeled naked in a wheelbarrow across the stage at the 1963 Drama Festival at McEwan Hall. Oh, horrors! Not surprisingly, that tickled Robert's sense of humour into satiric verse.

25

A New Buzz

THE EARLY DAYS at the Traverse provided a cornucopia of excitement. The bar was a demotic yet literary and sociable meeting place; there I got to know the Liverpool poets who gave readings, Roger McGough, Brian Patten and Adrian Henri; Angie Rew and Dave McNiven were the innovative music group Bread, Love and Dreams; the plays were adventurous and stimulating, and sometimes controversial.

The brilliant and versatile Tom McGrath's play, *The Hard Man*, was about the brutal Glasgow gangland figure, Jimmy Boyle, and with its nudity, its depiction of excrement-smeared prison walls as a mark of Boyle's protest, its excessive language and violence, it didn't delight everyone. Jimmy Boyle had, through the campaigning of such as Tom McGrath, Ricky Demarco and others, been transferred to an experimental art therapy unit in Barlinnie, where his meeting with his psychiatrist, or psychiatric therapist, Sarah Trevelyan, had eventually led to their marriage, which was a further factor in his eventual release.

My one meeting with Jimmy Boyle, who was of course a national cause celebre because of his release from the redemptive Barlinnie unit, tickled my sense of humour. I was visiting a friend of mine, Polly, in Dundas Street at the same time as he was. I introduced myself and to my amusement he said, 'Yes, I've heard a lot about you.'

For me, a lover of drama, the Traverse provided a constant stimulating repertoire. There I saw *The Caretaker*, Jean Genet's *The Maids*, John Byrne's *Slab Boys*, John McGrath's *Laurel and Hardy*, Donald Campbell's *The Jesuit* and plays by Stanley Evening, CP Taylor and others.

The origin of this recipe of cultural feasts the Traverse set up was the result of great idealism, perseverance and the serendipitous meeting of kindred spirits.

From New Orleans Jim Haynes had fallen in love with Edinburgh when he was stationed in the US airbase in Midlothian during the war. He returned to Edinburgh and on the corner of George Square in 1959 set up the Paperback Bookshop with its iconic rhino head outside which I well recall; it was relaxed and welcoming as Jim himself: coffee, browsing, discussions, readings, little theatre productions. These featured Jane Quigley later star of stage and screen, and at the time Jim's heartthrob.

Ever adventurous, Jim opened the Howff in the High Street. This venture was torpedoed when his partner, who ran the folk club, sold the Howff and left town.

When Tom Mitchell came to Edinburgh he met Jim Haynes, who told me that Tom and he had been friends since Tom's earliest arrival in the city. Tom was an unlikely, but as it turned out, dramatic contributor to the cultural life of Edinburgh in the '60s. He was already a legendary sporting figure as manager of the British cricket team that won the Ashes in Australia in 1958. In Edinburgh, he bought a dilapidated six-story building in Lawnmarket at the top of High Street, which was used as a doss house!

The triumvirate was completed by Richard Demarco, artist, entrepreneur and catalyst. Ricky had been approached by the Cambridge University Review and so he facilitated their use of the building where they served coffee and mounted a review with John Cleese in the cast.

By 1963, with a little help from their friends, at Tom Mitchell's rent of £1 per year – eureka! – the Traverse had its grand opening with an invited audience to see Sartre's *Huis Clos* and Arabel's *Orison*. These were the seeds of an international reputation for contemporary innovative drama. I recall climbing the narrow stairs of the licenced bar, which was a-buzz with a variety of theatre enthusiasts, vibrant conversationalists and folk like myself intoxicated by this new cosmopolitan vibration.

For me, another memorable off-stage moment in the Traverse is a highly comic one. The play was *Ruby Tuesday*, a zany play by John Bett. Barbara McLean was accompanying me, and being engaged in finishing a conversation, asked me to keep a seat, which I did in the front row of the U-shaped tiered seating. By the time the lights dimmed and the play was about to begin, she had not come back. The lights came up on a startled Barbara, sitting mid-stage on a sofa facing the audience. As she scuttled off backstage, frightened rabbit fashion, she passed a marvellously unfazed Juliet Cadzow entering and speaking her first lines as she took the place on the now vacant sofa. Barbara, it turned out, then spent the first Act until the interval huddled in an off-stage cupboard.

When the Traverse moved to its Grassmarket site, it retained the wonderful, tiered intimacy of the original theatre and the congenial social whirl of a more spacious bar. This more spacious bar was the scene of another memorable event, recounted by my friends with glee, which casts me in a most dismal light. I had been drinking too long and too excessively, and added significantly to my state of consciousness or unconsciousness by having smoked a joint – there was in the Traverse at that time a discreet source of cannabis and grass.

I recognised in the bar a young attractive woman and said to her, 'I know you, don't I?'

'You should,' she replied, 'we were married.' It was my former Danish wife, Ina.

Not to be alone in my discomfiture, I recall late one other such evening, the well-known girlfriend of a well-known actor pouring beer over his head as he was kissing a man at the bar.

Amongst the habitués of the liberal Traverse Theatre at that time was a Grassmarket vagrant. He was grizzled in appearance, like the poet Sydney Goodsir Smith's meths drinker: 'Bleerit e', unrazit cheeks, lips bricht crammasie, and slaverin' crozie mou.' He was known for his making of little rattles of woven cane, put together with handles, the rattle provided by metal beer tops. These he sold for whatever your price was. In the dying fall of my Christian persuasions at the time, this state of mind considerably accentuated by a bit of drink, I felt a compulsion to accept physically and fully the existence of everyone, including this vagrant, so that one night when in his gratitude for my purchase of a rattle, he decided to kiss me with his grizzled face and slobbering lips, I felt it a necessary bond of humanity to accept this slavery greeting. It was putting my money where my convictions were.

My natural empathy was enhanced when I fell in love with Dostoevsky. I became Raskolnikov or Prince Myshkin. I lived in the pages of *Crime and Punishment* and *The Idiot*, half my life was there. I was in two worlds and donned a long woollen coat, and sipping a drink in the Traverse or a Rose Street pub I'd lurk in a corner undercover, in Russia.

Prince Myshkin was my huge moral hero. When the scoundrelly and foxy Lebedjev came weeping to the Prince begging some roubles to save him from the peril of his debts, I followed every turn of phrase and thought, and when Lebedjev realised the value of his tears to move the Prince to pity, I was in an exultation to find that the Prince, seeing the moment that this weaselly suppliant was using his tears, nevertheless, helps him.

This wayward obsession led me into further instructive lessons about the naivety and simplistic notions I was following. On another occasion, just by the Royal Infirmary in Lauriston Place, a woman, ample, middle-aged and drunk, had collapsed on the pavement. I bent to help. The reek of nicotine, alcohol and vomit-soured stomach was hard to thole, but I decided I would escort her home, which with difficulty I did, making little of her sporadic outbursts as I supported her erratic course towards Tollcross. At length, we arrived at a basement where, after several loud knocks, a man answered the door and they both turned to me and said, 'Fuck off! Just fuck off!' I was getting the message.

Such charades as the man at the bar or my Grassmarket vagrant are not to be encountered in the bar of the Traverse in its latest incarnation, with the Usher Hall and the Royal Lyceum as its neighbours.

I don't think it is nostalgia or geriatric grumpiness that laments the loss of the more demotic clientele that characterised these former Traverse Theatres, but the present bar is thriving, busy, offers a good food menu and the Theatre maintains the adventurous innovation and boldness of previous days. A series of talented directors has attracted the best of actors and playwrights, consistently winning Fringe First awards and encouraging new writers, and so still glitters. I don't know if actors still have incensed partners pouring beer over their heads.

Theatre in Edinburgh was burgeoning. The Royal Lyceum had a series of fine directors and presented usually a more traditional box office repertoire of great American, European and British drama from Shakespeare to the present day. Political drama was hovering in the wings.

> On the evening of Saturday, 7 April 1973, the George Square theatre in Edinburgh witnessed a remarkable event. The occasion was a reading re-hearsal of the 7:84 Company's play, *The Cheviot, the Stag, and the Black, Black Oil*, which was a contribution to the conference 'What kind of Scotland?' run by the magazine *Scottish International*. Between three and four hundred people attended... It finished in a whirl of song and dance... the entire audience rose to its feet clapping and cheering as if electrified.

The radio arts programme *Orbit* made the above remarks about that first open reading of *The Cheviot, the Stag, and the Black, Black Oil*.

At that performance I was among the people who rose to give it a standing ovation. It was a stunning, innovative piece of drama, deeply embedded in Highland history and culture, and brought forward an era of events that had been neglected in Scottish education – notably the dire events of the Highland Clearances of which I, as a pupil educated at George Heriot's, had been taught nothing.

The format presented by a talented cast of actors and musicians – Bill Paterson, Johnny Bett, Dolina MacLennan, Liz MacLennan, Alex Norton and Alan Ross, made a jubilant occasion by reinhabiting and recreating the Highland and Island ceilidh house ethos and form.

This form emerged from John McGrath's conviction expressed in an article in *New Edinburgh Review* (August 1975) for the Company to be

> finding the way to present certain specific people certain specific facts about their lives using an equally specific form (the West Highland peo-ple and the ceilidh form much imbued with the native experience and insight of Dolina MacLennan and a multi-talented cast).

Subsequent to the roaring success of *The Cheviot* and its Highland tour came a series of left-wing productions – *The Game's a Bogey*, *Boom*, *My Pal and Me*, and finally, *Little Red Hen*.

These I viewed with increasing disappointment as the political propaganda became not sharper but more insistently bludgeoning until it degenerated into the hysterical vilification of the SNP that characterised *Little Red Hen*, in which Wilma Duncan played the part of a simple-headed typical SNP supporter. Against the accumulated wisdom of the *Little Red Hen*, its humanity and socialist idealism, is set this mindless wee thing, keen but hopeless, without the benefit of knowledge or experience as worthy an opponent as a poor feckless gomeril.

On the opening night of the *Little Red Hen* at the Lyceum, I was seated with Barbara in the front row of the Grand Circle. Witnessing this unbalanced derision of the SNP, of which I was a supporter, and considering the drama to have vanished behind the propaganda, I became increasingly incensed until I leapt to my feet and loudly and clearly arraigned the stage beginning, 'How dare you present this as drama?' and continued my anger-infused rant berating its dramatic and polemic failures. Concluding with, 'I am leaving!' I began to make my way out.

As I reached the end of the row, John McGrath, who was sitting further back in the Circle, stood up and said, 'So, you won't give the play the benefit of seeing it through?'

Realising that my case would be seriously weakened if I didn't see it to the end I said, 'Very well,' and made my way back and sat down, whereupon the stage, which had been like a frozen frame in a film, as if by magic came to life and the reanimated actors continued where they had left off.

After that show, John's wife Liz MacLennan, who had played the Little Red Hen, refused to speak to me; John, much more generous of heart, took my outburst as part of the ongoing polemic; some of the folk in the foyer applauded me; some thought I was part of the performance. Douglas Gifford and I, in an article written that same year for Chapman magazine surveying the increasingly propaganda-loaded plays of 7:84, concluded:

> We were able to regard and respect the socialist commitment of the McGrath *The Cheviot*, but a view of humanity which fails to regard and respect the sincere effort of others to find their own way loses its art and replaces a real sense of fun and living with a sour kind of laughter.

McGrath's politics were of an international socialism and furthering that ideal the aim of the 7:84 plays, yet perhaps the most tangible legacy of *The Cheviot, the Stag, and the Black, Black Oil* was to revitalise the cause of home rule because, as Dolina MacLennan says in her autobiography, *An Island Girl's Journey*, and few would disagree:

> I think it was a nationalist play... After the next General Election there were 11 SNP MPs in Parliament, and I think *The Cheviot* had a lot to do with it, because it stirred people to think for themselves and also raised

consciousness about the land question.

For me and many others, it furthered a growing engagement in a fuller understanding of our country's unique culture, history and character, and the need for these to be fostered and determined by the people living in Scotland.

A defining characteristic of Scottish culture is our legacy of the deep-rooted Celtic tradition of hospitality and internationality. In 1947, Edinburgh's Lord Provost Andrew Murray encapsulated that sense of welcome with the ideal of bringing the world together in peace by celebrating and sharing the arts, hence the Festival was born.

I recall in 1948 as a 13-year-old, being enchanted by an open-air production of *A Midsummer Night's Dream* in the grass-tiered seating in Edinburgh Braidburn Valley Park. Before the lawn stage, which was surrounded by trees, was a stream. I loved the magic, this production one of the seeds of my devotion to drama and ultimate careers.

So it was that when Allen Wright on the recommendation of my benign boss Sinclair Aitken invited me to become an Edinburgh Fringe drama reviewer, I was like a fish in its watery element.

Often I would be seeing and reviewing as many as three plays a day and into the night. Here was a realisation of Lord Provost Murray's vision of worldwide performers sharing their culture. The Fringe began with seven or eight companies and by the time I was writing reviews, there were hundreds and it kept growing exponentially each year.

26

The Society

ON THE THIRD Tuesday of each month, at 17 minutes past seven, a group of argumentative Scots and congenial others meet in the backroom of Clark's Bar, Dundas Street, Edinburgh. This meeting has been happening in various locations with various members since 1968.

The society was born in Milne's Bar in Rose Street, Edinburgh, one of the many bars there that attracted an entourage of writers, artists, actors, artisans and assorted boozy raconteurs of varied backgrounds.

A few friends – myself, Sean Damer, with his touch of the blarney stone, Brian Lang, later Dean of the University of St Andrews, his friend Roger Johnston, and brother Ninian, were the original core who met regularly in one of the horseshoe enclosures in Milne's. The disadvantage of meeting there, hallowed as it was by the great literary figures, was that our own debates were constantly interrupted by friendly, but intrusive, revellers, and so we decided to find a more suitable venue. We settled on the St Vincent Bar in Edinburgh's New Town.

We were following in a notable tradition of the 18th century Scottish Enlightenment. Edinburgh, during that age of initiation, discovery and enquiry, spawned a tavern tradition of robust debates and mighty drinking which could conclude in semi-conscious under-the-table camaraderie. These clubs, such as The Speculative Society – still going today and of which one of our number is a member – and The Select Society, attracted the best minds of the time: writers, artists, philosophers, advocates and professors, Adam Smith, David Hume and Allan Ramsay, among others. They espoused such aims as 'Poking up sluggish intellects to fire.' Examples of topics they debated were slavery, divorce, the role of women and the price of whisky!

We decided to christen our club 'The society', which could be interpreted as modesty or sheer pretension. We agreed on virtually no rules, but a format by which at each meeting one of the members or an invited guest would give a talk on a subject unannounced beforehand, but contentious. It turned out over the years that no subject failed to be contentious. Almost 60 years on, this is still the ethos.

As we appoint a chairperson for each meeting, and a secretary to take Minutes, there is a record of these evenings. No kudos or acclaim accrues from membership of this eccentric society, and new members arrive by common consent when they meet general approval, usually after they have offered a speech as a guest.

The original all-male cast, with some reluctant mutterings and mumblings, eventually agreed to invite interested women to become members, a glowing enhancement it is now acknowledged. As the initiator of this society, and following my natural impulse from childhood to form gangs, I was designated the founder by Owen Dudley Edwards, an accolade that has stuck. The Minutes penned by successive secretaries were often as, or more, entertaining than the talks, following the tone of robust flyting – playful but erudite mockery.

The roll-call of members over time makes a colourful kaleidoscope: a mountaineer /joiner; a couple of actors; a BBC radio producer; a hotel-restaurant manager; a tour guide; a Green MSP; a Scottish writer; a poet/architect; university lecturers; a titled gentleman; a noted photographer; a playwright; and a list of guest speakers as varied and remarkable, and possibly as idiosyncratic. A certain robustness in either role was a sine qua non to survive the verbal onslaughts and flytings.

Subsequent to our sojourn in the St Vincent, we found a congenial home in Stewart's Bar, Drummond Street. During our period of meetings there, we were hosted by its golden proprietor Peter Cunningham, his wife, Val, and the amiable barman, Jimmy. As a token of our welcome and regular occupation, David Bathgate's portrait of Robert Burns adorned the back wall of the back room where we held our meetings. This portrait had an itinerant existence, being stolen once, recovered from a Miner's Club by Peter Cunningham, abandoned in the cellar of Stewart's Bar when Peter died and the bar taken over to become the Brass Monkey and the society ejected. David Bathgate, however, recovered it from the cellar and it now reappears annually to sanctify the annual society Burns Supper.

Our Stewart's host was regularly celebrated in the Minutes:

As often happens, the most splendid contribution to the evening was the proprietor's, since Peter brought in a tray with a large glass of malt whisky for everyone present, and two trays of crusty ham rolls.

Peter and his wife, as a gesture of our appreciation, were honoured guests at the society Burns Supper.

For many years, these Suppers were as distinctive, and frequently as excessive, as any meeting. They were held in the drawing rooms of the homes of members, the Founder, John Bishop, Chris Ferrard, George Brown and Barbara McLean. One glittering evening in Barbara's house was kept aglow, apart from the quantities of malt whisky, by contributions from our guests, the acclaimed folk artists Aly Bain, Michael Marra, Owen Hand and Rod Paterson. These were followed by members offering a traditional Burns Supper toast: To the Haggis, Immortal Memory, toast to and reply from the lassies, and a brilliant telling of 'Holy Willie's Prayer' by Barbara's husband, John, in the character of a Glasgow wide boy addressing God. A traditional ceilidh followed with amusing readings from John Herdman, poems by Stanley Roger Green and songs by Robin Harper.

Although many Minutes remain, much from the '60s to the '80s is lost. The society meeting of November 1990 laments this gap:

> It would be difficult to overstate the significance of this meeting in the history of the society. For immemorial occasions the penetrating insights, witty observations, ingenious obscenities and occasional moments of trespassing into common-sense have been either lost or left to flap like autumn leaves in the wind without the safe home of a minute book. This minute is the first to be fully and faithfully recorded in the new minute book provided by the beneficence of our Secretary David Bathgate.
>
> Threats on the life of Salman Rushdie pale into insignificance compared to the vows of exacting all the pain of hell on Robin Harper in whose custody the old minute book has remained for as long as any member's memory could serve. Indeed, the topic of the recovery of that minute book threatened to occupy the entire evening and preclude the likelihood of a talk from our speaker.
>
> The various manners in which Robin might encounter an early death should he fail yet again to produce the old minute book forced the speaker for the night, an Irish copywriter by the name of Pat Maguire, to drink another double vodka in preparation for his talk.

Alas, it might be added that no excesses of vodka precluded the speaker's own address from being savaged by the unimpressed members and guest:

> Not the tenor, not the content nor the sentiments within the speaker's talk met with any sympathy or agreement from the members or guest, and at its conclusion Chris Ferrard sprang like a hungry rat for the speaker's throat with the beginning of a lengthy and convoluted question. Alas, not if Chris had been shot at point blank range from a blunderbuss could he have been more effectively silenced. R Barnaby Hawkes, the evening's Chairman, detecting within the first syllables of Ferrard's utterance (or splutterance) its irrelevance and unsubtle preamble to yet another of his Turkophile effusions, slapped it down with a stentorian, 'Out of order!' and thereby forced on the Ferrard physiognomy a look of disbelief that has not yet left him!

The society, nevertheless, over its now 60 years' existence, with various members leaving and dying, has attracted brilliant and polemic talks and speakers from many spheres – the professions, the media, the Arts, science, business, academia, memorable literary figures – Norman MacCaig, Alastair Reid, Liz Lochhead, Alasdair Gray, Richard Holloway, Richard Demarco. And over the years amongst others, lawyers and advocates, theatre directors, cosmologists, Humanist and Christian ministers, an Olympic fitness coach, an archaeologist, immunologist, an historian, a newspaper editor. The talks inevitably from time to time have been political, the majority of members being of a Scottish Nationalist, pro-independence persuasion. Quirky topics such as hats and the importance of grumps elicited surprising responses of wit, serious discussion and heated polemic. No bone thrown to the society failed to be nibbled clean. In the early days, illiberal quaffings of whisky and beer inflamed discussion.

This heady cocktail occasioned a disgrace. Owen Dudley Edwards and myself met in what Norman MacCaig called the University 'Stiff' Club for a pre-meeting drink but became so immured in argument that we were considerably late in getting to Stewart's Bar for the meeting where we should have welcomed the guest speaker. This discourtesy was compounded by the fact that each of us had invited a speaker for the night, Owen the QC Lionel Daiches and I, Iain Crawford, Publicity Director of Edinburgh Festival.

These two were acquainted and when they met in Stewart's Bar, discovering that they had both been invited to speak, generously determined to give a joint address. However, when no one appeared to welcome them, they decided to leave. Owen and I arrived to be informed by Peter that they had gone. Owen promptly offered an obsequious apology to the QC and assured him that so deep was his chagrin that he had tendered his resignation from the society, forthwith. Owen and I offered our own grovelling apology to the members and in poor recompense gave a joint talk about our own education. We were merrily cheered by a welcome donation of a bottle of whisky from our gentleman proprietor.

From the outset, along with the no quarter arguments, has been a generosity of spirit, camaraderie and mutual support. This ethos motivated the introduction of new members: when the noted Everest mountaineer David Bathgate, who had survived a night bivouac 28,000 feet up Mount Everest, fell from the crumbly sandstone cliffs 50 feet up the crags of Arthur's Seat, he broke his leg. Barbara McLean suggested the society could be a helpful distraction while he recovered. This brilliant distraction gave the society a multi-faceted asset.

Equally, when Chris Ferrard, a considerable Turkish scholar, was disappointed when he failed to get a Lectureship at Edinburgh University, Barbara once more put him forward as a member and so provided the society with a colourful and thankfully dramatic and sometimes explosive character.

Yet another benign, quirky, truly Renaissance man was suggested by a long-time friend, Annie Slora. This was her husband Dr John, a General Practitioner revered by his patients and adopted with enthusiasm by the society. After Dr John's death, his place was filled by his son David, whose organising ability has been a blood transfusion for the ageing members.

Apart from the fun of the robust monthly meetings and occasional outings to places associated with Scottish literary figures (Lewis Grassic Gibbon, Walter Scott – the Mearns country, Abbotsford), the society has fostered lasting friendships and a supportive care for members.

The society continues in robust health. The remaining collected Minutes are in the custody of Chris Ferrard in preparation to being offered to the National Library of Scotland for the curiosity of posterity.

27

A Ceilidh Decade: Dundas Street in the 1980s

MY MEMORY OF the '80s in Dundas Street is a kaleidoscope of marvellous meetings, people who have entered my life, sometimes briefly, but whose incandescence has left a forever afterglow.

Eddie Stiven, part of my BBC *Kilbreck* writing team, the artist Kate Downie and her theatre director husband Pete, actors David Peate, Ronnie Letham successively played musical rooms. Overnight friends periodically occupied the cuckoo's nest, a cosy attic space above the kitchen.

My congenial BBC boss and friend Sinclair Aitken suggested Craig Sharp as a scriptwriter for my radio schools programme, *Questions of Living*. Craig was a truly Renaissance man, ranging from being a highly qualified vet, to fitness coach to the British Olympic rowers, Professor of Sport, and with a wide-ranging knowledge and love of Scottish poetry, especially Robert Burns. He was also a great letter writer to friends and to *The Times* on diverse topics. He scripted for my programmes amongst others a highly imaginative and readily digested programme of how the blood system works in the human body.

He thought, wisely or not, that the Dundas Street environment with its entourage of passing musicians, poets and actors would be a good place for his daughter Carol who was a student in Glasgow at the Royal Scottish Academy of Music and Drama.

So Carol came to commute from college to a room in Dundas Street, a house of colourful transients, constant visitors and late-night parties. Her first impression was that she had landed to a cocktail of Mardi Gras and the House of the Rising Sun.

The environment was creative and eventful. Norman Chalmers was a talented multi-instrumentalist playing concertina as a member of Jock Tamson's Bairns, a group which won the Folk Band of the Year accolade. Carol had met Norman in the flat and asked him to teach her the penny whistle. His response was to say, 'If we gather a few folk, I'll teach the group.' And so, myself, Barbara McLean, John MacInnes, Militza Maitland, Carol Sharp, David and Julie Bathgate, all total beginners, formed the basis of the group, with occasional contributions from Liz Horobin, Ann Ward, Mary McGookin and Ali Millen. We assembled regularly in the flat and Norman announced as a challenge that we would play a gig in six months. Six months later we performed our first gig with tremulous success in the King's House Hotel, Glencoe, with our repertoire of songs and music from the Scottish tradition. Our little mixed instrumental band was patriotically named after

Hugh MacDiarmid's poem, 'Scotland Small?'. It was in that band that I learned to play the melodeon and the mouth organ, which would be usefully incorporated into my subsequent storytelling.

Previous to this, I had with Barbara taken up an enthusiasm for black and white photography, bought a single reflex camera, and converted two hall cupboards in the flat into a well-equipped dark room. Our photographic skills and knowledge were developed with the patient, expert and practical tuition of Robin Gillanders. Robin, an ex-pupil of mine from Royal High School days, was our photographer for the Fort Knox enterprise, and was already well known, later to take the official photograph of the opening of the Scottish Parliament. He was also an affable friend, generous with his time and knowledge, and with him we spent many exciting hours in his dark room seeing the images miraculously emerge like ghosts becoming material from the development trays. My photographs were a record of the habitués of the Abbotsford, a gallery of a phase Barbara, Carol and I had for nudes and travelogues of holiday jaunts, such as our annual midsummer encampment in the beautiful Glen Etive with a company of friends.

Threesomes with the best will and deepest mutual affection are at least a challenge, occasionally a triumph, and often a disaster, however laudable the aspiration and ideals. If the course of true love is never smooth, the course of inclusive love can be a rocky path.

Such was the latter with the relationship between Carol, Barbara, and myself. Barbara and I accommodated one another's different lovers as initially it was with this liaison, but inevitably these were fragile threads, and when Barbara met John MacInnes, we parted and my relationship with her took the form it has today of a lasting friendship.

A diverse entourage of colourful transient residents arrived by various routes. At a party in Rose Street one evening I met Alison Millen, whose vivacity and compassionate story so attracted me that she entered the flat and my life.

She was at once an astonishment and a delight, champagne and dewdrops, a punk diva. A natural storyteller, her narrations to the flatmates of her day at work looking after old auntie Kitty were artistically fashioned with moody shifts, comedy, affection, consummately constructed and concluded.

On my 50th birthday, in disguise as a charlady with becapped tradesman 'husband' Eddie Stiven, she affected to gatecrash the party. Before anyone tumbled to their identity, she seated herself at the piano and with Eddie lustily sang a witty new-minted birthday song. In the midst of this, she turned around, and to the amusement of the party roared out, 'Eat yer heart out, Norman MacCaig!' to his delight. They were identified and applauded.

In the dying fall of our relationship, we made a valedictory holiday on the Island of Rùm. She loved the sea and this kindled in her a love of the islands so that she later for a time looked after the café on the pier at Eigg. From there, her letters and poems gave a vivid and often dramatic account of the life and characters on the island.

Another colourful visitor to Dundas Street at this time was Charli, or Charlotte Lownie. She was a dauntless, exuberant lady I met in the BBC Club in London while I was on a radio production course shortly after I had joined the BBC Radio Schools Department in Edinburgh. By then she had retired. By her make-up and dress, manner, voice, she might have slipped out of the 1940s. In fact, she was a BBC production secretary during World War II, consorting with such literary luminaries as Dylan Thomas, Louis MacNeice, et al, whom she held affectionately and dramatically in her memory. If she seemed anachronistic or eccentric it was because she was wholly, refreshingly, and as I later found, startlingly herself.

It was years later, in the 1980s, that Charli happily reappeared in my life. I was sitting at my desk when my secretary said, 'There's someone called Charlie on the phone for you.' Her voice was unmistakable.

'David, have you time to meet an old geriatric for coffee?'

'Delighted.'

'Oh, you divine delinquent.'

We met in what was then the wine bar in Hanover Street.

'How are you Charli?'

'Oh, you know, nae hair, nae breists, nae teeth, nae wit.'

'Nothing wrong with your wit!'

By now she had a fine flowing blond wig, apparently false teeth, and according to her, 'Nae breists.' What she fulsomely had was energy for a talk.

To Alison she seemed dramatic, probably frightening to some. And to some she certainly was.

'I was in Jenners amongst the twinsets and tweedy ladies, having a peaceful afternoon tea, when a couple sat down with a screaming brat! I simply walked across, put my face two inches from the brat, and said, "Shut up!"'

Apparently the 'brat' did; and presumably, also, the other frequenters of the restaurant. Meeting Charli was to find yourself in the midst of a play. This is Carol's account of her visit to our flat.

'Helloooooooooooooooooo! Chaaaaaarrlii here!' called a distinctive old school RP female voice from the hall. David's pal Charli was on a rare visit from London. By the time she reached me in the living room of 33 Dundas Street, she had already been introduced to resident Ali, singer, storyteller, with whom she entered arm in arm in high spirits.

'Helllooooooooo Carol. Wonderful to meet you. So nice to see David again, and Ali, beautiful Ali.'

And with that she promptly sat herself down on the piano stool and began to plink plonk on the piano keys an improvised song which went something like this:

'Oh, it's so nice to meet the beautiful Ali, we really are getting along, so pally,

And Carol dear is here, with her welcoming home-made barrel of beer,

And David to bring us cheer,

And Charli, that's me, the old dear, very old, ancient dear,

Falling apart, with golden heart

And wonderful Ali, we really are pally...'

Plink plonk, plink plonk.

I thought Charli was the Director General or a BBC producer, such was the theatrical power of her being, when I found out that she had worked as a secretary.

Charli's candour was mischievous and with a full consciousness of its understated drama. Talking of her deceased husband, she said, 'Oh Sheughie was a good father to the boys, but frankly David, his lovemaking never amounted to much more than tum tum te te tum tum, snore snore,' announced with a sense of resigned ennui.

'What did he die of?' I asked.

With an even greater sense of exaggerated weariness, 'Oh, everything.'

When her rheumatism and advancing years prevented her from climbing the two flights to my Dundas Street flat, she was welcomed by Barbara and John in their ground floor flat in Eildon Street. Their two teenage sons fell in love with this feisty and iconoclastic octogenarian.

John responded readily to her perpetually youthful spirit. When he and Barbara were going out one evening, and she was to be left alone in the flat, he informed her that there were two young, handsome, muscular West Indian dancers in the flat above that she could invite down to 'entertain' her. 'John,' said she, 'I'd need a gallon of cod liver oil.'

She enrolled in a summer school on modern poetry. When the family delivered her to a spartan room in Edinburgh University Halls of Residence, the boys could scarcely hold back tears. They needn't have worried – I can't imagine how her tutors responded to her original and dismissive views on some of their beloved poets. I am sure they loved her.

I was attending a storytelling course at Emerson College in Sussex when she died aged 88 in August 2000. I was about to attend a singing class when a friend took me aside to tell me of her death. I loved Charli and had often written her a birthday poem. This is her posthumous poem:

For Charli

Laugh and be glad though time's a flying
banish all sorrow
and welcome to-morrow.
'Da Pacem Domine'

This year's birthday poem is when
you are no longer here
I hear you, hear you telling me,
'Get on with it. Get on!'
Of course you did not mention
the urgency
was because
you would be gone
to where you could no longer
hear me speak it.
I should have known
you'd choose to slip away.
You who could make mayhem
in a tea room
would have no fuss at parting
not even in the usual way
and certainly take no fussy
last farewell.
So, 'No flowers!' you command.
Understandable,
but Charli, just because you
are safely hidden and silent
don't think that I
delinquently
won't shout and shower you
with flowers of words
and make as well
a fussy spray of tears.
I can be as out of line as you.
Decorum never was your code
so I'll indecorously decorate
your memory
with gouts of tears
unruly celebrations
and loud bibulous laments

till you yell out 'Stop your nonsense!'
from beyond.
And furthermore you are to know
that when, this sunny afternoon
I heard you'd died
I wept
and then I sang.
Got on with it.
Took you with me in
the faltering notes
and ones that bravely rang.
Yes, I got on,
took you with me
in my song.
So don't pretend we weren't glad
delinquent we
both you and I
that together we caused
just a little
fuss.

28

Passionfruit and Pangkor Island

Jessieca Leo

Leo   Yok   Shiam
Jade Beauty
The jade is at its ugliest when it is taken out of the ground but the longer
it has to mature after that, the more beautiful it becomes.
Porcupine
The pig with the arrows sticking in it.
Moonface

MID-MORNING I was sitting at my desk in my BBC office in Abercromby Place
in Edinburgh. At her desk opposite, my secretary Carol answered the phone.
'A call for you, David.'
'Who?'
Her hand over mouthpiece, 'A woman, she didn't say.'
'Why not?' I wondered.
I lifted the phone. 'Good morning!'
'David Campbell?'
'Yes.'
And with no further preliminaries: 'You took some photographs of Ivor
Cutler, I believe. He's coming to the Edinburgh Festival and we wondered
if we could use a photo for publicity and how much it would cost.'
'Well, if you pay me more than I got for the one on his book cover.'
'How much was that?'
'Nothing.'
She laughed and her voice puzzled me.
'Where are you from?'
'Can you guess?'
'No! I tell you what; you can have what you want for £25 delivered in
cash, by hand when you come to the Festival.'
'Fine,' she said.
I didn't know at the time, 1982, but the owner of this mystery voice,
along with David Jones, one of the directors of Serious Music, had taken
five productions to the Edinburgh Fringe, one of them Ivor Cutler's show.
They needed a publicity photo and had been told by Ivor that I had the right
one. I sent the photograph.

I forgot all about the phone call. A wet Festival had begun, late August. I was alone in my flat in the early evening when the bell rang. I opened the door to see a small silken oriental woman, smiling like sunshine.

'I have come to deliver your £25 by hand as agreed.'

'Come in.'

Jessieca Leo, Jade Beauty, Moonface, Porcupine and I sat in my drawing-room. She took £25 from her handbag.

'Thank you. When did you get here?'

'An hour ago.'

'Have you eaten?'

'Not yet.'

'We'll spend the £25 on a meal.'

And so we did. You could still more or less do this with that sum in 1982.

This was a lively, spirited entrepreneurial young lady, resourceful, full of fun, attractive and ingenious. She was interested to see a recording session of *Kilbreck*.

At two o'clock on Sunday afternoon, the silken Jessieca floated into our studio raising eyebrows and curiosity amongst actors, audio assistants, sound engineers, secretaries. We rehearsed and recorded each episode in two hours; ten episodes over the weekend. It was concentrated and busy work requiring total attention.

With an episode 'in the can', I showed Jessieca to the front door of 5 Queen Street, the BBC Radio headquarters at the time.

'I have something for you,' she said, 'give me your hand. Don't look. Walk ten yards, open your hand.'

I did as asked, walked ten yards, opened my hand and there was – a passion fruit!

I turned. Jessieca was still at the door. She smiled, winked and left. The most elegant invitation ever I had. I kept it until we fulfilled its promise together. We were joyful companions, lovers, became great friends and as my friend Alan Rowland put it, a colourful Festival 'item'. Jessieca recalls:

The Fringe was exciting to say the least, but meeting a real Scotsman in a kilt was most intriguing. Yes, the first question that came to mind was, 'Do they or don't they, underneath?' The image of our meeting that has been etched in my mind is one of David in his kilt with a miniature umbrella that fits perfectly like a hat, and me in equally flamboyant pseudo-Asian attire complimented by a New Age Afro hairdo – dancing down the main street in search of sustenance. I think everybody thought we were characters promoting a show.

My mother, who later met David at my wedding, taught us that you can always tell the character of a person by the friends they kept.

I will always remember David's friends who gathered in his house on Dundas Street in the early evening – Alison, Carol, Alan Rowland and a few others, whose names now escape me. Whisky flowed and poetry sprouted from those golden gatherings like nectar out of the soul of a hidden spring. Their renditions and bravado touched something in me and I learned what it means to be proud of being who you are and the art of doing things with love, passion and conviction.

Memory is a fickle creature, conflating and intertwining strands. It was either then or before then that Ivor Cutler stayed with me for a few days. I never met any man more constantly and nakedly himself. You could meet him on the street, talk to him in your drawing-room and the exact same personality would walk onto the stage in the Albert Hall, or into a classroom of children. He loved mischief and honesty. Of Ivor, you could really say that his eyes twinkled. It was a canny Scottish observant twinkle that brewed fun, and behind that, compassion and uncompromising honesty.

I remember visiting Ivor in his London flat, an anachronism. In time gone by, Scottish miners would have a metal tub on the floor filled with water from pans and kettles. Ivor bathed in such a tub.

As we talked, I saw a handsome pair of tweed plus-fours and remarked how I admired them.

'I'm sorry to hear that,' he said in his distinctively articulated poker voice, each syllable clipped, clean, clear and Scottish.

'Why sorry?'

'I bought them in a market thinking that I would enjoy wearing them, but I found that I am larger than they are, and now because you have admired them I will have to give them to you. Otherwise I will feel mean and guilty.'

He wouldn't hear my protest. No, I had to have them and he refused to take any money. At length I suggested that I might come across some suitable item of barter. This was acceptable and later my friend and his, Barbara McLean, told me he fancied a Scots dictionary. He sent me a courteous brief and witty note of gratitude when I sent this:

19 February 1986

Dear David,

I don't remember ever receiving a gift that understood what would please. I'm deeply grateful for your thoughtfulness. It was enhanced by being totally unanticipated. There was no need to have done such a thing. The trousers are better hanging from your loins than waiting for me to get thin. I'll be in Edinburgh for two weeks for the Festival – see you then. Now back to the buik to look up more dusty words, gratefully Ivor.

On another occasion Ivor and his friend Phyllis were staying with me in my flat in Dundas Street. Once more August, Festival time. I had been invited to give the first of a series of lectures for the Fringe. I chose as my subject to present Scottish writers of our time. I was working at the BBC and had edited together many archive recordings and selections from programmes I had produced. I enlisted the help of the enthusiastic audio engineer Gregor Robertson. He would play excerpts to illustrate my talk which was allotted 90 minutes, talk and question time. I had taken care to prepare the presentation meticulously. The venue was the hall of the former Edinburgh University Men's Union, a venue I fondly recalled from my university days as the forays to student dances. The large wood-panelled hall was now arranged to accommodate 200.

Gregor and I arrived early to set up equipment. The event was to begin at 1.00pm. Punctually, Ivor and Phyllis sat in the second row. At ten past one a young woman took a seat at the back. With this audience of three I began my talk. After ten minutes, Ivor and Phyllis left. Gregor and I now outnumbered the audience two to one. On the principle of the mustard seed, and for the benefit of the one woman, we made our presentation. At its conclusion the woman, an Australian, thanked us, expressed her enjoyment and assured us she'd tell everyone she met to come. Unfortunately, this was the first, last and only 'performance'.

When I returned home, Ivor and Phyllis had tea and biscuits ready. 'I'm sorry we had to leave, David, but I was sitting in a draught.'

I should have guessed. Previously when I had asked Ivor if I could interview him for an arts programme for Radio Scotland he had agreed but forewarned me that the interview might be interrupted by the necessity of his removing or replacing garments due to the hypersensitivity of his skin to changes of temperature.

'I feel a draught if a mouse breathes.'

During that interview I concealed my amusement as he successively removed, replaced hat, jacket, pullover. These actions he accomplished with unsmiling earnestness but I was never sure if he was smiling within. At the conclusion with his customary punctilious grace, he thanked me for my patience and hoped it was what I was looking for.

'Beyond my wildest dreams, Ivor.'

'Yes, I thought so.'

Ivor died in 2006. He had a cult following. Those who enjoyed his work, his humour, his whimsy and subtlety became addicts. For those who are not acquainted with his recordings and books, I would advise them to taste and I would be surprised if they do not then dine lavishly on his fun and philosophy.

When he died I wrote this poem:

For Ivor

A pencil seems right
and words a few
to say 'Good-bye Ivor.'
Economy and whimsy and truth
and in small doses
huge mischief
is how I remember you
and wearing no clothes
but your own
although naturally they
were second hand
but actually you were naked
naked as I knew no other
man to be
and naked with skin
almost translucent
so that I could see
through to the bones
and never any difference
a sitting room, the Albert Hall
a kitchen
each you entered as yourself
and each you lent a little
mischief
and left an echo that said
and said and said
'Be naked ... please
it is the only way'
and for this, 'Thank you Mr Cutler'
the echo echoes
your ghost walks naked
as a child, an innocence
a bravery.

Writing of Jessieca's visit to the Festival prompted these recollections of the unique Mr Cutler. At that time too, I met Sean Murphy who was then Ivor's agent. Sean was a lively, enterprising, resourceful entrepreneur. Like his countrymen, great craic in the pub, a mighty raconteur and a robust adversary in argument and the Celtic art of flyting.

I first met him when I drove him to Brownsbank Cottage when he was making an LP recording of Norman MacCaig interviewing his friend Chris Grieve (Hugh MacDiarmid) to elicit a selection of the great man's poems. The charm of that recording, apart from the affectionate rapport between the two poets, is the ambient soundscape of birdsong.

Sean Murphy evokes two particular memories that recall the flavour of the time. Amongst the legion of artists and performers who came to the Edinburgh Festival Fringe was an American director called Cyndi Turtledove, fully as flamboyant as her name, adventurous, dauntless and cheeky. Cheeky because one night at a party in Marchmont she asked if she could borrow my car, a little green Morris Minor, for 'an hour'.

I didn't realise that it was the kidnap vehicle in which she and Sean were to disappear for the entire night and leave me to walk home, probably no bad thing considering the alcohol in my bloodstream.

My flat was an almost permanent ceilidh house especially at Festival time and Sean who had one evening been particularly acquainted with various beers and whisky, volunteered to sing. I never could have imagined a song could be sung so slowly nor the words and notes so extended. The song was, 'She Moved Through the Fair'.

The preparation for this 'performance' should have served as a forewarning. Sean settled himself on his seat, spread his knees, closed his eyes – reminiscent of Joxer Daly's closed-eyes mode in *Juno and the Paycock* – moved his mouth, made some experimental vowel sounds and eventually a prolonged 'mmm' which evolved into the first note of the first word 'my'. The rest of the word, the 'y' became a lengthy 'i' 'ee' diphthong with an interminable 'ee' eliding into the 'y' of young which word hung lovingly onto the 'ng' and thence to a long liquid 'l' of 'love' so that in the time it took to sing the first line, 'My young love said to me, my mother won't mind', another singer could have completed the entire song. Whether stunned in wonder, sedated by the pace or lack of it, or through grace and politeness, everyone listened and applauded this remarkable presentation. Shortly afterwards, Sean fell soundly asleep in the chair where he sat, so deeply asleep that not even a high octave dramatic rendition by a young woman soprano singing 'Summertime' at full volume, awoke him.

His sublime unconsciousness also spared him the role of prisoner to the intense histrionics of her presentation as she kneeled before successive guests, clutching them by the arm and gazing soulfully and meaningfully into their faces attenuating certain words for dramatic effect and then abruptly shifting her position to honour another guest with her electric performance. The denouement was to give a dramatic reprise of the first verse and conclude by rising to her feet opening wide her arms to encompass the entire company as she lingered meltingly on 'So hush little baby, don't you cry.'

By now the company was immune to anything and applauded the

rendition in the lavish spirit in which it had been given. Sean might have appreciated it.

It was as a consequence of Sean's being Ivor's agent on that Festival visit organised by Jessieca that he became a colourful part of the high days and long nights of the Festival that year. My connection with the colourful Jessieca continued in a breezy correspondence, so I was delighted when my sprightly friend revisited a subsequent Edinburgh Festival:

In 1985 (or 1987) I was living in Singapore and working for the Singapore International Arts Festival and I visited the Edinburgh Festival again. This visit was to change the way on how I look at love. I arrived in the afternoon and was welcomed by David and his beautiful girlfriend, Alison. We had tea and caught up on our stories. Then the most unexpected thing happened.

Alison said, 'I have changed the sheets and made the bed. I am spending the night at a friend's house. You two have a lot to catch up on.' To say I was flabbergasted and touched deeply was an understatement. The wonderful, generous, beautiful Alison came back in the morning and brought us tea in bed. For me that was the ultimate definition of selfless love, which is too often expressed in clichés.

Jessieca was a great world traveller and ever afterwards from her various destinations kept in touch, first by letter and then by email. One day came another elegant and exciting invitation: her wedding in Malaysia, the wedding to be followed by a mystery jaunt. An irresistible invitation, an adventure. The guests who assembled in the hotel in Kuala Lumpur were like an assorted Agatha Christie gathering without the murder – celebrants from New York, Munich, Memphis, Paris, London, Santa Fe, Kuala Lumpur, Tokyo, Edinburgh, Rome – with her extended Chinese family and friends. From Kuala Lumpur we made a bus tour to a Buddhist Temple.

By force of magnetism, my companion on the bus was Ferda from Istanbul. Ferda was petite, lean, electric and surprising. At the Buddhist Temple, together we ascended what seemed hundreds of steps and entered the wonderful and awesome vastness of the temple, our first shared exhilaration.

The wedding ceremony in the jungle village was a flamboyant ritual; the groom led to the bride by giant multi-coloured lions, four men forming the legs and accompanied by drums, gongs and cymbals. At the wedding banquet, along with the 16 foreign guests were 450 Chinese relations and friends; the feast merry, long and lavish with tasty dishes and drink-what-you-like. The groom, Thomas, and bride Jessieca were part of a beautiful and calm tea ceremony, which contrasted with the spirited dance of the lions, the Karaoke, songs, music and laughter at every crowded table.

Jessieca devised more surprises: we were invited to the honeymoon! Pangkor Island. Pangkor was a jungle green dream island. With neither of us objecting, Jessieca conspired to have Ferda and myself share one of the beach hotel chalets. Ferda rightly chided me for this interpretation of events:

'David, it did not happen quite as you write it. Well, of course, what do I expect from a storyteller? Your Bible, at least a major one in the history of storytelling, is One Thousand and One Nights, which follows the 'matryoshka' pattern, one story coming out of the previous one. But, David, it didn't happen quite as you have written it. I mean don't put the blame on Jessieca, s'il vous plaît. In that case I will have to recite 'To His Coy Mister' to you.

It sounds as if we were so, so innocent and passive and poor Jessieca, in the midst of all that brouhaha, had no other concern than matching us. She had nothing to do with it apart from inviting us all to her wedding. If you need to know the real story you may have to pay dear!'

The ferry crossed a quiet sea on a starry night with a little cusp of crescent moon and it was tropically dark when our little wedding crew disembarked and found our way to the chalets. We had hardly thrown down our bags when Ferda said, a little challenge in her voice I thought, 'I'm going for a swim.'

Impelled by the challenge, intrigued and attracted I followed her through the dark to the glistening water. I am a poor swimmer. Ferda threw off her clothes, plunged in and swam confidently far out to sea in an easy crawl. Following Ferda I divested, luxuriated in the warm water and, in contrast to her skilled crawl, gently breast-stroked closer to the shore.

A swell of waves arose as Ferda swam closer to me and then – no romantic Hollywood movie could have bettered this scene – tumbled by the waves our tangled bodies were rolled ashore.

Iguana night on Pangkor Island

Slim Lady moon lies on her back,
Amphibious you, sloughing land
                enter the ocean's hush
Seamaid soundless among stars
                            lure me
Into the swimming warmth.
Scales of silence glitter
                        between us
        Wave-laved
            our bodies tangle
                at the water's edge
Borne landward by the tilting tide.

Next evening as all the guests dined outside together in the warm air, Jessieca invited from each of us the story of how we met her. This, with some consequences of my meeting with Jessieca, Jade Beauty, Moonface, Hedgehog, woman of surprises, is that story.

Recalling Jessieca's lightsome mischief, the passion fruit, and Ferda's incisive editing of my account of our liaison, and reflecting on other meetings (and matings) I have concluded that it is naïve and myopic to consider that in affairs of the heart males are either the real instigators or decision makers. Jessieca averred that her visits to Edinburgh 'changed the way I look on love.' These meetings changed the way I perceived the dance of courtship, and for Jessieca, Ferda and myself were the ground for future adventures and explorations.

29

Eurydice

IT WAS EDINBURGH splashing with rain, the Festival and Fringe in full swing and folk dripping on the castle esplanade at the Tattoo. I was played out with excessive Festivalling, excessive socialising, excessive drinking, excessive everything. The flat was unusually empty, and I was having a lone convalescent evening. Eddie and Carol and Ali were somewhere in town.

It was take-down-the-garbage night and so I tied up the black plastic bag and descended the two flights to the common front door of 33 Dundas Street to find an attractive refugee from the rain sheltering within.

'I hope you don't mind,' she said.

'The only sensible thing to do,' said I. She was waiting for a bus at the shelter-less stop adjacent to our door.

Maggie was five foot seven or eight, handsomely built, with an open cheerful rain-glistening brightness, abrim with life and easy laughter. In the ten minutes we waited for her bus, I learned her name, of her recent return from the States where she had assisted at a Girl Guides camp, and then I noticed and told her that her bus was approaching.

She boarded and as the bus receded Eurydice waved from the rain-misted windows and Orpheus stood dismayed and recalling Frank Sinatra's 'The Gal That Got Away' and Humphrey Bogart watching Lauren Bacall vanish into the skies. I was cursing my folly for not inviting her to my imminent birthday party. 'Ah well. So be it,' thought I.

But the flashing smile in the lit bus receding into the night recurred, and recurred like a film spool on a loop, even in the next days. And so I hit on a naughty scheme to retrieve Eurydice. From the BBC I phoned the Scottish Guides Association to suggest we were considering doing a radio documentary on the work of Scottish guide leaders abroad, and informed the lady at the Association that I was looking to trace such a one I had recently met returning from a guide camp in New England but that all I knew was her first name. Courteously, the lady offered to set enquiries afoot but after a week informed me that they had drawn a blank.

Then I had my next mad idea.

I should say at this point that my relationship with the golden-hearted Ali was on the ebb. Like many things, clichéd as it seems to say, it had run its course, as it had been with teaching, as it was soon to be with my work in the BBC, as it had been when I left Scotland to go to Germany. Internal changes became certainties, and certainties prompted action.

My second mad idea was to advertise for my faded ghost in Scotland's national newspaper, *The Scotsman*, and so I took out a 16th-page advertisement with the limited information I had, inviting her to phone me.

What I did not foresee were the phone calls from many Maggies. One I vividly recall.

'Are you looking for a particular, special Maggie?' she asked. The tentative and plaintive tone of the enquiry dismayed me.

'Yes,' I said. 'Yes.'

'Well, I wish you good luck.'

'Thank you,' I said, and wished I could supply some congenial other David or whomsoever for her.

It happened that I had a BBC meeting in Glasgow after which I adjourned to the BBC Club. I particularly remember that overindulgent evening in the Club for a story someone told me about a BBC producer who had become so inebriated that he had to be helped out to a taxi by a solicitous companion. The last thing the Samaritan heard, as he helped him into the taxi, was the taxi driver enquiring 'Where to, Sir?' and the drunken response, 'Mind your own fucking business!'

I stayed too long in the Club, drank too much, inebriated as much with the banter as the drink, and was lucky to catch the last train back to Edinburgh. Sedated by alcohol, I fell asleep and woke up on the Marie Celeste. The carriage was empty and the train was going in the wrong direction. It slowed to a halt and I looked out of the window into the dark in what seemed the middle of nowhere.

'Hello?' I shouted into the night and further down the line an exasperated engine driver leaned out of his cabin.

'Are you a fucking passenger?'

Yes, I was a fucking passenger.

'Get down and wait.'

I alighted in that middle of nowhere – somewhere west of Edinburgh and the train shunted the carriage out of sight.

After a while the engine itself reappeared and I was invited into the lofty engine room. In this grand carriage I was conveyed in amenable and forgiving company back to Edinburgh where I alighted on Platform 19, Waverley Station.

It was after 1.00am when I opened the door of my flat in Dundas Street to be met by Eddie Stiven with the greeting, 'Maggie phoned.' As we were both habitual jokers, I made clear my scepticism.

'But no, she lives round the corner in Great King Street and has been at Drama College in Glasgow and has left her phone number.'

Maggie was found, but it was now too late to ring.

Next day however I arranged to meet and dine with the long-sought-after Maggie. Not only was her presence and conversation champagne but our interests and enthusiasms were identical: love of poetry, drama, walking mountains, plunging into icy Scottish rivers and lochs, travel, explorations of many sorts, and fun. On this heady cocktail and lavish libations we skipped down Dundas Street and around midnight arrived opposite my flat and at a moment of decision (and a road not taken). Were we to go around the corner to her flat for 'coffee', or to mine to meet my lover and friends? Things may have been much different had we taken the road to Great King Street since we were warmly mutually attracted and the coffee could have lasted the night.

This may be the place to outline the attitudes and ideals that drove my actions which my friends considered unrealistic, and more likely insane. My idea was simply the equation that if people showed a love or affection for someone, then the people would have that love and affection for one another. In the world of mathematics, it made perfect sense, and perhaps so in a perfect world, but in the workings of the human heart it does not compute. Many times with varying degrees of success and disaster I had attempted these reconciliations in my long marathon of exploring the meaning of love.

Consequently, in the euphoria of meeting Maggie, I felt it would be fitting to share that joy and introduce her to Ali, one love to another, and to my friends Eddie and Carol. So we came to my flat in Dundas Street. No one seemed to be about, so I knocked on the door of the bedroom occupied by Eddie and Carol.

'Come in!'

In we came. In the bed were Eddie, Carol and Ali. The reason for this cosily tucked-in threesome was that Eddie and Carol were comforting Ali who was, unsurprisingly, distressed knowing that I was with the Maggie I had dramatically advertised for in *The Scotsman*. What Maggie thought at that moment I don't know, but I was still full of inebriated bonhomie and bent on furthering the plan of a joyful meeting, so gaily invited everyone into the front room to meet and sing. I'd found that Maggie was a good singer and Ali had a varied and fun repertoire.

Eddie and Carol greeted Maggie like the shepherd his lost sheep, and Maggie realised that Ali's reception, though courteous, was less fulsome. Nevertheless, we all toasted the meeting, drank some more, shared a few songs, some chatter and ultimately Maggie went home and I never had that coffee.

Subsequently, Maggie and I met a few times – a concert at the Usher Hall, a folk song gathering or two, but the dying fall of my relationship with Ali, Maggie's having synchronously met the man who was to become her husband, meant that the drama ended, not with a bang, but a comfortable sizzle: the end of an affair that had never begun.

For a time Maggie met with a frolicsome female entourage in 33 Dundas

Street who styled themselves 'The Hags' and were a colourful coven. Maggie, with nostalgic delight, recalls the frequent ceilidhs of inventive games, song, music, poetry, chatter and nonsense.

The postscript is that she and Carol made an enduring friendship: in Carol's vexing and complex health problems of recent years, Maggie has been a vibrant support and encouragement. And Eurydice and Orpheus meet from time to time for lunchtime catch-ups and chatters.

30

Bert

I FIRST CAME across Bert the Tramp at the Lane Sale. These open-air auctions were exciting events where gathered seasoned sharp-eyed dealers, second-hand furniture shop owners, curiosity mongers and folk like myself.

Bert was the perfect picture of the kind of figure of the road that might have captured the imagination of Richmal Crompton's dishevelled schoolboy hero, William Brown. Bert was grizzled, tousle-haired, scuff-booted, baggy-breeked and had bright alert blue eyes. He wheeled an old black push bike, on and around which were secured bags and various items. He seemed always to be coming or going, never static, minding his own business, except on one occasion when I saw his eyes and tongue blaze fire in a volcanic burst at someone who had clearly offended him in the Lane. It reminded me of Donald Pleasence's irascible explosion as the tramp in Harold Pinter's *The Caretaker*.

The Bert I came to know was much more peaceable. I greeted him outside the door of Henderson's Bar in Thistle Street, which was adjacent to the BBC premises where I worked at the time.

Pinteresque, he announced: 'Eggs, would ye like some eggs?' It would have been churlish to refuse and I thought perhaps he needed the money.

'A minute,' and he disappeared round the corner into Thistle Street Lane North, reappearing with a half dozen egg box. I fished in my pocket for some payment – 'No, no! They're for you!' he stated flatly and firmly. And that was that, no questions. I thanked him and thereafter from time to time we'd engage in a little chat and the same transaction.

One evening I met him by chance outside my flat in Dundas Street and invited him up for a cup of tea. I was so surprised when he sat at the piano and vamped a tune that I took a photo of this incongruous spectacle.

His conversation was always sporadic, in the present, and he revealed nothing of his history. He became an unusual friend, and I gathered that he liked me. When some friends and I met him on our way to the famous Khushi's curry restaurant, which at that time was next to Stewart's Bar in Lothian Street, we invited him to accompany us. He always seemed completely at ease.

My last and most dramatic memory of Bert is remarkable for more than one reason. I had never known Bert to drink but one early evening as I came down Dundas Street with my Danish friend Annamette, he hailed me. He was sitting on the stone steps leading up to a flat, affable and loquacious with drink.

'Come to visit Star.' 'Star' was expressed with an extended vowel and rolling 'r'. 'My girlfriend, Star.'

'Why not?' I thought.

'Where?' I asked.

'A taxi, we'll get a taxi.'

Annamette and I were game for this unexpected turn of events. I had a half bottle of whisky in my pocket so we were ready and hailed a passing cab. Bert directed the surly driver to a complex housing estate, his instructions not helped by his vociferously uttering 'right' and pointing left. However, we arrived.

'I'll pay,' said Bert. Another surprise.

Annamette and I got out while Bert lengthily fumbled while the driver's grumpy scepticism turned into polite gratitude when Bert peeled off an excessive note or two.

We followed Bert through a grey concrete yard, up a concrete stairway to a door of a first floor flat where Bert knocked at the door. No answer. Bert knocked at the door of the neighbour opposite who informed him that Star had gone to the club in the basement.

Thither we trekked through bare concrete. A woman answered and informed us that Star had gone home. We retraced our steps feeling this was to be an abortive jaunt, but when Bert knocked once more at Star's door, it opened and there was a neat woman, Star, in a blue dressing gown.

'I told you to go! Told you it was finished.'

'I've brought these friends to see you.'

Star, seeing us standing there, clearly embarrassed, invited us in.

More surprises. Star was warmly welcoming, took us into her sitting room, brought glasses and while Bert talked to Annamette, she beckoned me into an adjoining room. It was a museum, a mausoleum. Silver cups and trophy shields everywhere, and photos of a young man clad in a judo outfit holding a large cup, her son. 'Murdered,' she said; her other son was in Saughton Prison.

We returned to join Bert and Annamette. Pinter could have scripted the rest of the evening.

'I told you it was finished,' said Star.

'You took down your knickers! Here on this floor. You took them down for me here! Your knickers!'

It was time to go. We took as rapid and polite a farewell as possible and made our way out of the housing estate labyrinth.

The postscript to this is a testament to the powerful way in which story works in the wonder house of the imagination. Shortly after this I had described this visit to my girlfriend Liz Horobin. Subsequently Liz insisted that she had accompanied me on that visit. She says so to this day. At storytelling workshops I often cite this as proof of the power of story to replicate life itself in the imagination.

31
Camphill

I FIRST MET the remarkable Catherine Lockerbie at a lecture on Hugh MacDiarmid given by the musician and composer Ronald Stevenson. I was sitting with Norman MacCaig. Every time the speaker, in Norman's view, mispronounced MacDiarmid's name, Norman under his breath testily corrected it.

Catherine at that time was a highly gifted student at Edinburgh University and was in fact just about to graduate with a Double First. She had a passion for literature and Scottish poetry, so was delighted when I introduced her to Norman, who of course with an eye for beauty, reciprocated the pleasure.

Catherine was to become a lifelong friend, but I soon found she could well be epitomised by MacDiarmid's avowal in a 'A Drunk Man Looks at a Thistle' when he states he is 'Nae hauf way hoose, but aye... whaur extremes meet.' From the earliest time that I knew her, Catherine had on the one hand a great empathy and desire to help those with physical and learning disabilities, and on the other to offer opportunity to the highly gifted. This latter impetus was to make her a creative and valued member of the Heretics community and hugely successful in directing and developing the Edinburgh International Book Festival.

While I was working in the BBC, I asked Catherine to put together a programme about the three young people with severe learning disabilities that she was looking after in the Camphill Community in Aberdeenshire.

In order to make the programme and understand the ethos and nature of the Rudolf Steiner-inspired community of young people with learning disabilities and their carers, I camped for a week in the grounds and joined in the life and meals of the community.

This experience profoundly affected me and changed the way I viewed anyone with disabilities of any kind.

One day, a young teenage girl whom I was told habitually banged her head dangerously against walls, saw me and ran at me full tilt, leapt up, legs circling, arms around me, she gazed deeply and intently and questioningly into my eyes.

Suddenly I realised that she was in her own way speaking to me, and I felt a total companionship and a great inadequacy.

The script Catherine wrote was to be the second part of my radio programme, 'It's not fair; what's not fair?' for my audience of teenagers. The first part featured young people and others complaining about what they did not have. The second part showed Catherine's extraordinary empathy in speaking from within the mind of her charges, and illuminating the unique gifts and qualities they had.

Shortly after this visit, I was invited to review a play for *The Scotsman* to be performed by young people with similar learning disabilities from St Joseph's School in West Lothian. My feeling that I would need to make allowances was dramatically contradicted by the experience – the commitment, sincerity and power of the actors. One young girl with Down's syndrome was providing a drum accompaniment, and her absolute and compelling concentration elicited this poem:

Thank You Rosie`

I never till now saw
a drum beat like yours.
As if waiting with love to waken
the sound,
you hover suspended and intent.
And then your wrist, a snake
about to strike
full of grace, no menace,
in the slowest, slow motion
I ever saw,
plucks sound from the drum
like a delicate note,
struck neat as a bite
clear and benign.
And at once you are intently
waiting for the drum to
ask for its next plucked resonance.
What accuracy and sweetness in your
intent drumming.
You taught me something today
that I still don't know
and I, like the drum, must wait till
it resonates in me with a
meaningful sound.

These two experiences furthered my conviction, fostered also by attending Buddhist courses of meditation and teachings, that the greatest human virtue is gratitude.

Knowing Catherine's fluency and gift as a writer, from eloquent and prolific letters she wrote me when she was studying in France, and knowing her commitment to Scottish writing and drama, I suggested to Allen Wright, arts editor of *The Scotsman* and friend of my BBC boss, Sinclair Aitkin, that Catherine would be a good drama reviewer for his Festival Fringe coverage. It was not surprising that her success was such that she soon became leader writer for the paper, nor that in 2000 she was chosen to be the Director of the Edinburgh International Book Festival.

During Catherine's nine years in that role, Charlotte Square Gardens became the book lovers' mecca of the world, welcoming folk of every age and clime through its gates for three enchanted weeks each August. Of her legacy, former poet laureate Carol Ann Duffy wrote:

Catherine has been a literary director of integrity and vision, compassion and inspiration, and writers and readers everywhere are forever in her debt.

32

In the Listening Place

WHEN I REFLECT on the story of my life, it is impossible not to conclude that there is 'a destiny that shapes our ends, rough hew them how we may.' As I closed one door, another opened and as I gave up the BBC, aged 52, I fell sweetly and naturally into storytelling, this fostered by two significant meetings and subsequently many more.

I had almost closed the BBC door when I fell in with the legendary Tinker-Traveller storyteller, Duncan Williamson, and Linda Bandelier, a singer-storyteller, who was to become my second wife. With my own credentials as an ex-teacher of English, lover of poetry and BBC radio producer of drama and folklore, I was apt and ready for a new world.

When I met Alan Heriot, the illustrator of Duncan Williamson's *Fireside Tales of the Traveller Children*, he exhorted me to meet Duncan, saying we would be fellow spirits. As I'd fallen in love with the story 'Mary and the Seal' and wished to broadcast it for my schools radio audience, this was a timely piece of advice.

In the late summer of 1987, in my dusty, dilapidated Ford Transit van, I drew up in the backyard of Lizziewells Farm Cottage, by Auchtermuchty, Fife. He stood, John Wayne-style, at the back door scrutinising my approach with his vivid blue eyes, lacking only a holster and a six shooter.

'Duncan Williamson,' he announced.

'David Campbell.'

'BBC?'

'Yes.'

'You want to broadcast my story "Mary and the Seal" on the radio?'

'Yes.'

'But you don't like it the way it is!'

'I love the story. I just don't think it will fit into my 20-minute radio programme, but I love it.'

Stepping forward, he seized me in one of the hugs I came to know so well.

'David Campbell, youse and me are going to be great friends. Come in.'

'Wait a minute.'

I returned to the van and fetched a bottle of Glenfiddich.

This ceilidh was the beginning of my friendship with Duncan Williamson, a friendship which predicated many colourful events, journeys and meetings.

In my two volumes, *A Traveller in Two Worlds*, I have chronicled this remarkable Scottish Tinker-Traveller's life story along with our complex friendship, a topsy-turvy journey and eccentric love affair. Duncan later was to symbolise our unlikely companionship by presenting me with a ring of appropriately unidentifiable metals. When, in one school, we were telling stories and playfully flyting and insulting one another in the classroom, a teacher remarked, 'You two are like an old married couple.'

This first meeting led to a dazzling apprenticeship. Invited to accompany Duncan on his school storytelling visits arranged by his multi-talented wife Linda, and acting as his chauffeur, I learned from the master storyteller. What I most learned, and have subsequently carried into my own practice and mentorship, was the total importance of 'Hello'– 'Make friends, David, and folk will listen to your stories.' At first I was bewildered by the time, with five or 95-year-olds, that Duncan would take having fun, teasing, playing, riddling, chatting to whatever audience. Then the magic of the story!

Soon after I began to accompany him, Duncan, ever happy to elevate my credentials, announced, 'David Campbell, manager of the BBC, is going to tell you a story.' Abruptly baptised thus, and gathering my wits, I told the story of 'Mary and the Seal', the story I had found in a collection of his stories compiled by his enterprising wife Linda. Afterwards, Duncan said, 'David Campbell, you told that better than me. It's your story now.' There were no half measures with Duncan.

From that time, we travelled Scotland visiting schools from the Borders to Orkney, the Hebrides to Aberdeen, in my Volkswagen van for transport and bed, I in the upper-level bed suffocating from Duncan's incessant smoking! These journeys, enlivened by sturdy flytings, endless song, and story, and jokes, cemented our friendship.

I had always kept an open door at Dundas Street with parties featuring everything from frivolous games to splendid musicians, singers, actors and writers. In the years I spent with Duncan, the emphasis moved from literary soirees to Traveller-style ceilidhs with Duncan as self-appointed *fer an tigh*, the constant being liberal alcoholic libations, Duncan's preference being what I considered poisonously powerful Carlsberg Special lagers.

His appetite for company was insatiable and I used to feed him people and leave them mesmerised by the ancient mariner in the front room while I took a snoozy respite in my bedroom.

In the changing ethos, my storytelling and singing were nourished by getting to know, board and entertain others of the Travelling people and their disciples. In Scotland we had the fortune to learn 'Eye to eye, mind to mind, and heart to heart' as Stanley Robertson would say, from Willie MacPhee, Sheila Stewart, Duncan himself, Essie Stewart, Betsy Whyte, and islanders like Laurence Tulloch and George Petersen from Shetland – a stellar galaxy. Andrew and Sheila Douglas, Barbara McDermott and her daughter Heather, Alison Millen, Paraig McNeill, Linda Bandelier, Ruth Kirkpatrick, Claire McNicol, James Spence and myself, were amongst those who were fortunate to know and learn from these great artist carriers of the legacy of rich folk tradition of story and song.

I had also got to know Hamish Henderson, arch Druid of the Scottish folk revival. I met him first of all of course in Sandy Bell's Bar where he held court in his demotic way of unostentatious wide-ranging scholarship, and deep knowledge of Scottish and world folklore. Chris Ferrard, a Turkophile friend of mine, told me that an Ethnology student from Turkey announced to him that he'd had a meeting with Hamish Henderson in the School of Scottish Studies. He thereupon proudly showed Chris his photo of the venue. 'That's not the School of Scottish Studies,' said Chris, 'That's Sandy Bell's Bar!'

My first conversation with Hamish was not about folk matters but about motorbikes; why I don't recall except that I had one, and that took Hamish to reminiscing about motorbike despatch riders in the Second World War. I was by that time an avid follower of the mushrooming folk scene in Edinburgh. In the upstairs room of the Waverley Bar, Dolina MacLennan sang Gaelic and Scots songs, and famously Sandy Bell's was a little mecca. Stuart MacGregor had started the Edinburgh University Folk Club. At the inaugural occasion Hamish, the guest of honour was asleep. He awoke to Stuart's strident introduction. Doubtlessly sedated by a bibulous session in Sandy Bell's, he climbed groggily to his feet, began to sing 'Tail Toddle' and was soon in full erudite flight.

So singing and storytelling became part of my repertoire and the content of CDs I produced with musicians and singers. Amongst those, on a visit with Duncan to Glasgow, we boarded with a compelling singer and dancer, Ruth Frame, and her husband. Ruth I later met whilst I was hosting a session of writers and storytellers in the Eden Court Theatre, Inverness. Seeing Ruth in the audience, I asked her to open the second half. Fragile from having parted in a fractious way from her husband, she refused, but encouraged by a friend of hers, I persuaded her to sing 'The Twa Corbies'. From a wavery beginning, this became an eerily, atmospheric rendition and the beginning of her recovery she said. This led to future musical and storytelling collaborations and a close loving and creative friendship.

The Williamsons were to become a second family for me. Duncan frequently stayed in my house, comfortably camped on a sofa bed and covered by a large Campbell plaid which he christened his 'Broonie blanket'. He was, he averred, part Broonie, the Broonies being little human-like creatures, neither good nor evil, whom you spurned at your peril and welcomed to receive their unsolicited help and gifts.

Both of Duncan's children by his second marriage, to Linda, stayed with me while they attended university. Betsy – flamboyant, confident, determined and focused – attracted a coterie of friends and followers. Without documenting in detail her meteoric rise to millionaire riches earned by her business acumen and success in owning a financial management and head-hunting business, it is enough to suggest she inherited the cream of her father and mother's genes. She also established her brother Tommy in a lucrative Edinburgh dog-walking business which suited his love of the outdoors and follow-where-the-wind-blows amiable and easy-going nature.

If, in a sense for better or worse, I was 'married' to Duncan, Linda Williamson is my wordwife. We are bonded not only through being wedded to Duncan, but through our huge mutual affection and admiration, our profound love of poetry and belief in the holistic eloquence and wisdom in story. Linda herself is a story large and multi-faceted. My encapsulation of her in Volume II of *A Traveller in Two Worlds* expresses my regard and admiration and enjoyment of her:

> Slender, demure, a hidden hurricane of energy, Cinderella, princess, hag of the ridges, spiritual nomad, kitchen demon, benign Svengali.

Now, like myself, she carries on Duncan's legacy. She with her story eloquence and song, emulative of Duncan's flair, adds her own laser beam scholarship and depth of Eastern mythic tales and poetic expression.

With Duncan, I took our Scottish heritage of tales all over the British Isles, to Canada, Israel, Holland, Iceland. I myself carried the lore and tradition to Germany, the States, New Zealand, Australia, Japan, and with Claire McNicol and Ruth Kirkpatrick, nourished the dormant Iceland lore into a lively resurrection of a great tradition.

Riches of our Scottish oral tradition inherited from the Travelling people are a priceless legacy and to this day permeate the ethos of storytellers in Scotland. Something of that lives in the Guid Crack Club monthly story gatherings. It was Duncan who suggested to me, 'David, why don't you start a storytelling club?' so that's how the Guid Crack Club came about in the late '80s.

For me, the power and importance of the told story are central tenets of my belief and practice. My long-time mentor and turbulent friend, Duncan Williamson, still speaks to me from the grave, as he does in the faithful continuing of his songs, stories and spirit by his widow, Linda.

His wisdom for me is encapsulated in these edicts:

'David, if you make friends with people, they will listen to your story.'

'Stories was wir education.'

'Here's a present for you, David. It will never break, it will never wear out, you will never lose it, you can give it away and still have it, every time you give it away it gets better, if you don't give it away it's no use. What is it? A story, the best thing my daddy gave to us long, long ago, in the tent.'

The wonderful Traveller Sheila Stewart was asked in a workshop she was conducting in London, 'What skills do you need to tell a story?' She answered, 'Skills? Shite!' By this she meant, in agreement with the practice and belief of Stanley and Duncan, you need to love the story or the song and give yourself totally to it, a mode the Travellers call the *Coinneach*. And you need to want to offer it as a gift. You serve the song and the people. My own absolute belief accords with this – you must love the song and love the people and love the service of giving it. Skills follow.

islands, mainland and the northern islands.

At John Bett's wedding, Doli, with her usual sense of drama, announced, 'David Campbell is invited to the floor.' And there she stood, and had instructed the band to play 'Moonlight in Vermont', and so we started off the dance to that melody.

Thereafter a hasty pursuit of passports and visa credentials, and we were off. The film showing on our flight to the States was *Crocodile Dundee*. Doli and I were to epitomise the naivety of its protagonist. We should have boarded a connecting flight to Boston where we were to be met, but the bumpkins failed to fathom the connection, and ended late in the evening in the airport hotel, sharing the one available bedroom.

Our morning flight to Boston was met by Linda Bandelier. As she drove us to Geneva Point Centre, we discovered our young driver was a singer, storyteller and Methodist minister, who was presently helping at the elder hostel for which we were bound.

'What kind of stories do you tell?' I asked.

'I composed a song and story telling the creation story with Eve, the person who dignified mankind with autonomy.'

We were later to hear this story. I was more than surprised as I had just given a talk to the society on the subject of Eve as a metaphor or story of the emergence of self-consciousness.

While Linda filled the car with gas, the coincidence of my Society speech with her story and song evoked my exclamation, 'Fuck me!'. 'There'll be none of that David,' said Doli, 'She's a minister of the Church' – surprisingly, Doli was to be proven wrong.

The campus was like a fairyland delight. Little wooden individual cabins, customised; a little smaller, and they could have been for woodland elves. These cosy cabins surrounded a sward of green and were themselves encircled by trees. A path led through the woods to beautiful Lake Winnipesaukee about which of course there is a love story, a native American legend about an intrepid Brave who swims under the ice to gain his sweetheart.

On the first night, Doli and I were welcomed by the director of the centre, his wife, and assorted worthy officials, volunteers and staff. We were dangerously plied with drink and, at one stage, it behoved Doli to reply to the director's address by recounting our inept Crocodile Dundee-style passage from Scotland, concluding vividly, 'and David Campbell and I in the airport hotel shared the same room, the same bed,' and then lilting every letter articulately in her Lewis island accent, 'but we have never fucked,' the last word seeming to have two syllables very clearly; causing glasses to be held in mid-air, and jaw-dropped reactions from the respectable guests. Doli's utter charm, however, made immediate converts and fans.

They say the way to a man's heart is through his stomach. Not mine.

Mine is through song. Linda had a rich and mellow voice. On the porch of the community building the next evening in the soft light of the red fading sun, she with guitar was singing to a charmed company of youthful elderly Americans. I, too, was entranced, not by the voice only, but by her unaffected attentiveness and warm connection to the audience.

The days sang sweetly by. My sessions on regional Scottish lore and writings, Doli's island childhood, were palpable hits, as were our evening ceilidhs of song, dance and story, with participation in these from our audience.

One such invitation to participate won my heart, and literally, lifelong love. In our audience was a slim, elegant, elderly lady, and I announced, 'There is someone here I've fallen in love with. It is you Zilfa.' Her name was Zilfa C Braids. 'And I would like you to give us all a wee story, a poem, or a song.' Zilfa rose, and said with ease and composure, 'My father told me, "Zilfa, stand up to be seen, speak out to be heard, and sit down to be appreciated."' With that she resumed her seat and confirmed her place in my heart. We subsequently exchanged letters, favourite poems, news until I had a letter from her daughter five years later informing me of her death. I still have her photo on the pin board in my office, amongst all the other deceased friends and loves, each whispering their own memories.

Edinburgh and the BBC were forgotten in the sweetly occupied and leisurely days on the campus with woodland walks, swims in Lake Winnipesaukee, interesting company, the vivid companionship of Doli, and a developing relationship with the Methodist minister, a development that was to take me by surprise.

Doli, Linda and I were off to the famous Loon Mountain Highland Scottish Games with tents and sleeping bags. My consciousness that Linda was a Christian minister made me keep my approaches modest and platonic. Not for the first time in my life, I was to learn that the real initiators are women, not deluded men thinking ourselves the leaders in the game.

We gleesome threesome shared a large tent. After the long day's Highland Games and few drinks, Doli fell asleep, and Linda, with what I see as her American women's candour and forthrightness, invited me to consummate our relationship under the sheets.

At the end of four weeks, Doli and I flew home. Linda was going to travel to Israel to explore Biblical sites, and I invited her to visit me at Christmas en route. One morning, an Airmail letter arrived in the flat from Linda, the last two words of which were, 'Marry me!' I cannot fathom my response. Tears filled my eyes, which I took to mean I should say, 'Yes.' That night, I phoned her in the States and, miscalculating the time difference, I had rung in the early hours of the morning. Not wishing to offer my response to an answering machine, I was about to hang up, when Linda's sleepy voice answered. 'I got your letter,' I said. Silence. 'I accept.' Longer silence. Later, she asked herself, 'What have I done?' But that understandable doubt soon dissolved, and we planned her short Christmas visit to Edinburgh.

My mother, still spry and vivid aged 87, was once more alarmed at my precipitous behaviour, and yet more so when Linda arrived and we discovered that with astonishing bureaucratic sympathy and delivering documents late night, at the 11th hour, we could marry the day before she was due to leave for Israel.

On top of Arthur's Seat at sunrise on Christmas Eve 1989, Ken Froud, the minister who had presented the Scottish religious service programme I had produced on radio for primary schools, married us. The drama had leaked into the *Evening News*, so a few curious observers appeared, along with pals who gathered in the chill dawn summit of Arthur's Seat. My faithful friend Alan Rowland acted as best man whose thoughts of the affair I couldn't fathom. Doli MacLennan, companion of our American jaunt and witness of the genesis of the affair; Norman Chalmers, musician, friend had carted a harmonium to the top, and provided a musical accompaniment, along with Robin Harper, later the first Green MSP and Green Party leader. Robin heralded the event with a flamboyant trumpet solo, and two lads who were my next-door neighbours in Dundas Street, McLeod pipers from the island of Skye, played a stirring introduction and conclusion to this ceremony.

My mother and sister joined a small wedding breakfast party at Prestonfield House Hotel. My mother demurred the invitation to the evening ceilidh in my flat in 33 Dundas Street. She had by now however quelled the worst of her doubts about the consequences of my impulses and rash actions.

Our honeymoon lasted one day, Christmas Day. The next, Linda flew to Israel. My sceptical friend Chris Ferrard, I was informed, gave the marriage one year. His prophesy was a bit out.

I continued to do some freelance writing and production for the BBC whilst Linda was in Israel taking up a post as general factotum in a Biblical resources company. This organisation was led by a tidy American red-haired dynamo called Jim Fleming, a bundle of energy, knowledge and erudition whom I was to find knew everything from the life cycle of the fig tree to the archaeology, geography, history of the Holy Land, a walking Biblical resource encyclopaedia. After six weeks, I joined Linda and her group on my first visit to Israel and the Palestinian territories. I later, as part of my freelance work for the BBC, made a bitter-sweet radio programme about this schizophrenic, scarred and turmoiled country in the Middle East.

34

A Torn Land

FIRST IMPRESSIONS: FIRST day in Israel at Tantur Biblical Resource Centre. The houses are recent, concrete, and although they are built on a hill, spiritless. The day cascaded rain. Under cement sky, mud dust, muddy rain, and intermittent eerie scraped lead light, heralding hail, lightning, a dark at noon sky, I was introduced to Israel. But warm and friendly at the Centre was the welcome by resource workers, Rhonda and Don, and my new wife, Linda. We transported Scottish ceilidh to Israel with wine and song from Linda, myself, and others in the company.

The electric Jim Fleming led us on my first excursion to the tomb of Lazarus where little Arab boys begged from an American pilgrim who offered them half a shekel. 'One shekel, one shekel,' barked the diminutive, imperious beggar, 'One shekel.' Another American woman offers the boys a green back American dollar. Hands like a pack of jackals bewildered the woman who stumbled backwards. Two boys, to elicit charity, bore tiny goat kids, depriving them of a hand to snatch with; a wizened old Arab seeing diminishing returns for these boys, kicked the backside of one of the goat bearers all the way down the street.

Below in the seclusion of Lazarus's tomb, a Franciscan sister, Marina, reads John's account of Jesus raising Lazarus from the dead to hushed pilgrims. Inevitably, opposite this tomb is a gift shop bearing every kind of tawdry religious emblem and symbol.

A Jewish extremist pamphlet nearby exhorts the State to expel all Arabs, and forbids sexual relationship between Jewish men and Arab women. In the Church of the Holy Sepulchre in Jerusalem, founded by Constantine, religions cluster like bees for the holy honey, each claiming a corner of the holy hive: Greek Orthodox, American, Roman Catholic, Coptic, Syrian, Orthodox and rejected to the roof, the Ethiopian Church.

There are great lessons to be learned in these holy places. I went out to an adjacent Arab shop to change the batteries in my BBC Uher tape recorder, and hurrying to catch up with the party of pilgrims from Denver, I found my money, passport and driving licence gone. The ingenuity that poverty elicits.

All the passengers in an Arab bus are expelled by a Jewish Army control by the roadside. An old man is told to remove his shoes, which the soldier throws away for the old fellow to fetch. I wonder what I would have done if the old man was my father. An Arab woman, chocolate brown dress, head covered, fishes in a Jewish rubbish bin looking for things that have been thrown out.

Linda and I walked through the Jaffa Gate, through the old city of Jerusalem, down the Via Dolorosa and past cross-bearing pilgrims of various nationalities and denominations singing, praying, while the Arab merchants advertise in English, German and French 'Four Stations of the Cross t-shirts, 99 per cent reduction!'

I met a retired Liverpudlian in a café here. She'd been here for eight years. She quips, 'Do you know how to make a small fortune in Israel? Bring a large one!' I grew pale when an American during the Arab strike says, 'Killing these people is not murder.'

At Easter, Frieda Morrison a co-producer in the BBC Education Department, joined us for a visit to the Church of the Holy Sepulchre. She and Linda were below in the main church, while I was on the roof during the Ethiopian church service. There I met Martine, French, and like me, compelled by the quiet intensity of the worshippers relegated to their small space on the roof. Somehow we fell into step, and bewilderingly caught by a surprising intensity of shared emotion, we kissed, descended and joined Linda and Frieda. Martine thereafter became part of our company for excursions, parties, and one other once more surprising kiss.

It was the occasion of her leaving to return to France. We met, not really by chance, in a shopping mall in modern Jerusalem and sat drinking coffee. Before she left, no words, nothing to declare the intention, we leaned together, our lips met and time ceased. Here is what I wrote there as I sat after she had gone:

Circles
For Martine

Across the dowdy mall
Inside the ramshackle modernity
Of a shopping centre,
I see the blades of a metre high
Model Swiss Army Knife open and close:
The scissors cut the air
And you unstrange stranger
Have gone, cut the air
Kissed me as if we spent the night
And gone into windy Jerusalem.
I look at the silly time on my watch

I sip my vodka and write on.
I know we spent a lifetime married this afternoon,
A lifetime the rascal clock
Tells me we never spent;
It is his hands not ours that lie.

When I left that dowdy mall with scraps of paper shifting in the wind, I returned to Tantur, the Biblical Resources Centre, and told Linda of the strangenesses of the afternoon. I was exhausted, as after a long and wakeful night.

That evening, we were intending to go to a Biblical Resources Centre party. I lay down to sleep and asked Linda to waken me for the party. I woke next morning. She said I slept so soundly she did not wish to disturb me.

Doubtless this land, with its pervasive past, and present intensities, passion and violences, heightens the senses.

Nowhere, perhaps, expresses the historic war-torn nature of this patch of the Near East as Megiddo, from which we appropriately have the word 'Armageddon'. Megiddo is the scene of Lord Byron's *The Destruction of Sennacherib*:

The Assyrian came down like a wolf on the fold
And his cohorts were gleaming in purple and gold
And the sheen of their spears were like stars on the sea
When the blue waves roll nightly on deep Galilee.

Perhaps fuelled and fevered by the pervasive simmering and eruption of violences around us, I devised a foolhardy story, more like a method acting workshop, that Linda and I would present for Christian pilgrims from Denver on a journey to that place of terror and destruction. To the pilgrims gathered around the stone ruins of Megiddo, I began our address:

Friends, pilgrims, we meet in this haunted place, this place that has given its name to the ultimate Apocalyptic disaster for all mankind, this Armageddon layered by successive graves of dead civilisations, this place of grief and blood, this microcosm of human savagery. Here we invite your imaginations to travel backwards, through the present, and forwards to empathise with the vulnerable briefly flickering lives of some of the people who once inhabited these ruins, those heaps of stones amongst which we stand. We invite you to enter the wonder house of imagination to see these ghosts rise from the stones, to whisper their stories. There are rumours of war.

We then invited the men and women to inhabit characters, some within the safety of the city walls, some outwith, farmers, herders. Those outwith were to plead for shelter in the overcrowded city.

Then my risky gamble. That morning, I'd given a young American a script I'd written of a radio news broadcast. He recorded the announcement of a state of High Military Alert which meant all passenger flights from Israel were cancelled, and that one provision had been made by the Israeli Government for one air freight mail flight from Tel Aviv that would leave that evening. Other flights to be suspended indefinitely. Linda and I then supplied writing material for the pilgrims to compose letters to their loved ones.

On this hillside, redolent of generations of war, the pilgrims wrote and what ominous sign should suddenly occur but that a flight of military jets thundered across the sky. When their letters were written in a strange calm intensity, and all was revealed, there was a consensus that this whole Megiddo enactment had been the most deeply moving experience of their Israel pilgrimage; big relief for me and Linda.

One of my enduring memories of Israel was a visit to Masada, a towering rock city fortress that was the last Jewish outpost against the Roman invasion, almost impregnable. Finally however, Roman ingenuity in hoisting a fire-bearing scaffolding and a change of wind direction forced the embattled Jews to make a suicide pact, in which only ten survived.

On the bus journey to Masada I sat beside an elderly American, Mary Ingenthorn, who recounted a remarkable dream she had had. This dream, I said to her, should be a story. 'You make it into a story, David.' I subsequently did, and it became a radio broadcast, for me, a talismanic tale that is published as the last story by the St Andrew Press in *Tales to Tell*. As she told me the tale, I was holding her hand as I am wont to do, and she said, 'David, no one has held my hand since I was married 50 years ago, except my husband, but I don't think he'll mind.'

I visited Mary and her husband when I was in the States and gave her a copy of the tape of the broadcast and a copy of the book.

Both Linda and I at this time witnessed both the trials endured and violence done to the Palestinian folk, and their great hospitality. We befriended a wonderful Old Town merchant, Ali Bedouin, who took us and a small retinue, including our friend Frieda Morrison, on a spectacular jaunt in which we waded thigh deep up a wadi, camped on a rock shelf under the stars, sang and exchanged life tales, and ate luxuriously a chicken stew, prepared by Ali on an open fire.

During my time in Israel, my BBC connections introduced me to Schmuel and Mimi Huppert. Schmuel, a child survivor of Auschwitz, was now Head of Cultural Programmes for Israeli radio. Schmuel and Mimi were liberal folk, lamenting the state of affairs in the country, but bearing the deep psychic scars of the Nazi horrors. Later, on a visit to Israel with storytellers Duncan Williamson and Michael Kerins, Schmuel conducted us through a harrowing museum graphically chronicling the deaths of children in Nazi extermination camps.

Horrific as this is, my own conclusion is that if individuals or peoples constantly keep alive the wounds of their past, they live in the mindset of victims and frequently re-enact the behaviour of their abusers, something I see sadly evidenced in the ethos of Israeli politicians and religious factions.

When I was producing *Kilbreck*, our research into abusive families demonstrated so often that the abused become the abusers even down generations. I saw at close quarters the way the Palestinians are humiliated, deprived of rights and dignity, in an ever increasingly apartheid society, encouraged by America. Of course, I met many worthy Israeli folk, but the ethos and actions of the Israeli state I find abhorrent and I never will buy goods from that country.

35

On a Quest

WHEN LINDA RETURNED to Scotland and 33 Dundas Street, life was busy and creative.

Linda and I made motorbike journeys throughout Scotland telling stories, as far north as Orkney. Returning from that journey, through icy winds, we arrived at Duncan and Linda Williamson's farm cottage, Lizziewells, in Fife with me, the driver, frozen. Duncan's solution was to ply us both with large whiskies. These put Linda more or less to sleep on the sofa, but rather less than more, for Duncan announced to me, 'David, aren't you and me so lucky to be married to two beautiful American Lindas!' From the couch came a not so somnolent minister's utterance, 'Yes, fucking lucky!' An expression that totally changed and loosened Duncan's opinion and appreciation of his Methodist pastor guest.

Bent on improving our range and skill in storytelling, Linda, Paraig McNeil, Alison Millen and I formed a close-knit foursome – Storyteller Scotland. In this pursuit, we had weekly meetings and workshops, as well as designing and presenting to the Scottish Arts Council, criteria by which storytellers would be eligible for the same Arts Council funding as writers. This was accepted and made a significant change in the recognition of the art of storytelling, and was a foundation of the later multi-directional expansion of storytelling in Scotland. This change was signally inspired by the creative and administrative brilliance of Donald Smith, then director of the Netherbow Arts Centre.

This preceded the conversion of the Netherbow physically and culturally into the Scottish Storytelling Centre. Donald suggested that I establish an administrative office in Dundas Street for which a secretary was appointed.

Apart from travelling the whole of Scotland with Duncan Williamson, and beyond to Europe, Iceland, Canada, America, and Israel, I, by mistake, won a yarn spinning contest which took me to Australia. By mistake it was because, being busy, I agreed to supply the Australian organisers with the names of storytellers who could take part. They phoned again to say they were still short, and persuaded me to take part in a preliminary heat, with the result that they invited me to be in the final. I had arranged to go to a Mark Morris Festival dance performance with Linda on the same date. Linda, with what I see as American 'Go for it!' attitude, suggested I tell them I could attend only during the half-hour interval in the dance performance. At half-time, kilt flying in the Edinburgh east wind, I rode on my motorbike from the Festival Theatre, through Festival traffic, and parked on the pavement

33
More New Worlds

I WAS 52, and my mother was, as she had been when I left teaching, dismayed that I had left another secure position, this time in the BBC. But, for me, it was the sure choice between stagnation and possibility. I had also the idea that I might write; an idea that had to bide its time.

Returning one afternoon to my flat at 33 Dundas Street, I was greeted by an enterprising German lecturer friend, Reiner Koelmel who later became a wealthy and generous film distributor.

'I hear you have given up working in the BBC. How would you like to go to America?'

A stunning suggestion. Most interesting.

'Why?'

'A friend of mine and his wife were going to work in an elder hostel, but his wife is ill. You would need to take a woman with you.'

Intriguing.

'Tell me more.'

The job was lecturing in a campus in New England on an aspect of Scottish culture to retired Americans for a month.

It appealed. Now, to find the appropriate partner for this enterprise. She serendipitously appeared. I'd arranged to take my fiery red-haired girlfriend Liz Horobin to Perthshire to climb, and had also arranged to stay with the spirited multi-talented Dolina MacLennan, who was then married to the writer John Herdman, and running a very well thought-of guest house in Blair Atholl.

Doli and I had been invited to the wedding in Edinburgh of the actor John Bett, whose off-stage life was fully as dramatic as his thespian career. So, my Blair Atholl visit had the double purpose of climbing and driving my long-time pal Dolina to the wedding.

Our conversation on the car journey to the festivities ran something like this:

'Doli, I've been invited to do a series of talks in New Hampshire on an aspect of Scottish life and culture, and I have to take a woman with me. Interested?'

'When would it be?'

'In about three weeks.'

'I'll tell John we're going when I get back.'

Bingo. Deal done. Doli would talk of growing up on the island of Lewis, and I on 'Voices of Scotland' as expressed by the Scottish writers on the in front of the Assembly Rooms in George Street. I entered in time to hear, 'And our last finalist contestant is David Campbell.'

I won, the prize, a mighty ball of wool, which I cradled between my arms on the bike on my return journey, and... a trip to Australia! Great was Linda's surprise, and that of my friend Pam who was sitting nearby, to see this giant arm-stretching ball of wool I was hugging.

This Australian trip was to take me back to World War II, memories of my childhood in Fraserburgh, and a request from my sister Anne. When I told her I was going to Australia:

'Maybe you could find Vick and Bill.'

'Where are they living?'

'I think in, or near, Melbourne.'

'When did you last hear from them?'

My sister showed me a thin letter dated 1945 from Bill Carstensen with the lines, 'I have been to see the ruins of Pompeii, but they are nothing to the ruins of Bill.'

Investigating ex-Servicemen Clubs in Australia drew a blank. Fortunately, I mentioned my imminent trip to an ex-colleague in the BBC who said that he had friends in Melbourne who would be delighted to host me.

My plane touched down in Melbourne at 7.00am. By 8.00am, I was breakfasting on the lawn with my hosts and telling them of my quest for the two airmen. My host's husband, John, disappeared for a few moments and returned to say, 'There's a V Tennant in the Melbourne Telephone Directory, not far from here.'

I phoned, and soon established this was indeed Vick, who had been stationed in Cairnbulg airport training near Fraserburgh and had been a frequent visitor to our house. My mother kept open door for the young trainee airmen. And, yes, he remembered my sister. 'Come over.'

An hour later, my host drove me to the tidy house and tidy wife of Vick Tennant. He was full of memories, and greetings, which I tape-recorded for my sister. His wife's brow thundered when I mentioned his fellow crew member friend, Bill.

'A bad lot.'

Only when she left the room did I hear more. They had survived a crash. Bill had married and had eight children; Vick none. One of Bill's sons was in Melbourne. Bill's whereabouts he didn't know. He showed me a photo of their plane and crew.

After I left their orderly house, manicured lawn, clipped bushes and Vick's woodworking hut, I phoned Bill's youngest son, Phil.

'Lucky you phoned me. None of the rest of the family talk to Bill.'

Next day I was welcomed into the house of Phil, his wife, Norma and a baby son.

Bill had been an unpredictable, irascible, and violent father and husband. The youngest son had escaped the worst of his father's excesses.

Later in my Australian journey, I met Bill's sister. One sentence expressed what she saw had happened to her brother: 'Bill left like a young angel and returned like a devil.'

Bill's son had given me a postal address for Bill 'up country'. I sent a letter to this address containing my itinerary. A big surprise then when one morning the hotel receptionist phoned me to say there was a call for David Campbell. It was Bill.

'Could we meet?'

Curt. 'Any idea how big this country is?'

'Some notion.'

'I'm going to a doctor's appointment in Murray Bridge.'

I could get on a bus, so we arranged to meet.

My early morning bus from Canberra arrived about midday in Murray Bridge, a dusty one street, one hotel-pub town, the street empty but for a dog or two, and Aboriginal children idly playing. I saw a few Aboriginal men at the bar and, leaning on a sill looking out the window, a grizzled, lean white man. I entered, surmising the man to be Bill.

'Are you Bill Carstensen?'

'Yup.'

'David Campbell. Would you like a drink?'

'I got a drink.'

Strangely, at once I liked this, to say the least, economic character.

Fights, a nomadic life, and trouble was his narrative, shot through with a very combative humour. He'd called his mongrel bitch dog Helena after the small town mayor's wife. He'd given his name at a court case as Yal Cunt, to hear it called out in his trial.

We had an amiable and lively afternoon in which he asked fondly after my sister who had a big liking for Bill, but he refused to give a recorded greeting.

Task completed, I returned to Canberra and to the Comedy Festival that was supposed to be the peak of my prize trip. The stand-ups were Scottish, English, Irish, Welsh, Australian.

I was ready to deny my nationality when I heard the ugly, misogynistic, invasive performance of the two Scottish comedians, and took my chance to escape.

My final destination on the far west was Perth where I was invited to stay with Keith and Frauke for whom I had been a matchmaker 30 years before. Here, too, I was welcomed by Aboriginal storytellers with great tales and bitter ones of the devastation of their peoples, the separation of parents from their children to 'civilise' them, the desecration of the land and culture.

On my return to Scotland, I was phoned by a girlfriend from the past,

Catriona Murray. On hearing her voice, back came a flood of memories, flighty heydays of the Abbotsford. Amongst the habitués was Sharon Levinson, a theatre agent whose actors like Robbie Coltrane I used in my radio broadcast. I became a big confidante for Sharon, vexed by the fickleness of her clients. Catriona was Sharon's flatmate. These two were each radiantly attractive and spirited, a contrast in beauties; Sharon a sheen of black lustrous hair, Catriona's a cascade of golden red, an immediate enticement for the Campbell, recalling Rita Hayworth of adolescent adoration.

These had been lightsome times when I was amongst Catriona's boyfriends as she amongst my girlfriends, but our meeting planted a Jack-and-the-Beanstalk seed.

Now I learned she had been working, dancing, travelling in the States, and had returned to Edinburgh to nurse at Edinburgh Royal Infirmary. The number on her driving licence happened to be the same as my unchanged phone number by which she had phoned and found me.

This meeting up again had many consequences. One was that she asked her father, former production director of Glenfiddich Malt Whisky – my favourite tipple – if he could get the company to sponsor myself, Linda, Paraig and Ali on a storytelling trip to South Africa. Retired now, he had been a successful and popular worldwide ambassador for the company, and to our delight arranged an all-expenses paid itinerary in South Africa.

36

A Land in Transition

PARAIG, ALI, MYSELF and Linda were a motley group to step off the jumbo jet in Johannesburg, Paraig in the full great kilt, me in the philabeg, or short kilt, Ali in striking blue dress, and Linda in tracksuit.

Our first taste of British settler Africa was the lavish welcome when we reached the first leg of our storytelling journey in Grahamstown. There, my Aunt Connie and her Afrikaner husband Bill greeted us with a meal cooked by their black maid, Doreen.

We had ten days of morning, afternoon and evening storytelling sessions thereafter in Grahamstown Arts Festival – schools, Caledonian societies and theatre.

Our colourful Scottish programme of tales and songs met with ubiquitous enthusiasm.

Bill insisted on driving us to these venues as he considered buses, which we favoured, would be unsuitable because they would be crowded with 'non-reflectors'. Such attitudes were a rude introduction to aspects of the colonial culture and in consideration of my aunt's hospitality meant that we had cause at times to bite our tongues.

Bill generously drove us to our onward journey, Port Elizabeth, from where we took a surprisingly comfortable ten-hour bus journey to approach Cape Town down a mountain pass from which we saw Table Mountain jump abruptly 3,000 feet into the sky.

I had arrived at collapsing point with a fever, but recovered sufficiently to host the first half of our evening concert in the Caledonian Club. After a week of storytelling we explored Table Mountain, the beautiful Botanic Garden, and the luxurious seafront restaurants. Of the extensive, crowded shanty townships outside Cape Town, we saw nothing, only learned of the unsurprising hazards involved in passing through, even in a taxi.

Mandela had been freed from prison in 1990, two years before our visit, but in this time of transition, our experience was that the white European colonialism still held its insular authority, apartheid and attitudes prevailing as expressed in my aunt's husband, Bill. The attitudes of superiority in some of the white settlers was to us anathema. In two years, when Mandela became president, things were to change.

Next, we flew to Durban where our visit was pure fun and holiday, an idler's paradise. Scottish roots were everywhere and we were lavishly welcomed by a Scottish family, given a luxury flat overlooking the Indian Ocean, and the seafront Golden Mile where Zulu women traders sold their wares of cloth and carvings at such low prices as to make haggling for us out of the question. To their music I could not resist dancing which evoked their applause and flashing white-toothed laughter.

The glorious warm ocean was to hold a nightmarish experience for me. One morning, at 5.30am, we took a deep-sea fishing trip. Our introduction in the cool light of dawn was ominous: the upbeat black skipper welcoming us on board with, 'All those gonna be sick on this side, all the fishers on that side.' We slid out of a flat calm harbour and at once the craft began to rock and roll, and immediately I knew that whatever was left of our Greek feast of the night before was ordained for the fishes.

For perhaps the most wretched and retching ten hours of my life, an endless meditation of nauseous suffering, the hands on the clock stopped. Linda shared my fate and ashore we both wobbled off to bed. Ali and Paraig had caught enough fish to provide next day's breakfast by which time we had sufficiently revived to enjoy the meal.

Of our trip now, Johannesburg, Sun City and Kruger Park remained. Courtesy of our sponsors, we had entered Sun City, a gambling city of perpetual night, and were given bedrooms, the main feature of which was a high-security safe in which to keep gambling money.

Everything was aglitter, from chandeliers to the sparkling free champagne handed out freely by Africans incongruous in Scottish kilts and offering also crystal tumblers of Glenfiddich whisky. From these excesses we demurred, for we were immediately, after a lavish meal at which we pecked, to offer a performance. This turned out to be considerably daunting. We were placed on a small, elevated stage behind curtains, essentially a theatre setting, except that when these curtains were magically opened by the kilted stage crew we saw that our audience was, apart from half a dozen folk drinking, engrossed in gambling machines.

Before attempting to sing our opening song, 'Come By the Hills', both me and the would-be audience were jerked to attention by Ali's powerful soprano pitch in good Glaswegian Scots, 'Hey, youse! Quiet! Listen, we're gaun tae sing!'

Upon this cue, we burst into song, and in this place of endless night, glaringly lit in every corner, the audience were clearly as bemused as we were.

A yet worse suggestion by the organisers was that we could tell our stories at the roulette tables. We could only imagine the reception of the gamblers, distracted by some weird interloper saying, 'How would you like to hear a wee Scottish story?' We declined the invitation, and the next suggestion was that we try the bank area where the customers were exchanging cash for chips. This was hardly a success, and before we returned to our security locked bedrooms we took generous drams of Glenfiddich.

Johannesburg and Kruger National Park were to offer yet more of the astonishments of Africa. The generous hospitality of our hosts Liz and Nicholas Ellenberg, who was the director of Theatre of Africa, was a luxury, which contrasted disturbingly with what was outside the guard dog and gated entrance of their house. Outside was threat and danger, unsurprisingly heated by the abyss between the haves and the have-nots. Accordingly, we were in a comfortable prison made uneasy by the knowledge of two adjacent worlds.

Kruger National Park, our final destination, was an exhilaration and wonderland, a filtered glimpse of Eden and evoked in me reflections as to where I was at this time of my life. At Kruger, I was addicted to each new astonishing sighting of elegant creatures, injecting a flush of excitement as the sun climbed round the whole sky in a twinkling while we gazed and marvelled full of affection for such as the bush comedian, the gremlin-like warthog with his busy, casual ways, and skinny tail vertically jaunty, the lanky sedate giraffe with her graceful gallop, and the awesome, prowling, intent leopard. Humbled by these marvels of creation, I was reminded of Robert Burns's outrage in his beautiful love lyric 'Now Westlin Winds' of 'tyrannic man's dominion'. It was, however, the warthog, that prompted a poem of sorts that clarified for me my sense of the confines I felt in my marriage to Linda. As recorded in my journal, it was the attrition of many tiny criticisms of my behaviour that led to this feeling:

Shrivels my soul to drier dust than the soil of drought-thirsty Africa, reminds me of the sacredness of being myself.

The Warthog

Even in drought and thirsty
plains of Africa
the beautiful creatures
still keep their spacious eyes,
the elegance of their freedom.

The ugly comical warthog
rooting at desiccated tussocks
tells me, by the absurd assertion
of his skinny vertical upright
and lovely tail:
'Say what you like,
think what you will,
but I am unambiguously me!'

I remember my mother telling me that as a toddler crawling up the stairs in front of her she had said, 'Hurry up, hurry up, David,' to which I, with a similar spirit to her own, replied, 'I do as my likes,' and I never liked being told what to do or how to behave. So, the warthog, like the tortoise explorer, was a hero in his individuality. As my relationship with Catriona deepened, it was freeing to find we each prized spaciousness in our closeness, acknowledging the beauty and wisdom in the words of the prophet Kahlil Gibran, 'Let there be spaces in your togetherness, the pillars of the temple stand apart.' A corollary for me is Samuel Beckett's cautionary: 'Habit is the great deadener.'

37

In the Footsteps of Robert Service

IT WAS ON the recommendation of my friend and ex-pupil from my English teaching days at the Royal High School, Tom Pow, that I arrived at a storytelling festival in the Yukon. Tom, now a celebrated poet, had been performing in Whitehorse at an arts festival, where he met its vivacious and dynamic director, Michele Emslie.

Charismatic, she forgot nevertheless, that she was to greet me in Whitehorse, and was far to the north in Dawson City where she was socialising with what, I was soon to learn, was her customary live-in-the-moment joie de vivre, and extravagance. And so it was her obliging friend, Laura Lee, who met me and took me to the hospitality of Ken's house, where my planned stay during the festival was to be unexpectedly curtailed. Reminded and informed of my arrival, Michele made a non-stop, helter-skelter, high-speed car journey from Dawson to arrive late in the evening at Ken's house. It was not too late however for the gypsy festival director, a burst of wood-fire flame, to clatter through the door, and before any greeting, hit my breast with a glowing hug, bone to bone, a solid tremor. Nor was it too late for a party while the Yukon midsummer dark never came, and we three drank whisky, smoked cannabis, excessively into the wee small hours. When Michele was about to drive home, 'No!' said Ken, 'Not now, you're not!' and offered her a lumpy sofa. Whereupon I, tired and sedated, as I left for my comfortable bedroom, said, 'You're welcome to share my bed.'

I was reading myself to sleep when the door peeped open, and we luxuriated in the comfort of companionable cuddles. Remembering our clattering meeting, I wrote this poem:

Poem for Meeting

I remember in the Hebrides,
When Tiree blew cold springtime,
I sat before the island children,
Six proud years old with faces
Washed by scouring winds,
        intent and listening
While my story told itself within
        their vivid eyes;
My tale complete, I sat and sighed.
A little fair-haired girl

Observed that sigh and said,
'I can give you something to help,'
and flew to me
Thumped bone to bone against my chest,
Six years wrapped into a total hug.
Instantly, I was transfused
with love and life,
And gratitude for such innocence.

Now, here in the Yukon,
Far from blowy Tiree,
The story tells itself again.
You, bone to bone, come
Clattering against my breast,
Fuse with the fair-haired island girl
And I am burned alive with memory
And this new and fiery you.

Next morning, apparently daisy-fresh, startlingly efficient, she had arranged for me a busy schedule of interviews with the local press and radio.
After this, a tour of Whitehorse, meetings with staff and other storytellers,
looking at venues. She kidnapped an unresisting me from Ken's house; in
her battered car, drove me over dusty roads, through a forest track to her
lakeside log cabin. Here I remained for the course of the festival, at which I
was to meet the brilliant Jewish-American storyteller, Laura Sims, who was
to facilitate an unexpected turn in my storytelling career.

In the Whitehorse Festival, I told and sang my hour-long version of the
Great Orkney love story of the 'Selkie of Suleskerry'. I was gratified at its
reception, when one of the audience told me that after the performance she
had gone down to the riverside to weep.

Meantime, I was captivated by Michele. Everything about her, from her
Slavic, heart-shaped face, high cheekbones, flare of temperament, suggestions
of unbridled sensuality. And yet, that face could look hauntingly ancient,
beautiful, wistful. I soon got to love her loping walk, sexual mischievous-
ness, sharpness in flyting and good-heartedness. Vivid, delighting in story,
song, adventure, the unexpected, and living contagiously in the moment, I
christened her, 'The Immediacy Monger'. This quality required mountains
of patience from her friends, 'I'm on my way!' being small indication of
when she would clatter in.

This spontaneity took us many places. By chance, one evening, we met her
friend, Moira, who led us to a strange cathedral of concrete, marvellously
graffiti-ed with the ornate hieroglyphics of some local artists. We followed her

through miracles of light, yellow fires in the clouds, an irradiating rainbow, past huge blue and orange metal drums in a yard, illumined by the late brightness of the endless Yukon sky, splashing a red-orange glow on our faces, faces already radiant with the adventure, and a new-found dizzy companionship. We three created a cathedral ceilidh in the echoey, lavish concrete acoustics, water dripping, rain galloping on the roof. Moira sang a feeling version of Tam Lin, and Michele and I sang the Highland Fairy Lullaby, and some of Michele's favourite singer-songwriter, Sandy Denny, in the sweet coincidental communion of the night, continuing in this baptism of rain, rain, rain as we walked out into the glittering evening where no dark falls, and the sun had returned again.

Another spontaneous manifestation of the flexible storytelling festival's arrangements was a jaunt in a borrowed battered thunderbird car to legendary gold-rush town, Dawson City. With only three hours sleep under our lids, Michele raced the thunderbird the 485km road in her record time of five hours; a hairy, exhilarating drive for me.

We go back in time, and drive down a dirt track road with a boardwalk, and the architecture of gold-rush times, past wood buildings bearing legendary names – Diamond Tooth Gerties, Klondike Kate. On the scarred mountains, and stone rubble hills, we see dredged up at the roadside evidence of the impetuous hunger for quick fortune. These were to inspire the Scottish bank clerk turned rhymester, Robert Service, to make a fortune from the characters and events from that heady past.

I have had from childhood an ability to memorise or recite poetry. In my school teaching days my rendition of Service's famous verse ballads 'The Cremation of Sam McGee' and 'The Shooting of Dan McGrew' could cast their long-proven spell on any class and keep a drowsy afternoon wide awake. My love of Service, deepened by visiting his haunts, found an enthusiastic reception to a show devised and performed by myself, Barbara McLean and Wendy Weatherby at the Scottish Storytelling Centre.

In Dawson, Michele and I found lodgings in a fine rickety wood house. Here, as we lay quietly, she told me of her great sadness. With the inheritance of her illegitimate birth, the resulting Catholic guilt and shame, and her 'dad's' beatings, I find her sparkling, generous, adventurous spirit all the more amazing.

After midnight, we drove to the top of the dome, a hill above the town, where I was stunned with wonder to gaze down on where the rivers, Yukon and Klondike, joined in two glittering, golden seams, lit by the ever-present sun. It was like the mother lode come to the surface.

In Dawson that evening, we met up with Michele's ex-lover, Michael, who had now fallen in love with Michelle, spelled with two 'L's. I liked Michael at once, and we agreed we had our love for Michele as a common bond. It reminded me of the line from Tennyson's poem 'Ulysses' – 'We are part of all that we have met.' This understanding, so simple sounding, is yet in relationships so hard to live. And so it was disappointing, but not surprising, that when Michael phoned Michelle to ask her to meet us, she said that would be too difficult.

However, having discovered that next day was Michelle's birthday, Michele and I wrote a brief birthday card and delivered it to Diamond Tooth Gertie's pub where Michael was playing piano for the guests. At night, when Michele and I had returned to her lakeside cabin in Whitehorse, I was teaching her ballroom dancing when the phone rang. Michael, and Michelle, who with wistful sweetness said, 'Why did I not join you? Now I would love to meet you both.' Sometimes, perhaps, amor vincit omnia.

My return to Scotland appropriately book-ended the Yukon visit with a phone call from Tom Pow to ask me to join him on his visit to Norman MacCaig. To Tom, I am grateful for the many wonders of the Yukon.

38

An Independent People

The Feasting Halls of Valhalla

I have been in the feasting halls
of Valhalla
Aglow in caves of ice where the
cold earth boils
and bubbles
I have been the guest of ancient men
And women straight as birch trees
Folk who live in times long gone
and yet to come
There I have heard the speech of rocks
the prattling grass of spring
Dainty pebbles gossip on the shore
I have seen and heard the laughter of the earth
A terror of delight
And when night crawled across the sky
I saw hieroglyphs of wonder writ
So when I slept
the mightiest miracles
that dreams could make
Seemed wispy shades and shadows
and I longed to wake
and live once more
the wonder of that place.

(Written 27 May 2000, leaving Iceland on flight KLM 2083)

TWO ELVES WERE a fitting prelude to my love of the land and people of Iceland.

October 1999, I happened into the corner booze shop for a bottle of malt whisky, elixir for storytellers and friends during the Edinburgh International Storytelling Festival. There were two fiddle-bearing young elves in the shop – Karen and Kate, clad in green, wearing pointy turned-up shoes: elves for sure! Were they going to the Storytelling Festival? They had not heard of it. 'Come up to my house, and meet a story wizard,' I said.

Duncan was as intoxicated to have this elvish audience as they to drink the magic potion of his tales. A few stories, a few fiddle tunes, an afternoon ceilidh.

Karen was my introduction to these feasting halls of Valhalla – Iceland. As a tour guide for a party of Icelandic teachers, she suggested to them an evening with David Campbell, an old Scottish storyteller. Out of deference to their young guide, they agreed, determining to make this visit to the old fogey as brief as possible before returning to the congeniality of, for them, the inexpensive Edinburgh pubs.

When they arrived to find their kilted and affable host had already two bottles of fine malt whisky on the table, their spirits rose.

Following the Celtic tradition of first story or song from the host, I sang my favourite ceilidh starter song, Colum Sands' 'Rest for a while, the night is young'. Little did I realise how young! Teaching them Traveller style, eye to eye, mind to mind, heart to heart with gestures for them to follow made a good participative beginning.

Liberated by a few drams, their Icelandic songs began to pour out. One teacher, Helga Lilja Agustsdottir, told a chilling tale of the Deacon of Myrka River, and suddenly it was ten minutes to ten, ten minutes to closing time! I suggested another visit to the corner shop for a bottle. Another bottle wouldn't do; they wanted two, and returned from the mission with three, which ensured the completion of the ceilidh mantra, 'stories and songs from the guests until dawn'. We were consanguineous spirits!

Johanna, athletic and statuesque, later to be christened 'the Viking princess' by Duncan, stated that it was her intention, whilst in Scotland, to discover what was worn under the kilt. I informed her, 'Nothing is worn under the kilt. Everything is in perfect working order. A viewing can only be arranged by private appointment.'

That evening began my love of Iceland, which was to become a rich relationship with the land and its people. Helga Lilja's invitation to Iceland resulted in exciting storytelling initiatives, exchanges and several warm friendships.

I was met at Reykjavik airport, not as I expected by the 'Viking princess', but by her new partner, Oli Schram. He was the owner of the Highlander Tour Company and is a powerful, eloquent, knowledgeable guide to the wonders of his beloved Iceland.

Oli introduced me to one of these wonders of Iceland, taking me to an art gallery craft shop to meet Helga Lilja Bjornsdottir, tall, lean, warm, welcoming and multi-talented. She was to become a firm and precious friend. Like the many Icelanders I met, she was artistic, athletic – a swimmer, a skier, mountain trekker – a tour guide, deeply knowledgeable about all aspects of her island, from the geology, the history, the caves, the archaeology, to volcanoes, topography, literature; she was a gracious and modest woman.

She had an erudite mother, two talented daughters and a son Oli, reputed to be one of the best handball players in the world who led his country's team of this tiny population to the Olympic Handball Final. Another Icelander was crowned the strongest man in the world.

The land, the resilience, hardy nature of the people inherited from their Viking-Irish ancestry is captivatingly captured in the novel *Independent People* by Iceland's Nobel Literature Prize-winning author Halldór Laxness. It is one of my favourite novels, deepening my love and respect for the land and its people.

Helga Lilja Agustsdottir arranged for me a storytelling tour round the east coast and as far north to her hometown of Akureyri, 12 miles from the Arctic Circle. I was welcomed there by the dazzling spectacle of a celestial sky show, the Northern Lights, and Helga Lilja's tenderest lamb that I'd ever tasted, from a breed native to the island. Nothing was usual. My taxi was a hotel-sized pantechnicon wagon, into which I had to climb to the passenger seat next to a young Viking who seemed to think that he was driving a racing car! At breakneck speed, we would skim over bridges that seemed too narrow, across precipitous river gorges. This more than exhilarating round trip concluded with my performance in a theatre in Reykjavik.

Before I left, I was invited by a fine entrepreneurial gent, Rognvaldur Gudmundsson, to return to Iceland to give storytelling workshops.

One of life's greatest pleasures is to introduce friends to friends and thereby hatch new friendships; no better way than to share stories for truly 'by their stories shall you know them'. This adapted adage of mine is as true for a person as for a culture. So, I needed no more than Rognvaldur's prompting to invite one of my favourite storytellers, close friend and companion workshop leader, the gifted singer-storyteller Claire Mulholland to accompany my next visit to Iceland.

We were met at the airport by the elegant Helga Lilja Bjornsdottir, who welcomed us to her home, a fine meal and after modest libations a comfortable night's sleep. The next day, she discerningly introduced us to a spry scholar-priest, man of a joyous God, Geir Waate, an Icelandic Hamish Henderson. Like Hamish, he carried his scholarship and knowledge lightly, and left us so astonished and humbled that when we left this encyclopaedic man of Iceland, Claire exclaimed, 'What have we got to tell these people?' But we discovered to our surprise that in this saga land of heroines and heroes, the storytelling tradition had become dormant, but like sleeping geysers and volcanoes, was not far below the surface waiting to erupt. So when our storytelling participants gathered, it was little effort to reignite the fires, and release the geysers. For in the first workshop were folk who were to become notable storytellers. Amongst these, in the workshop we held at Reykholt in west Iceland in 2000, were Sigurborg Kr Hannesdottir,

Ingi Hans Jonsson and Thora Grimsdottir, all of whom subsequently became well-known and well-liked storytellers. Sigurborg was a warm and efficient organiser of events but when I told her to participate in the workshop, 'I was terrified but ended up loving it,' she said. Our workshops, she said, gave a few pioneers the courage to pursue their love of stories.

I, unwittingly, became the catalyst of a successful marriage. Ingi Hans, a divorcee, was a stocky, humorous and eager student. I didn't know of his partiality for Sigurborg, whom I christened, because of her smooth complexion and soft hands, 'Silky Skin', and one day, in extravagant and fun mode, I said to Ingi Hans, 'Oh, I love Sigurborg, Silky Skin.' This so alarmed him that he forthwith proposed to her.

When Claire and her husband Fergus had a baby, I had to find a new story mate. But I was not short of another wonder – my good friend, sister story-teller and workshop leader, the feisty North-East quine, Ruth Kirkpatrick.

Ruth and I were equally creative workshop leaders and leading by example told stories we loved enhanced by Ruth's fine ballad singing, my spicy jokes and a general sense of camaraderie. Our visit was enriched by a trip with Johanna's tour guiding husband, into the interior highlands, where we unleashed a party of reticent Belgian storytellers into an all-night ceilidh where they became revellers in the timbered Viking longhouse. Their lavish contribution of assorted beer and spirits soon popped open an unexpected fizz of robust song and merriment.

My technicolour memory is that we camped by a hot, bubbling, crystal-clear river, pyramid hills on three sides, one charcoal black, one iridescent green of moss, and a bright rusted red. Such a dramatic island, such quiet yet dramatic people. What greater gift for friends, than to introduce them to this island of lunar landscapes, mountains, volcanoes and glaciers, wonder skies, and a hospitable, independent, proud people?

Later, in 2007, Ruth and I were featured storytellers and workshop leaders in a Nordic storytelling seminar in Reykir, in the north-west of Iceland. There, we held a frolic and fun storytelling session in an outdoor thermally heated swimming pool.

In the same vein of introducing people whom I love to one another, I took to Iceland the storm-force gift of master storyteller, Duncan Williamson. Along with his storytelling, Duncan's great gift was his contagious warmth and living his own adage, 'a stranger is just a friend you haven't yet met'.

So, wherever we travelled to visit Helga Lilja Agustsdottir in Akureyri in the north, Johanna, the Viking princess and Helga Lilja Bjornsdottir in Reykjavik, Duncan was a hit. For me, as usual, he was a delight and a vexation. A delight as company, and a vexation trying to ensure that his pre-performance alcohol intake did not extend his stories to full-length sagas. Everyone, of course, loved him and his stories willy-nilly.

Part of the European project Storytelling Renaissance was to fund an Icelandic storyteller's visit to Scotland. And who should be chosen but the mischievous troll, Ingi Hans Jonsson? And so, discerning that he would be a twin spirit, I set him on the path to meet Duncan Williamson, in his Fife fastness.

Ingi Hans, who had never been on a train before, was met at the station at Cupar by Duncan, who asked, 'Are you Mr Jonsson?', to which Ingi replied, 'Yes.' Duncan's next question being: 'Did you bring some whisky?'

'David Campbell warned me not to bring any whisky.'

Duncan: 'You should never listen to that bastard.'

Here followed a four-day spree of stories, smoking and whisky. Ingi Hans said that in all his lifetime, this was one of the toughest experiences he had survived but 'to get to know Duncan was invaluable; I have learned much from David Campbell, but Duncan was my master.'

The connections and friendships made in Iceland made a lasting legacy, a sentiment shared by Sigurborg:

The connection with Scotland was very, very important for us – and still is. Whether it has been in workshops or storytelling evenings here in Iceland or in unforgettable ceilidhs in David Campbell's living room at Dundas Street. If I try to find one word that symbolizes the approach that we have learned from Scottish storytellers, it is generosity, a spirit we found boundlessly in David Campbell, Duncan Williamson, Claire Mulholland, Ruth Kirkpatrick and Donald Smith.

I conclude this section with two glittering memories.

Courtesy of Johanna and Oli Schram, my partner Catriona and I rode as if on wings on a snowmobile over the icy snow of Vatnajökull glacier, and yet in this exhilaration there is a sadness for mankind's self-inflicted wound of global warming is rapidly melting the glacier away.

If the glacier provided the peak of physical excitement, Sigurborg and Ingi Hans made a home-from-home welcome for Catriona and me by hosting a joyful ceilidh in their house inviting me to tell a couple of tales to a small gathering of Icelandic storytellers from the recently established Storytelling Association in their area. The company was warmed in the tradition of the Celtic rune:

Yestreen a stranger was at my door
I put food in the eating place, drink in the drinking place,
Story, music and song in the listening place.
And the stranger, he blessed myself, my dear ones,
My cattle and my house

     For often, often, often, sings the lark in her song,
       Goes the Lord of all in the stranger's guise.

For me a farewell blessing for our Iceland visit was a medieval Icelandic hymn performed by two sisters, Dagbjort and Silja, daughters of Runar, who by the ethereal spirituality of their singing lifted my heart as never before.

39

A Lucky Break

THIS WAS ANOTHER time of changes. Linda and I found our priorities and preferences were essentially different: her tiptoeing into extra-marital relationships left her uneasy, and tolerating mine, equally so. This, and our open house to transient visitors which she at first welcomed, palled. So, we mutually and amicably agreed to part. Our storytelling work with Paraig and Alison, continued with the Storyteller Scotland office still operating from Dundas Street. Linda and I, with invited storytellers and musicians, performed the ever-popular Supper with Burns, an annual dramatised life of Burns with the traditional accompanying meal.

However, the dual role of storyteller and co-ordinator that I now occupied became increasingly uneasy and schizophrenic. My unease became intolerable when Paraig, in a ranting acrimonious letter, accused me of misusing my position.

The protagonist in the traditional fairy tale is rescued at the nadir of his fortunes by a fairy godmother or other such saviour. My fairy godmother at this low point was Pascale Konyn, a visiting storyteller from Newcastle. In the course of our conversation when I was outlining my disquiet, she said, 'David, you should go to the storytelling course at Emerson College.' But this 12-week residential course costing £2,000 was beyond my finances at the time.

However, with the waving of a wand, I was invited to New York to stay with Laura Sims in her house on Broadway. Laura was a brilliant storyteller I'd first met when I was telling stories at a Festival in Whitehorse in the Yukon.

One evening she announced we were to tell stories to representatives of the advertising agency McCann Erikson. Driven upstate in a limousine and boarded in a suite each in the hotel we were to tell our tales after dinner. After pre-prandial drinks, of which I drank sparingly, we had a lengthy sumptuous dinner interlarded with speeches, and it was late when their group leader announced we would proceed to the storytelling suite.

To my astonishment Laura and I told one brief tale apiece when the leader thanked us and announced it was time to retire. Rather dazed at this huge extravagance for one small story, I was dumbfounded when Laura told me, 'You won't be disappointed with the fee.' $2,500 dollars each. Almost the exact fee for the Emerson College course.

My storytelling was given a vitalising and deepening dimension by my enrolling, in 1995, in the developing Storytelling School at Emerson College in Sussex, led by the visionary and skilled storyteller, Ashley Ramsden. This 12-week residential course in beautiful grounds in a college inspired by the philosophy and educational precepts of Rudolf Steiner was an in-depth immersion moving from world myths to fairy tales and jokes, the whole gamut of the narrative genre. Alongside were the associated skills, the crafts and related graphic and musical arts. These were led by dedicated and experienced mentors for international students of various ages, myself aged 60, being the oldest.

Whilst at Emerson, I made several rich meetings. Music was central to the Steiner philosophy that Emerson College espoused. Sasa Salinasova was a beautiful singer and when we met was interested to hear of the Scottish folk tradition. Under a leafy oak tree in the grounds, I, a better teacher than singer, taught her 'McCrimmon's Lament' which she sang feelingly and beautifully, a sweet christening for our friendship. Later, coming to live in Scotland, this friendship continued along with her exploration of the repertoire of Scottish song.

A propitious meeting at the college was with Ken and Mio Shapley who were to become fast friends and play a colourful role in storytelling in Scotland. Encountering me and because of our warm rapport, they decided to come to live in Edinburgh. There, Mio, who is Japanese, now plays the clarsach and piano aboard the Royal Yacht, in Edinburgh hotels, and more widely afield, as well as conducting tea ceremonies in her beautiful kimono. She is also an exuberant storyteller with an effervescent sense of fun.

Ken, fascinated by other worlds, fairy lore and magical tricks, punctuates his storytelling by his skills on the Didgeridoo. His love of other lands, cultures and wanderlust along with the recognition that their marriage had run its course, means that they happily mutually parted.

When I was invited to tell stories in Japan and tour six cities there, I asked Mio to join me. Together we toured, led by the elderly dynamic and ever fast-moving Miki Sakurai, President of the Japanese Story Foundation. My stories with harp introduction and alternating Japanese versions told by Mio made a popular marriage. Between times we stayed with Mio's hospitable mother and mischievous father, who took me to the sauna, happy to verify that under my kilt I had a 'sparrow'.

During this trip, I extended my story repertoire by telling some Japanese stories that in theme and plot could have been Scottish cousins, two island peoples, particularly sea and supernatural tales.

Subsequent to being a student at Emerson, I was invited to spend a week contributing a unit of Celtic stories within the 12-week course. Having conducted this week on my own, I invited Claire McNicol to co-lead the course in the following year and then, when she became the mother of Freya, I was joined for two further years by Ruth Kirkpatrick. These joint workshop weeks were a delight and highly popular. They also deepened my friendship and admiration for these two remarkable and talented women.

In the tradition of freely passing on this wealth, married to my own experience, I was excited to give a course in Edinburgh, invited to the idea by Janis Mackay, now a successful writer of children's fiction based on the riches of Scottish lore. Janis had returned to Scotland after a varied career, notably teaching Speech and Drama at a cousin college to Emerson in Sussex. We made a good match, and conducted a 12-part course sharing our knowledge and expertise. Perhaps a dozen of our participants became seasoned, much travelled and notable storytellers, including Andy Hunter, Bea Ferguson, Ailie Finlay, Claire Mulholland, Audrey Parks and Senga Munro. Janis herself has become a seasoned and skilled storyteller and has been instrumental in nurturing emerging storytellers through the apprenticeship programme at the Scottish Storytelling Centre. As a 'tribal elder' of the storytelling community, I have held mentoring courses for these fledgling storytellers. This has given me the satisfaction of passing on my 30 years in the art and craft

40

Elegies

MY MOTHER WAS assiduously fair in avoiding any show of favouritism for her children. Our relationship, perhaps her own sense of mischief and her fondness for the rascal, meant we always had an intuitive closeness of spirit and understanding. I loved writing letters to her on my many travels knowing the expressions of amusement and sometimes even surprise that would delight her and flicker across her face.

I still feel gratitude for my mother's selfless nourishment of the family, and hear my father's wise patient words. When I reflect on our family, I see clearly how close and how separate were the siblings. We were four – my brother John (killed in the War), and my sister Anne from my mother's first marriage were as different from one another, as were myself and my brother Eric, from my mother's second marriage to my father. John and Eric were firmly centred at home; Anne and I were rovers.

The death of my brother John in World War II, when I was eight, still brings sporadic tears to my eyes, and I recall the years of companionship with my young brother, and my sister Anne's spontaneity and innocence.

These features of her character she expressed in her watercolour paintings, which attracted much admiration and sold rapidly in Edinburgh. Having seen the celebrated works of 80-year-old Grandma Moses in the American School of Naïve Art, I suggested she send some work for their attention, but she didn't get round to this.

She began to slip, indiscernibly at first, into the anonymity of dementia. When she announced at a lunch outing with my brother Eric, his wife and Catriona that she had won £250, we were delighted. When she later informed us that the doctor and the newsagent had conspired to embezzle it, we knew something was amiss. For a time, still living at her house alone in Braid Crescent, she began to be haunted by fears and fantasies which when I went to visit her and take her to a memory clinic prompted this poem:

Fading

My sister, you have gone wandering
Amongst the snakes that waited in the grass
To sting your age with apparitions
More real than me,
Who like one through a glass
Darkly claws to bring you close.

You frown at strangers that I cannot see,
And like one beyond the veil
Are visible only as an actress in a film
Playing a part in Celluloid.
A word flicks the reel of memory
And the reel relentlessly replays itself
And always returns
To where we came in.

Thereafter, it was fortunate that her kitchen ceiling collapsed, expediting her being taken to a care home which my brother found not far from where he and his wife lived in Dollar. Her condition had so far advanced by now that, to our great relief, she made the move without demur and with her nature's persisting cheerfulness. On our visits, however, she soon failed to recognise us, and yet retained that innocent delight in passing people and events. This made our visits, however strange, preferable to the times when she had been haunted by demons. These demons reminded me of my father's time of frightening hallucinations.

Witnessing my father and my sister becoming unrecognisable and un-reachable brought a harrowing sense of impotence, of being consigned to the role of spectator at the distress of those I loved.

Eric and I had a lifelong friendship and although vastly different in character and style, shared the same values and interests imbued by our parents. We golfed together, shared a pint and ranging discussions. While my mother was alive, she and I made regular visits to Dollar where my brother lived with his wife and four children.

Standing Ovation
In memory of Eric Campbell

You took life head on.
No petty tyrant daunted you.
Affronted by injustice,
careless of the consequence
you spoke out.

And yet, a Mister Chips.
You taught Mathematics
or how to measure
the ingredients for cakes
like a recipe for life.

No wonder your farewell
spurred the whole school
to a standing ovation.
You braved the dark days
with little fuss;
your religion: not beliefs,
but deeds.

By these fruits you are known
and, as the poet said, the 'little
nameless, unremembered acts
of kindness and of love.'

No richer memorial a man
can have:
the immeasurable love
of family and friends.
A standing ovation, brother.

41

A Fateful Day

AT 7.00PM ON 4 July 2002 my vigorous and enjoyable game of squash with John MacInnes was halted by a click and crick in my back and so I showered, dressed and rode my motorbike to dine with Catriona in her flat, four stories up.

It was only after the meal that I became conscious of a growing pain in my back and left leg but managed to ride home. Rapidly the intensity of the pain increased. Little did I know that I had ruptured two discs in my lower spine and that the inter vertebrae cushioning tyre of fluid was leaking onto the nerves. Soon the pain was so intolerable that I was sweating with a shooting pain down my left leg. I was lying on the floor trying to find a less distressing position when the doctor whom Linda Williamson had called arrived and injected morphine. By 8.00am in severe pain and vomiting, Linda's partner, John Slavin, visiting at the time, accompanied me in a taxi to the chiropractor I had attended in Torphichen Street. He at once let me know that no manipulation could help and that any interference could be harmful, and so began the long journey of heavy painkillers, hopeful therapies and helpful solicitous friends.

I was at first bedridden, prescribed large doses of co-codamol tablets. These, along with visits from friends and my attempts to play the penny whistle, were alleviating distractions. The guardian angel who arrived to be a nocturnal nurse and comfort was Catriona, who in the first days of painfully sleepless nights camped on the floor in my bedroom, brought me food, distracting conversations and books to read.

A great achievement at the time it seemed was when I could get down the two flights of stairs, walk 100 yards to a little park in Queen Street Gardens and walk 840 steps and do 20 squats. Pain invites many unlikely measures and so I tried Chinese medicine, various massages, therapies like drum sound massage, Reiki, acupuncture, and in memory of my father's experience, a visit to a spiritual healer and so on, but ultimately convinced also that surgery was too uncertain and invasive I took the advice of Dr James Hawkins: 'Walk.'

Patiently, Catriona had ferried me to all these different practitioners and now to the beaches on the east coast with me reclining on the campervan's beds. By extending walks I was healing and dear Duncan's advice was 'Shave off that ugly beard' and so tentatively back to school storytelling with Duncan, the therapy of the presence of children and his mischievous spirit.

A consequence of this injury is the need for constant awareness of the permanent damage, which leaves me with a recurrent numbness in my leg, an incapacity to lift any weight, to play golf and precludes my zippy rock 'n' roll dancing. But, as my good friend, Alan Rowland says: 'David, we need to cut the cloth.' And so I do.

The solicitous nursing of Catriona evoked this poem:

Silences

What is not said,
the silences
And secret places where
an understanding sits,
A wise elf beneath a tree
of knowledge
And one whose apples bear
not guilt but love;
Here is the walking place
Where hand in hand
We gaze in unsaid pleasures
At the passing wonders
of the ordinary and extra-ordinary world.
These are where my love for you
finds speechless sense.

42

Girl Friday and Robinson

Celine

Seeing my eyes blurred by her departure,
She'd have been brusque,
Made coffee, offered cake,
And a no-nonsense rebuke from the heart –
Without frills.
And we'd have laughed,
I know it,
Banished the gloom.
We'd planned a lunch,
Fuelled by gossip and liquor,
A mischievous heart-to-heart.
Plans fall apart, their timing cruelly derailed.
But I shall toast my strong, invisible friend,
Rejoice in our linkage of words –
Now done, but archived forever.

(Diane Cater, November 2015)

THIS POEM, ON the death of Celine Leuty, was written by Diane Cater, a woman she had never met except in an email correspondence. It speaks the radiance of 'Girl Friday'.

On Good Friday 2005, Celine, aged 65, walked into my house and my life, where she made a warm, remarkable and companionable presence until she died in 2015, concluding ten years of creative work, deep friendship and love.

It was Celine's spirited daughter, Sammy, who answered my advertisement for a computer literate secretary-assistant, and in our phone interview established three half days would better suit her mother.

In this roundabout way, Brazilian Celine appeared prompt at 10.00am on Friday morning in 2005 carrying, unknown to me, a bundle of impressive credentials and an even bigger bundle of varied experience and skills, many of which were to emerge and surprise me in the succeeding years. Her surprise was concealed but equal to mine when I enquired about none of her qualifications, but asked her to type a workshop plan to my dictation and to enquire if she could start immediately. That was that, the birth of ten years of mutual joy and work that was pleasure.

When the film-maker Leo Bruges was shooting a documentary of my life and asked Celine, 'Is David a flirt?' she laughed and said, 'Always, but a very charming one.' 'Does he flirt with you?' She was quick to aver that ours was a relationship of mutual respect, a clear demarcation of roles, though full of fun, and that I was the best boss she ever had, a sentiment I echoed in having Celine as the best Girl Friday ever! No one luckier than I.

Celine was Girl Friday, and far beyond any PA, secretary, administrator. She was advisor, creative critic, confidante, cookery coach, and source of traveller tales, virtually family member at parties, dinners and dramatic schemes. She starred as Mother Goose in our house Christmas pantomime, devised by my lodgers at the time, the puppeteer Andy and resident actor, Adrian. Like everything she did, her Mother Goose was full-blooded and colourfully costumed, a surprise mischievous package.

In Celine's colourful life, she had spent some years of her marriage in Africa, where amongst other intrepid adventures, she had been a rally driver. She liked to drive me to my storytelling performances where she either attended or found a place to read before she drove me home.

We practised guitar together, Celine admonishing: 'David, slow down! You've speeded up,' just as she'd say in mock despair about another of my failures with the computer, 'David, how many times do I have to tell you how to do that?'

So robust were our exchanges that Andy, overhearing, thought we were having a testy argument when it was our affectionate mode, as in a Scottish flyting.

Her African life had taught her great practical skills. One day when she arrived, I was making a few wooden shelves. She seized the saw, drill, screws, raw plugs, and relegated me to junior apprentice.

Everyone who visited loved Celine – Duncan Williamson, Linda Williamson, Catriona, successive lodgers, the entourage of passing storytellers and friends. Zizi, our Brazilian house cleaner, shared memories of their homeland and life stories. The close email friendship that Diane Cater had formed with Celine came about because, after a hiatus of almost 50 years, Diane found my storytelling website and sent me an email. She and I had met when Ron Wood and I were camping in the Highlands. Diane and her friend, Sandra, were great folk singers and joined us for a few merry days in our tent outside Pitlochry. I still remember and sing their versions of 'An Old Man Come Courting Me', and 'My Bonnie Laddie's Lang a-Growin.' We met subsequently in Edinburgh where we attended the Highland Games. Afterwards we lost touch until we began an unexpected and rich email exchange during which Celine came to know Diane who was now living in the south of England and working as a potter. She helped put together a beautifully crafted publication with my script for the Supper with Robert Burns show, and accompanying Scottish recipes which she'd researched.

When the first intimations of Celine's fatal illness appeared, her not so young doctor assured her it was a passing digestive problem and prescribed the ubiquitous antibiotics and at last said to her, 'Well, you're fine now.' She was far from fine, and in considerable pain. A young doctor at once discerned serious trouble, advanced cancer of the bowel, so advanced as to preclude operating. The palliative treatment did not much slow the advance. It was not surprising that her son and three daughters, as was I, were angry at the failure of her elderly doctor to heed Celine's frequent bulletins of distress, a woman far from given to complaints.

Myself and Catriona, a big pal of Celine's, visited her whilst she was courageously living out her last sad days at the house of her son, Philip and his solicitous wife, Maggie.

After her funeral, close friends and family returned to a reception given by Philip and Maggie in their house. It was a hard moment for me when Philip took me aside to give me Celine's guitar, which she had left me. Our favourite piece, 'The House of the Rising Sun', still plays in my head when I lift it, and I hear her admonition, 'David, you've speeded up again!'

43
West Coast Retreat

I FOUND A glorious second home, a caravan in the west outside Glenuig, looking out over the ever-mysterious island of Rùm, my fanciful Tir nan Og, mantled so often with clouds above the Viking peaks, Hallival and Askival. Nearer, the heartening island of Eigg, a triumphant buy-out by its residents: the island's sgurr rises like a thumbs-up for perseverance, cocking a snook at the iniquitous land-owned tracks of beautiful Scotland.

Forsay caravan site, contrary to much of the depressing history of estate management in the Highlands, is owned by the fair and helpful Robbie Clegg who succeeded his popular mother, Jean, and hands-on sister, affectionately known as Tich. The joy and virtue of the site, as well as its situation looking out to Eigg and Rùm, with its basic amenities – shower, toilets, running water, and no electricity, television or internet connection – is perfect for those like myself, who enjoy the refreshing return to simplicity, the camaraderie and pleasure in improvisation. When I walk through the gates, the city falls away like a weight I didn't realise I was carrying. I walk also into another family – friends – with the attitude of mutually helpful villagers. For me, it is the ideal writing retreat with the perfect peace of its surroundings, the soothing lapping of the sea, the view of the islands and leisure for walking, swimming, exploring; a place with a rich history, well-stocked village shop and amiable local folk.

At the time of writing, the attractive Glenuig Inn has been given a new lease of life under the ownership of three enterprising women: Kirstie Mann, Rona Yard and Rona Barr. Their aspiration is to recreate a vibrant community hub with a wholesome menu, popular beer, the welcome return of Guinness, chips in a bowl and live music.

My friends Barbara and John introduced me to this getaway haven, where I was luckily able to buy a caravan. And so I found myself with interesting companions, not only Barbara and John, but my next-door-neighbour George, a jack-of-all trades who would survive if every shred of modern living were blasted from the earth. For the survivors, he would be the generous Admirable Crichton of the play by JM Barrie.

Gathering round the fire built by the artist Gerry and his wife Carol at Hogmanay, frequently are myself, Catriona, our friend, writer Janis Mackay, the poet Liz Lochhead, assorted other caravanners and their guests. Afterwards, traditionally on the first of January, Barbara and John hold an afternoon party supplied with lavish Bloody Marys which lend extravagant bonhomie, loquacious memories and tales, songs extending long into the evening!

The delight of the site is the sociability and simultaneous respect for privacy which has provided a conducive ethos for the undisturbed writing of these memoirs.

Glenuig New Year

On the shelf of rock at Glenuig,
In the dark where light begins
Old year like the incessant waves
Breaks into the new
We sit silently knowing
That sure as the rock we sit on
Love had taken us
To a wordless sanctuary
A quiet celebration
For in our
Journey
We, in fire and crushing times
Have emulated
The geological eons that
Give us this rock place
A temple open to the skies.

I have always considered myself lucky, and I had not long begun the writing of these memoirs when, on my way home on the bus from my weekly singing class, I fell into conversation with Beverley Casebow, who had been attending a fiddle class. Shortly after this, on Christmas Day, I met her in the local grocery store and when I found out that she was intending to spend the day on her own, I invited her to come and join the Christmas party with my very close friends Ken and Mio, whom I knew would, like myself, welcome the stranger at the door. Duncan Williamson used to aver, 'a stranger is just a friend you've not yet met' and so this turned out to be. Not only a friend, but working at the National Library of Scotland, and a gifted writer herself, she became the wise editor and patient typist of my hand-scrawled memoirs. She is an intrepid cold-water Atlantic swimmer, sturdy walker and lover of the mountains, islands and Highlands, their history, literature and lore. Forsay caravan site and its community was consequently a cosy magnet where she could occupy the privacy of Catriona's caravan and work with me on the memoirs.

Celine used to say, 'I organise David.' For the writing, Beverley occupies this role, and is another member of the family of my companions.

The Sweetest Music

THE LEGENDARY FINN McCOULL and his hunters-warriors of the Fianna had spent the day hunting on the high hill and now at last rested on slopes overlooking the sun going red on the western sea.

Finn turned to his followers and said to Oscar, 'What, Oscar, is the sweetest music?' At once the great warrior replied, 'The sweetest music is the clash of spear on shield in the hot rush of battle.' 'Umm, umm' said Finn, 'and Caolte, what to you is the sweetest music?' 'The sweetest music,' said Caolte 'is the baying of the hounds in swift pursuit of the deer on the high hill.' 'Umm, umm' said Finn, 'and Oisin, great maker of words, what to you is the sweetest music?' 'It is the first call of the cuckoo in the springtime,' said Oisin the poet. 'Umm, umm' said Finn, 'and Diarmaid, brother of my heart, what to you is the sweetest music?' 'The sweetest music,' said Diarmaid, 'is the ripple of a girl's laughter meeting with her first love.'

'And then' said Oisin to Finn, 'what to you, Finn, is the sweetest music?' and Finn replied: 'It is the music of what is happening.'

Thank Yous; a Fairy Story

ONCE UPON A TIME, there was a mischievous elf. When our story begins, he had eight decades behind him. I should tell you, his earthling name was 'David'. On his 80th birthday, he began to tell his story. Was it really by chance that he met a word witch? Her name was Beverley. When she heard snatches of his long life's tale, she said two magic words, 'Write it!' And so the journey began.

All his lucky life, as in the best fairy stories, he met helpers at just the right moment. So it was 'I will help,' she said, and so they began to weave the tapestry. She magically translated his runes into printed letters, above all organising his random memories into sweet order as he recounted his quest through the spring, summer, autumn and winter of his days. On the tangled path, he told of the wizards, giants, dwarves, saints and sinners his steps had fallen in with. Everyone from the lucky egg from which he was hatched.

On the path through the forest of memory, many were the light and beneficent spirits, the Pucks and Ariels, who cleared the tangles, and in the darknesses held dancing ghost fires for his feet to follow.

In glades of wonder, those airy sprites gave him this treasury of tales, here unlocked. Here are some of the sprites who bestowed these story jewels: Ron Wood; Maureen Mellors; Gordon Allan; Mick Ridings; Tom Pow; George Robertson; Jim Goodall; Frauke and Keith Chambers; Ina Schierbeck; Dolina MacLennan; Robin Mackenzie; David Bathgate; Liz Lochhead; Carol Sharp; Stewart Conn; Pam Wardell; Eddie Stiven; Frieda Morrison; Jessieca Leo; Ferda Erding; Helga Lilja Bjornsdottir; Sigurborg Hannesdóttir.

Near the journey's end, once more came helpers for this lucky life. Sabrina Maesani, a sorceress, fathoming the mysteries of a technical world – patient, lucid, composed; Barbara McLean, wise word woman, a keen-eyed seer and companion advisor; the generous-spirited Robin Gillanders with his ever-ready expertise and photographic flair; and from his story grotto the word wizard Donald Smith, dispensing his wily wisdom. Much thanks also to Gavin MacDougall and his team at Luath Publishing; Anne Hunter and Catherine Lockerbie for their careful and helpful reading of the text; and Jennie Renton for her patience, enthusiasm and invaluable comments.

Along the many winding, sometimes tangled, paths, keeping the hearth of the heart warm, Catriona.

For all of these brother and sister travellers, much thanks.

Copyrights and Permissions

I would like to thank the following people for permission to publish these poems:

Ewen MacCaig and Birlinn for extracts from Norman MacCaig's 'Moment Musical in Assynt' and 'Praise of A Man'.

Stuart McGregor's family for his 'Prayer of the Country Whore Lady'.

Donalda Crichton-Smith for 'Beginning of a New Song' by Iain Crichton-Smith.

Linda Williamson for 'The Streaker from the Braes' by Duncan Williamson.

Diane Cater for 'Poem for Celine'.

George Brown for his poem written on the occasion of Stuart McGregor's leaving for Jamaica.

Luath Press Limited

committed to publishing well written books worth reading

LUATH PRESS takes its name from Robert Burns, whose little collie Luath (*Gael.*, swift or nimble) tripped up Jean Armour at a wedding and gave him the chance to speak to the woman who was to be his wife and the abiding love of his life. Burns called one of the 'Twa Dogs' Luath after Cuchullin's hunting dog in Ossian's *Fingal*. Luath Press was established in 1981 in the heart of Burns country, and is now based a few steps up the road from Burns' first lodgings on Edinburgh's Royal Mile. Luath offers you distinctive writing with a hint of unexpected pleasures. Most bookshops in the UK, the US, Canada, Australia, New Zealand and parts of Europe, either carry our books in stock or can order them for you. To order direct from us, please send a £sterling cheque, postal order, international money order or your credit card details (number, address of cardholder and expiry date) to us at the address below. Please add post and packing as follows: UK – £1.00 per delivery address; overseas surface mail – £2.50 per delivery address; overseas airmail – £3.50 for the first book to each delivery address, plus £1.00 for each additional book by airmail to the same address. If your order is a gift, we will happily enclose your card or message at no extra charge.

Luath Press Limited
543/2 Castlehill
The Royal Mile
Edinburgh EH1 2ND
Scotland
Telephone: +44 (0)131 225 4326 (24 hours)
Email: sales@luath.co.uk
Website: www.luath.co.uk

Contents

Acknowledgements

Thanks to the following (in alphabetical order) for their assistance and/or support in compiling this book: Roger Atyeo, Jim Barker, Josie Barker, Karen Boyle, Steve 'Biggsy' Bygraves, Ally Cubbon, Mary Cubbon, Stewart Cubbon, Paul Downey, Clark Gibson, Paul 'Green Dog' Greenhead, Shannon Chloe Greenwood, Angela Hewitson, Emily Hewitson, Neil Hewitson, Paul 'Jonah' Jones, Jim Loughran, Donnie McCleod, Leigh McQueen, Nick Mullen, Ben Purvis, Bertie Simmonds, Heather Temple, Pete 'Scouse' Whittington, Tracy Wisbee and to all at The Briars for keeping me sane.

A special thanks to Michael Doggart, Tom Whiting, Tarda Davison-Aitkins, Rachel Nicholson, Juliette Davis, Sara Walsh and all at HarperCollins*Publishers* for making this book possible.